Barbarians and Civilization in
International Relations

Barbarians and Civilization in International Relations

Mark B. Salter

Pluto Press

LONDON • STERLING, VIRGINIA

First published 2002 by Pluto Press
345 Archway Road, London N6 5AA
and 22883 Quicksilver Drive, Sterling VA 20166-2012, USA

www.plutobooks.com

British Library Cataloguing in Publication Data
A catalogue record for this book is available from the British Library

ISBN 0 7453 1902 5 hardback
ISBN 0 7453 1901 7 paperback

Library of Congress Cataloging-in-Publication Data
Salter, Mark B.
    Barbarians and civilisation in international relations/Mark B.
Salter.
      p. cm.
Includes bibliographical references and index.
      ISBN 0–7453–1902–5 (hbk.) – ISBN 0–7453–1901–7 (pbk.)
      1. International relations and culture. 2. World politics—1989–
I. Title.
      JZ1251.S25 2002
      303.48′2—dc21
                                                                    2002001236

10   9   8   7   6   5   4   3   2   1

Designed and produced for Pluto Press by
Chase Publishing Services, Fortescue, Sidmouth EX10 9QG
Typeset from disk by Replika Press Pvt Ltd, Delhi, India
Printed in the European Union by Antony Rowe Ltd, Chippenham, England

To:
my family, old and new

Contents

Acknowledgements

I would like to thank my family for their continuous and univocal support. When I asked for *Neorealism and its Critics* for Christmas in my junior year, my mother rightly guessed that I was *not* going to become a lawyer. My family has been the anchor for my many travels, and I could not have done this without their love and support. My West Coast family took me in as one of their own. My family has expressed constant optimism throughout the entire process, and I cannot express my gratitude. Thank you Stuart, Mary, Patricia, Hunter and Kay. My grandparents slipped me food, train fare and the benefit of their wisdom. My siblings kept me grounded. I would also like to thank the 'best people', Meredith Browne, Adrianne Gaffney, Sara Levin and Kaley Walker, for their close friendship.

The bulk of the research for this project was made possible through the support of the Social Sciences and Humanities Research Council of Canada. I would also like to thank the Department of Political Science and the Institute of International Relations at the University of British Columbia. I have presented versions of chapters 3 and 9 at the International Studies Association, which provided a much needed airing of some of these ideas. I was extremely lucky to have a superlative doctoral committee. Professor Kal Holsti provided essential feedback and consummate professionalism in his supervision. Professor Rob Walker provided intellectual guidance on those occasions when the project seemed too vast. Professor Brian Job provided essential direction in negotiating the process of finishing a doctoral dissertation. At UBC, Professor Sam Laselva was an invaluable source of inspiration and inquisition. I would also like to thank Simon Dalby for his help and support at the end of this project. Patrick Thaddeus Jackson and Jacinta O'Hagan were excellent sounding boards for the project. I would also like to thank Eddie Keene, who was the Editor at Millennium during my year at LSE. I also owe a great debt to J.P. Sewell for his early encouragement.

I would like to thank Roger van Zwanenberg at Pluto Press for his faith in this project.

I would like to thank Pamela Ritchie for her work formatting the typescript at a busy time.

For a thousand things, my wife Kate deserves a thousand thanks. She is the best partner anyone could hope for, and I am fortunate beyond reckoning.

Cairo, 2002

1 Introduction

On the Corniche, along the Nile, just outside the Luxor temple, is a traffic sign that reads 'Obeying the traffic light is a sign of civilization'. After five years of noting each invocation of the discourse of 'civilization', the traffic sign – in English – seemed to illustrate the end of the road. This exhortation, directed at the English-speaking tourists rather than the Arabic-speaking inhabitants, seemed to signify exactly what was at stake in the 'clash of civilizations' debate in International Relations. What I found in Luxor was not only the assertion of an Islamic identity *against* the continual flow of Western influences or the rejection of globalization. Rather, at Luxor, I found refutation of the inevitable 'clash' of civilizations, cultures or Islam and the West.

Luxor is a site that has gained prominence several times in its history. Luxor temple in particular is an excellent example of civilizational dialogue: it was started by Amenhotep III (1414 BC), added to by the Tutankhamun (1333–23 BC), defaced by the famous Ramses II (1290–24 BC), invaded by the Assyrians in the seventh century BC, and later by Alexander the Great (332–23 BC). Copts converted the inner sanctum into a church, defacing the hieroglyphics with Christian iconography in AD 200–300. After the Muslim invasion, a mosque was built into the structure of the pharaonic temple in the thirteenth century. And the temple is the source of the obelisk that now stands in the heart of Paris, the Place de la Concorde. More recently, in 1997, Luxor was the site of a terrorist attack against tourists at the temple of Queen

Hatshepsut. Currently, one might point as signs of globalization to the obligatory McDonald's, innumerable cruise boats continuing the flow of tourists that began with the French invasion and Thomas Cook, or the multilingual shopkeepers hawking copies of the artifacts that grace the Louvre, the Metropolitan Museum of Art and the British Museum. What is notable in Luxor (and in Egypt generally) is their complex relationship to the West and to Islamic extremism.

Let me start with the present. The terrorist attack, which killed 68 Western tourists and Egyptians, seemed to prove Samuel Huntington's construction of a violent Islamic revival. Because of popular and academic constructions of the Muslim as terrorist, supplemented by the image of the Palestinian *Intifada*, Western media interpreted this attack as a 'natural' or 'typical' manifestation of the 'fundamentalist' backlash against Western domination and/or globalization. Tourism, on which the local Luxor economy depends, dried up for nearly three years. Cut off from the global networks of capital and the consumerist culture that accompany it, Luxor was economically devastated.

There were several attempts to disavow the attack. The Egyptian authorities tried to dispel the image of danger with a 'funeral ceremony' at the temple one week later, complete with Verdi's *Tears of Anger* and candles.[1] The popular press blamed Islamist extremists for the attacks and the government for their failure to deal with the root causes of social alienation.[2] As one commentator argued, 'The only way to describe the perpetrators of the Luxor incident is that they are traitors [to the nation of Egypt].'[3] The group that claimed responsibility for the attack, *Al-Gama*, said through a spokesperson that the terrorists acted without organizational approval.[4] Particularly interesting, in view of Western perceptions of this attack, is the disavowal by Islamic religious authorities: 'The Grand Sheikh of Al-Azhar [Egypt's leading University/Mosque] Mohamed Sayed Tantawi said, "This is a criminal act. This act is opposed to the precepts of Islam."'[5] The government of Egypt recruited nearly 30,000 new police and instituted security measures to protect not Egyptians, monuments or heritage, but wealthy tourists. However, the claimed goal of the attack was the release of *Al-Gama*'s leader Sheik Omar Abdel-Rhaman, who is 'jailed in the United States for conspiring to blow up the World Trade Center in 1993'.[6]

While this raises interesting questions concerning globalization, tourism geography and political Islam, I want to focus on this site as an exemplum of the 'clash of civilizations'. In short, while moderate groups, such as the Muslim Brotherhood, find a great deal of support for their Islamist message within Egypt, radical Islamist groups are rejected on economic, religious and political grounds.[7]

However, within the Western imaginary, every Muslim is a potential terrorist. This is the image which Huntington repeats in his infamous 'clash of civilizations' discourse.

This project stems from a dissatisfaction with the critical engagement of Huntington's *Clash of Civilizations* argument. The 'clash of civilizations' thesis has become a touchstone for contemporary theorizing about the post-world (post-Cold War, postcolonial, post-structural, postmodern, post-Fordist, post-realist, post-bipolar: in short, post-). In his first short article on the 'clash of civilizations', Huntington proposed a theory that integrated all the anxieties of the post-world: globalization, culture, identity, religion, fundamentalism, barbarism and civilizational decline. He argues that cultural groupings will be the main actors and culture and identity the main axes of conflict. These conflicts are more insidious and intractable than previously rational conflicts like the Cold War, because identity and culture are zero-sum conflicts. However, the description of 'civilization' makes sense only with the construction of marginalized 'Others'. In the imperial discourse that Huntington disinters, barbarians are the natural enemies of civilization. In his cartography of the New World Order, Huntington represents Islamic civilization as youthful, fundamentalist, leaderless and, as such, barbarian. Huntington's description of the post-world also describes a place for the United States at the head of Occidental, or Western, civilization. He warns that unless the West unites under its leadership – and the US assumes that leadership role – the countries of Western civilization will 'hang together or hang separately'.[8]

Though many scholars have engaged Huntington's empirical claims, few have pursued the political implications or the imperialist legacy implicit in his rationale. The site of Egypt, and representations of the Luxor massacre in particular, place this discourse in a different, postcolonial light. In an effort to contest this representation of the post-world, this project borrows heavily from a group of International Relations (IR) scholars who have charted the analytical potential of the concepts of culture and identity for understanding world politics. The vanguard of this group, scholars such as R.B.J. Walker, Richard K. Ashley, David Campbell, James Der Derian and Michael Shapiro, base these interventions from a post-structural theoretical position.[9] In adding to this conversation, *Barbarians and Civilization* investigates the trope of the 'barbarian' in International Relations and the popular international imaginary to disinter the politics of Huntington's argument.

The trope of the barbarian is familiar: lacking in manners, language and morals, but not organization, barbarians represent a violent threat to the 'civilized' inside.[10] The space of the barbarian illustrates the limits of the political community – the figure of the barbarian – either alone or in a horde – acts as the 'constitutive outside' of the *polis*. Although this phenomenon is not uniquely Western, in this project I concentrate on the European/Western discourse of civilization and barbarians.[11] Jacques Derrida argues that binary structures play a primary role in Western philosophy, and traditional IR theory is no exception. In this work, I attempt to deconstruct the civilized/barbarian dichotomy and illustrate some of the sites where it has been mobilized in IR theory. The civilized/barbarian discourse also points our attention to imperialism, and the ways in which imperialism is at once central to our understanding of international history and international relations, and similarly absent from traditional narratives of sovereignty/anarchy. Furthermore, the 'barbarian' represents a rhetorical well from which politicians have drawn throughout the twentieth century and from which they still draw.

The resurrection of the 'civilizations' discourse acts as a new 'civilizational realism' which attempts to *re*inscribe imperial cartographies on the post-Cold War order. The dual function of this move is to render the 'West' unproblematic and to 'barbarize' the multiple 'non-Wests'. As Campbell and Shapiro argue: 'the imbrication of morality and cartography is historically evident in the way those who have employed the civilizational discourse have treated those outside of their "civilizational" boundaries with less moral solicitude.'[12] This project represents an attempt to trace the civilized/barbarian discourse through the nineteenth and twentieth centuries, and illustrate the political function of the discourse in post-Cold War IR theorizing.

Barbarians and Civilization is indebted to post-structuralism in its methodology. This genealogy stresses the shifts, disruptions and displacements in the 'civilization/barbarian' discourse. By concentrating on these discursive shifts, we see how the identities of Europe/the West/IR theory shift in turn.

This introduction indicates some of the theoretical conversations to which this project contributes. Chapter 2 explores the meanings and etymology of several key concepts to the argument: civilization and barbarians. In short, the presence of 'barbarians' at the borders of the community, which helps legitimize political actions within the community and at the borders of the community, has been consistent – if the 'barbarians' themselves have changed over time. An important aim of this project is to fill a lacuna in IR theory, the presence of the (post)colonial in the contemporary world. In an effort to show the pedigree of Huntington's discourse, I examine the use of the trope of the barbarian in European imperialism. Chapter 3 examines some important ideational aspects of European imperialism after 1798. It argues that imperial expansion was a central part of European identity, and that the civilized/barbarian dichotomy was an essential part of colonial discourse. In particular, I examine the case of Egypt as illustrative of the themes of demography, visuality and racial stereotyping. These anxieties about racial purity, demographic threats and visuality are reflected also in the colonial metropole. Chapter 4 plots how the tensions endemic to Europe at the turn of the twentieth century are reflected in the 'civilization/barbarian' discourse. In addition to a growing philosophical scepticism expressed by Friedrich Nietzsche, Europe began to lose confidence in its imperial rhetoric as evidenced by the work of Oswald Spengler and Sigmund Freud. The civilizing mission began to show signs of strain, and by the Second World War, had lost all claim to credibility. Hitler's self-proclaimed 'barbaric' German state barbarized Germany and Europe. Chapter 5 examines the unravelling of the civilized Europe/barbaric Others discourse. The connection that Nazi thought drew between International Relations and imperialism is of particular interest. This chapter also looks at Nazi atrocities through the lens of anti-colonial writers such as Aimé Césaire and Frantz Fanon, who reflected the 'civilization/barbarian' rhetoric back to the imperial centre. Decolonization had a profound impact on the world, and on the discipline of International Relations. Chapter 6 examines the specific theoretical moves that removed imperialism from the view of IR theory. Chapter 7 intervenes in the critical debate surrounding Huntington's 'clash of civilizations'. In addition to tackling Huntington's empirical claims, this chapter charts the popular analogues of Huntington's argument in Benjamin Barber and Robert Kaplan. Specifically, I argue that Huntington's civilizational realism reinscribes a (post)colonial worldview on the post-world.

Huntington has four chief policy prescriptions in his argument: the abandonment of African civilization, America's wariness of the Islamic–Confucian connection, the leadership of the US within Western civilization, the *re*nationalization of the US domestically. Only the first of these prescriptions has been evaluated by current writers on this topic. The conclusion suggests dangers of the mobilization of imperial tropes in the post-Cold War popular international imaginary.

In this, I am treading the path of a group of scholars who concentrate on the implications of imperialism and the 'postcolonial' condition on international relations. Postcolonial theory, or postcolonialism, is concerned with 'imperialism, Orientalism and culture' and, more specifically, with the roots and implications of imperial forms of domination.[13] Postcolonialism and IR theory often speak past each other, although they are concerned with similar relations of power and domination.[14] Philip Darby illustrates the utility of combining postcolonial theory's occupation with culture and ideas and Internation Relation's concern with power and material domination.[15] Scholars such as Roxanne Lynn Doty, Philip Darby, A.J. Paolini, David Blaney and Naeem Inyatullah have endeavoured to illustrate the impact of these concerns on contemporary world politics.[16] Darby and Paolini show the utility of some concepts from postcolonial theory in the evaluation of world politics.[17] Doty takes a similar tack, arguing that contemporary IR theory that uses the North/South dichotomy uncritically has the effect of reproducing colonial categories and stereotypes.[18] *Barbarians and Civilization* continues this argument, applying a similar analysis to the civilized/barbarian dichotomy.

One can characterize current encounters with the civilized/barbarian discourse in international relations in three fields. The first is the juridical field, examining the specific international legal context. Scholars such as Gerrit Gong take the legal discourse of imperialism and international society and interrogate it. The second is the foreign policy analysis field, in which scholars such as Doty examine the ways that specific (imperial) countries enact and reify the civilized/barbarian dichotomy. The third examines the discourse of 'civilization' itself, investigating the specific political uses of the term. Iver Neumann, Jacinta O'Hagan and Patrick Thaddeus Jackson have done work in this area. I would count this effort as operating within the third field.

My students in Cairo are very familiar with the basic argument

Huntington puts forward. They confirm that his characterization of the Islamic world is skewed.[19] But, as Huntington illustrates in his rebuttal to his critics, 'If not civilizations, what?', the empirical discrepancies are not the most important part of his argument. What is at stake in accepting Huntington's post-worldview is a *re*inscription of a nineteenth-century worldview on the world. This colonial *Weltanschauung* imposes closure on a host of arguments regarding development, global justice and the ethics of intervention. In tracing the evolution of the trope of the barbarian from its pairing with civilization at the turn of the nineteenth century to its most recent invocation at the beginning of the twenty-first century, I hope to open a discursive space for an inclusion of 'civilizations' without the assumption of clash, zero-sum encounters and the inevitable violence which this worldview endows.

2 Civilization and Barbarians

In the greater clash, the global 'real clash', between civilization and barbarism, the world's great civilizations, with their rich accomplishments in religion, art, literature, philosophy, science, morality, and compassion, will hang together or hang separately.[1]

Huntington's invocation of the clash between civilization – read as high culture – and barbarism illustrates the function of these terms as identity groups and the connections between identity, culture, civilization and barbarism.

IDENTITY

The concept of 'identity' is clouded in epistemological battles, academic wrangling and definitional ambiguity. Despite this conceptual ambiguity, 'identity' is clearly a central theme in political discourse and warrants serious analysis. Because individual and group identities are formed 'in relation to a world beyond themselves', identity politics are of prime concern to International Relations.[2] Huntington provides a provisional definition of identity that acts as a starting point for his argument:

> people define themselves in terms of ancestry, religion, language, history, values, customs, and institutions, [they] use politics not just to advance their interests but also to define their identity. We know who we are only when we know who we are not and often when we know whom we are against.[3]

Huntington offers a definition of identity that is singular, static, unchanging and based on a simplistic dualist structure of self/Other. He makes an important conceptual distinction between 'identity' and 'interest'. On the one hand, 'identity' is understood as who individuals believe they are and the limits of their community. On the other, 'national interest' – a slippery term at best – is understood as the goals and aims of a community. While these goals may include the protection of identity, Huntington defines identity as more than a conglomeration of interests. He also highlights positive and negative aspects of the process of identification, which I will elaborate below. While there may be a range of reactions to the 'Other' or outsider – from xenophobia to Orientalism – the 'Other' is by definition marginalized in or excluded from the community. Huntington continues: 'Psychologists generally agree that individuals and groups define their identity by differentiating themselves from and placing themselves in opposition to others.'[4] Post-structural and postcolonial theorists have taken up this view of identity as difference.

William Connolly lays out the post-structural position: 'difference requires identity and identity requires difference . . . doubts about self identity are posed and resolved by the constitution of an other against which that identity may define itself.'[5] The assertion of a group sameness or national 'identity' requires some elision or exclusion of difference. Communities are never homogeneous, and their populations are never obvious, stable or completely knowable.[6] McClintock expressed the empirical concerns about the definition of identity as homogeneity: representations of identity and difference often do not reflect empirical or material 'sameness' or 'difference'.[7] There is a large body of recent theory that is concerned with the relationship with the 'Other'. Often influenced by psychoanalysis, critical theorists have argued that while the 'Other' is excluded from the 'self', the 'self' requires the presence of the 'Other' to define its boundary.[8] A prominent scholar in Cultural Studies, Stuart Hall argues:

> Directly contrary to the form in which they are constantly invoked, identities are constructed through, not outside, difference . . . it is only through the relation to the Other, the relation to what it is not, to precisely what it lacks, to what has been called its *constitutive outside* that the 'positive' meaning of any term – and thus its 'identity' can be constructed.[9]

Because definition is determined by limits, at least in part, the 'Other' is a necessary component of the 'self'. Doty summarizes the post-structural position for International Relations:

> identity is [conceptualized] as a practice and an effect that is always in the process of being constructed through signifying processes that expel the surplus meanings that would expose the failure of identity as such . . . The spectre of the other is always within the 'self'.[10]

The 'Other' is both required and excluded in the process of identification.

The 'self' defines its boundaries in relation to some 'Other'.[11] That 'Other' may be multiple, benign or inconsequential. The 'Other' may be portrayed as inferior or fetishized as superior. The boundaries may be territorial, juridical, economic, racial, sexual or social. However, the 'Other' remains outside the community and accordingly is not granted the same rights as the 'self' inside.[12]

Much critical theory in the fields of geopolitics, security studies, political, human and cultural geography concentrates on the spatial aspect of identity.[13] Hall expresses this dynamic: 'identities . . . are more the product of the marking of difference and exclusion, than they are the sign of an identical, naturally-constituted unity.'[14] Because of the different representations of the 'Other' and the myriad of material consequences these representations may have – from assimilation to genocide – it is imperative that scholars be specific about the identity-discourse and historical context that they are studying.[15]

Critical theorists in International Relations have also examined the self/Other dynamic. Michael Shapiro provides an excellent explanation of Hegelian and Lacanian identity formation.[16] David Campbell summarizes a post-structural position of identity and identity formation succinctly:

> the problematic of identity/difference contains no foundations that are prior to, or outside of, its operation . . . the constitution of identity is achieved through the inscription of boundaries that serve to demarcate an 'inside' from an 'outside', a 'self' from an 'other', a 'domestic' from a 'foreign'.[17]

Post-structural theory's interest in power leads scholars to investigate the operations of power in and on identity structures. Michel Foucault describes how identity positions come to be constituted by psychiatric, medical, judicial and sexual discourses. However, he does not explore how individuals come to occupy these positions.[18] Thus, for example, there is a difference between believing one is a doctor and being a doctor, believing one is a judge and being a judge. While identity may be constituted by representation, we cannot ignore the institutional and discursive context in which identities are legitimized. This leads us to question the location of the 'operations' of identity.

The representation of certain identities produced within specific historical and institutional contexts becomes a central analytical focus, in part because they define the cultural forms identity may take. In addition, the specific textual and material occupation of those subject positions becomes equally important.[19] Thus, many post-structural analyses are not concerned with the empirical definition of a particular identity, but rather with how that identity is represented, performed and reified through social and political practices.[20] This notion of identity practices is connected to the practices of boundary policing, which is central to current thinking on the subject.[21]

In an illuminating work, Iver B. Neumann provides a valuable typology of the varied perspectives taken by different disciplines, all concerned with the same dynamic. He suggests four paths along which theorizing of the self–Other relationship has been developed:

1. *The ethnographic path*: based in studies of 'in-group' and 'out-group', this path is represented by scholars who study nationalism and the constitution of ethnic groups in International Relations.[22]
2. *The psychological path*: similar to Bloom's analysis[23] of social psychology, this path applies psychoanalysis to inter-group dynamics and ethnocentrism.[24]
3. *The Continental philosophical path*: largely tangential to International Relations, this path outlines philosophical contributions by Habermas, Taylor and other philosophers on the relationship between 'self' and 'Other' in the Western tradition.[25]
4. *The 'Eastern excursion'*: following Said, this path constitutes the majority of Neumann's argument on the identity of Europe and its specific exclusion of one of the many 'Easts' – Turkey, Russia and Northern Europe.[26]

These four paths represent the best contemporary summary of disparate fields which tackle the same general theme, although it should be noted that scholars working within postcolonialism, feminist studies and human/cultural geography have also engaged this problematic. *Barbarians and Civilization* follows Neumann's fourth path, focusing on the colonial or imperial East. I work from the assumption that the identity of a group claiming the status of 'civilized' – in this case Europe – requires a group that can be represented as barbarians against which to define themselves – in this case the colonial subjects. The status of 'civilization' is meaningless without 'barbarians' against whom to compare one's self in order to draw the limits of the political community.[27]

By tracing a specific permutation of the self/Other dichotomy, *Barbarians and Civilization* elaborates a specific instance in which identity is defined contingently and relationally. The ascription of civilized or barbarian is not a neutral, objective description. Rather, the civilized/barbarian discourse has specific, imperial overtones which should not be overlooked. Walker plots some of the relations between identity, culture and the civilization/barbarian dichotomies: 'culture, like civilization, becomes something we have, distinguishing us from the barbarians outside . . . The possession of "civilization" justifies the conquest of "barbarism".'[28] The possession of 'civilization' is marked by artifacts of culture.

CULTURE

As argued by Raymond Williams, culture is one of the most contested and complex words in the English language.[29] As Walker points out, 'culture' 'has been the site of serious philosophical and political dispute' in European political and social discourse.[30] In Huntington's formulation, 'culture' is seen as the inheritance of centuries of European/Western excellence. During the late Victorian era, culture was represented by Matthew Arnold as the 'civilization' of the upper, educated classes against the 'anarchy' of the lower and emerging middle classes.[31] On the other hand, *Kultur* is understood as a local, particular, nationalist identity.[32] Framed within a debate about the national identity of Germany, *Kultur* was described as the natural, *volkisch* historical particularity of the German people, often against an emerging technical, sterile and universal *Zivilisation*.[33]

Herder is one of the first philosophers to argue for the existence of multiple civilizations, instead of the theory of one single European civilization, a view that was popularized by Spengler.[34] Nietzsche argues specifically: 'Civilization has aims different from those of culture – perhaps they are even opposite.'[35] As a consequence, there is a certain historical tension between the claims of particularistic culture and universalist civilization. In many ways, Walker argues, 'culture remains associated with the insistence on diversity, fragmentation and relativism, on the celebration of traditions arising from particular communities against the claim of a universalizing humanity – claims that have tended to arise from particular, though dominant, communities.'[36]

In sum the definition of culture as national identity is tied to a larger philosophical debate surrounding universalism and particularism. Culture often stands as a code for particularism and relativism – perhaps suggesting the source of traditional discomfort with the concept. Culture, especially in Arnold's terminology, is taken to represent the 'best' a society has to offer and is coded in racial, class and gendered terms. Specifically, the academic tendency has been to concentrate on elite rather than popular culture. However, postcolonial and cultural studies have indicated the importance of popular culture to identity and political discourses.

In much recent critical and postcolonial theory, 'culture' is understood as the field of representations in which power and identities are constructed, reified, negotiated and resisted. In the first instance, this notion encompasses the previous definitions of culture – understanding the field of representations to comprehend the abstract ideas, history and values of a particular group, but also the specific textual and institutional ways these ideas are practised. It also widens the scope of analysis so that national, subnational and international cultural fields might be understood. As Sujata Pasic argues: 'a cultural approach enables us to leave behind unitary state actors, purely interactionist accounts, and unnecessarily limiting conceptual boundaries such as domestic versus international and state versus society'.[37]

In the second instance, this notion of 'culture' emphasizes the process of cultural dialogue over the assumed cultural consensus or 'product'. This prompts the theorist to analyse cultural practices within their specific historical, political and economic context. Seeing 'culture' as a dialogue also prompts us to 'resurrect subjugated knowledges', seeking those voices that resist the dominant discourse.[38] This view of 'culture' as a field of representations also enables scholars to see identity formations – such as self/Other and civilized/barbarian – in their discursive context. The discourses of race, class, gender and imperialism are mutually constituting and mutually implicating.

The study of popular culture is an important component of this position. Popular culture, it is argued, offers more discursive space for the analysis of resistance to dominant discourses.[39] Darby highlights the importance of popular culture to International Relations:

> The need to elevate culture as a subject of study in international relations directs attention to people as a neglected dimension of the discipline . . . what has been missing is people outside the circles of official power; people who in some way are expressive of their society and carry its values into other societies and the international arena.[40]

While not disputing the importance of diplomatic and state elites, the international imaginary of the population, the 'popular international imaginary', is also central to International Relations. What I mean by 'popular international imaginary' are the popular beliefs about the world outside of the state, the nature of that 'outside' – the international society, and the place of the state in that society. This is a slight modification of a term both Said and Shapiro use: 'international imaginary'.[41] An international imaginary is understood as the structural and symbolic framework that gives meaning to, and perpetuates the configuration of, sovereign states and their International Relations.[42] Shapiro continues:

> To analyze how things in the world take on meanings, it is necessary to analyze the structure of imaginative processes. The imaginative enactments that produce meanings are not simply acts of a pure, disembodied consciousness; they are historically developed practices which reside in the very style in which statements are made, of the grammatical, rhetorical, and narrative structures that compose even the discourses of the sciences.[43]

I plan to use histories, travel writings and IR theories that use the discourse of civilization/barbarian to explain and justify imperialism as reflections of the popular imaginary. This too marks a departure from traditional International Relations which, for the most part, has concentrated on elite perceptions of the international realm. Given this focus on popular culture and popular international imaginary, I will concentrate on histories that are exemplary of their cultural milieu, supported by other literary and popular texts.

CIVILIZATION

and discipline, that is, perfect cooperation, is an attribute of civilization . . . none but civilized nations have ever been capable of forming an alliance.[44]

'Civilization' has stood for several different ideas in its history, however Mill's description suggests the way in which 'civilization' was understood specifically as European civilization – a specific kind of European civilization. Mill's quote also indicates the way in which, at its inception, 'civilization' described the sphere of possible International Relations (that is, peaceful inter-European relations) and a sphere of imperial relations. From its inception, civilization was defined as the opposite of 'barbarism'.[45] In its first incarnations, 'civilization' stood for a process of 'cultivation' (linked to both manners and agriculture) and for European identity. The term first appears in English in 1772,[46] in opposition to barbarity, and in French in 1767.[47] The term was quickly mobilized in the imperial context – as both endorsement and critique of the process of European expansion.[48] In the nineteenth century, 'civilization' was taken to represent a mission of homogenization and 'improvement'.[49] Thus, the rhetoric of 'civilization' was quickly appropriated by imperial ideology to mean the 'civilizing mission'. It also came to represent European states as a group. European nations – as exemplified by the Covenant of the League of Nations – saw themselves as the 'civilized' world in stark contrast to the savage and barbaric worlds. Laws of warfare and the treaties of international organizations were based on the tacit or explicit value consensus which 'European civilization' represented.

For most of this part of its history, civilization was a political term, which was used to elide the differences within European communities, in comparison to those savage and barbaric communities outside Europe. I will elaborate the differences between 'savage' and 'barbarians' in the next section. European civilization was defined in part as the technologically superior, universal standard portrayed by Enlightenment thinkers. The distinction between 'civilization' and 'savagery' and 'barbarism' was also mobilized to distinguish classes within European nations. The term 'civilization' was also defined against groups *within* Europe which were labelled 'barbaric' and 'savage'.[50] In sum, 'civilization' has been a contested term used by both proponents and critics of the civilizing mission and the imperialism of which it was a vital part. However, 'civilization' has always been a characteristic that 'we' have, in contradistinction to 'them' – the barbarians.[51]

In the mid-nineteenth century, a model of societal development was developed by French and Scottish philosophers.[52] The development of a 'four-stages' model of the progress of human societies marks a formal distinction between 'savage' and 'barbarous' societies. Societies were placed within a hierarchical taxonomy based on their method of subsistence. 'Savage' societies – which were the most primitive – consisted primarily of hunter-gatherers. 'Barbarian' societies – which were more developed than 'savage' peoples – consisted of shepherds. The third stage of society was the development of agriculture. The final stage of society – which in this case represents a description of European society – is the institution of a commercial, capitalist market. However, even though other 'civilizations', such as Arabic, Turkic, Indian, Chinese, Japanese, could each be considered to be as evolved as the European in this taxonomy, divisions between European and non-European civilizations remained important in popular discourse. In 1750, Montesquieu specifically distinguished between 'savage' and 'barbarians' in the *Spirit of the Laws*.[53] By 1777, Burke would write:

> now the Great Map of Mankind is unrolled at once; and there is not state or Gradation of barbarism and no mode of refinement which we have not at the same instant under our View. The very different Civility of Europe and China; The barbarism of Tartary, and of Arabia. The Savage State of North America, and of New Zealand.[54]

This illustrates that, by this time, it was well established that civilization, barbarism and savagery represented different stages of societal evolution. Even when European authors praised the 'East', they did so within the discursive structure of Orientalism, which implies a power/knowledge structure that does not allow for symbolic equality between East and West.[55] Thus, the developmental model of evolution exists in the same discursive space as sixteenth- and seventeenth-century ideas about the 'Turk' and European 'civilization'.

Gerrit Gong adds to this understanding of the term that 'civilization' represented an expression of a single European identity, based on a notion of secular – rather than religious – unity.[56] He argues that, as a standard, 'civilization' reflected European culture's dominance over other societies. Just as identity is involved in the policing of boundaries, European civilization was also figured as a 'standard' in international law. The European standard of civilization, of course, conflicted with other societies that had their own sense of 'civilization' and 'barbarians'.[57] What is of particular interest, then, is how the European standard of civilization came to prevail over all others.[58]

Gong explains how the standard of 'civilization' was mobilized to distinguish those states that could expect sovereignty and those that could expect domination.[59] This juridical boundary between Western and non-Western states was patrolled earnestly. As Neumann and Welsh argue, the border between civilized Europe and the barbarous outside was integral to the European notion of self and Other.[60] The only non-European powers of account within nineteenth-century international discourse were those that imitated Europe: the Ottoman Empire (1856), Egypt (between 1801 and 1882), Japan and the United States.[61] The incorporation of these pseudo-Western states into the international society of Europe was the exception that proved the rule of 'civilizing', proving that it was possible for those that were not yet members to attain the status of 'civilized'.[62] There is a striking parallel between this ambivalent acceptance of non-Western states and Homi Bhabha's notion of 'passing' and colonial mimicry.[63] This distinction between civilized and barbarian spheres of International Relations had serious implications for the conduct of imperial powers in the non-European world.

A resurgence of the term 'civilization' can be found in Europe during the First and Second World Wars. 'Civilization' was mobilized in wartime propaganda as a characteristic that separated 'us' from 'them' – and every side employed the rhetoric. A decline of the use of the term 'civilization' in popular and academic culture accompanied the process of decolonization and the loss of European self-confidence.[64] Civilizations have received some attention by world systems theorists, but this perspective is chiefly concerned with the expansion of global capital. Jackson's criticism of this perspective as being essentialist is persuasive. Huntington's now (in)famous 'clash of civilizations' thesis from 1993 represents the resurgence of the interest in 'civilizations'. While Huntington's use of the civilizational concept has been recently examined, the imperialist echoes of this move have been largely unexamined.

In sum, while the meanings of 'civilization' have shifted according to the ideological needs of the dominant groups, it has always represented a standard that determines the boundary of a particular, often European, community. However, the specific permutations of this rhetoric illuminate the structure of the changing European identity over the past 200 years. Also, because so much of the civilized/barbarian rhetoric has been aimed at a popular audience, tracing the changing meanings of 'civilization' illustrates the potential of popular representations of international relations for critical IR theory.

BARBARIANS

Problem: Where are the barbarians *of the twentieth century?*[65]

Etymologically, the term 'barbarians' has its origins in the Greek description of foreigners whose speech was incomprehensible to them.[66] 'Barbarians' could not participate in Greek speech, which was the foundation of logic, philosophy and politics – and as such could not participate in the *polis*. Euripides indicates three uses of the term barbarian: '(1) unintelligible, (2) foreign, non-Greek referring simply to nationality, (3) foreign, with some implication of inferiority. This third sense coincides with the intensification of national consciousness and the corresponding hostility towards outsiders that arose during the struggle with Persia.'[67] Kristeva traces the history of the term 'barbarian', with extremely interesting results. Specifically, the meaning of 'barbarian' varies with Greek politics and is coded from its inception in gendered and national terms.[68] Aristotle describes barbarians as 'slaves by nature', which in turn legitimates imperial expansion.[69] As such, the trope of the barbarian was tied at its inception to concepts of self, nation and empire. 'Barbarians' are always described in relation to a standard of civilization, and are always defined in relation to a 'lack' of civilization. Barbarity is the mirror to civilization. As such, the 'barbarian' is gendered (as either masculine, androgynous or feminine), sexualized (a lack of sexual restraint or perversion), capitalized (as ignorant of capitalism and the class system, but wily and dishonest once introduced), surveyed (inscrutable, but controllable through statistics, demography and surveillance), indistinguishable (numerous and lacking individuality) and dangerous (both through open revolt and covert subversion of individuals). These tropes may be implicit or explicit, but conditioned much imperial and metropolitan behaviour.

While introducing the history of this trope, I want to reaffirm Bhabha's argument regarding repetition. Bhabha argues that colonial discourse rested on a foundation of philosophical fixity – which ironically requires constant repetition of the stereotype. Bhabha makes specific reference to the tropes of the 'noble savage' and the 'lustful Turk' to which I would add the 'barbarian'.[70]

During the Middle Ages, following ancient Greco-Roman symbolism, 'barbarians' were equated with the 'Other' of Christendom. This dichotomy was reified during the Renaissance, most often using the stereotype of the 'Turk' in *exhortatio ad bellum contra barbaros*. In Neumann's analysis of the evolution of the 'Turk' in the European imaginary, he notes a common feature of this rhetoric is that 'a logic of culture exists and must take precedence over a logic of *raison d'état*'.[71] Renaissance thinkers drew distinctions between Scythian barbarians of Central Asia and the 'monsters' internal to the wilds of Europe (or outside Europe), but used both terms.[72] It is important to remember that 'barbarians' and 'monsters', the 'Others' of Europe, are not just external. Jews, Sinti and Roma (Gypsies), and Eastern Europeans are each constituted as 'Other' from mainstream European identity, and, as such, are often the object of the 'barbarian' or 'savage' stereotypes.[73] Neumann and Wolff both provide excellent historical studies of how Eastern Europeans in particular are constituted as marginal members of European society and how that marginal identity functions to shore the identity of Europe itself.[74]

In part the separation of the 'barbaric' from the 'savage' coincided with the growing secularization of the European states system and of European states themselves. The term 'savages' first came to be applied in the sixteenth century. The 'Other' of Europe ceased to be defined in primarily religious terms during the fifteenth and sixteenth centuries.[75] The terms 'barbaric' and 'savage' are used all but interchangeably from the sixteenth century until the eighteenth century. In the eighteenth century, we see how 'savage' and 'barbarian' come to represent different 'Others'.

Information and images about non-European societies proliferated in utopias, dystopias, fiction, plays and epistolary novels and became extremely popular throughout the seventeenth and eighteenth centuries.[76] The exotic 'East' became a receptacle for European ideas – both about itself and its 'Others'. In describing its 'Other', either as superior or inferior to Europe, representations of the 'East' were used to elaborate the identity of Europe. The distinction between 'savages' and 'barbarians' has two chief sources. The first is the growth of knowledge about other non-European civilizations and societies and the systematization of that knowledge. The second comes from a 'four-stages' model of societal development, based on subsistence relations, popularized by Scottish and French theorists in the eighteenth century.

It is also important to look at the evolution of the notion of the 'savage'. While 'barbarian' has been a staple – if not stable – stereotype since Herodotus, the stereotype of the 'savage' is of relatively recent origin. 'Savages', coming from the Latin word for a wood (*silva*), was first used to represent men who lived in the German forests without any organized society. The 'savage' was conceived as either 'noble' or 'ignoble' – as either uncorrupted by 'civilized' manners and thus closer to the natural state or as entirely unrestrained by 'civility' and thus closer to an animal state.[77] Whether 'noble' or 'ignoble' – peaceful or violent – the 'savage' lived without the benefit of society and European 'civility'. The 'ignoble' savage was viewed as justification for the civilizing mission. The Romantics used the position of the 'noble' savage to criticize European civilization.[78] The 'savage' was represented both as an ancestor of the European and as an internal, primitive part of the psyche of a European.

Europe did not have a long-standing relationship to America in the way that Asia had existed in its historical imaginary. As such, with the discovery of the New World, the 'savages' encountered by the first explorers were symbolically *sui generis*. This is not to imply that Europe did not have a source of images to project on the native Americans. The description of 'savages' in the New World often coincided with ancient descriptions of 'monsters' – mermaids, dog-headed men, etc.[79] Todorov's *Conquest of America* looks precisely at representations of native Americans to elaborate a general theory of 'Otherness' because it was an 'extreme, and exemplary, encounter' with the Other.[80] However, we should note that 'the American savage' was *not* an overdetermined site on which to project the European view of itself. Those thinkers who regarded European 'civilization' well, condemned the 'savagery' of the Native Americans. Thinkers like Rousseau, Montaigne and Montesquieu, who viewed the benefits of 'civilization' with more scepticism, were more laudatory of society with civilized decadence.

Montaigne's 'On cannibals' and 'On the custom of wearing clothes', published in French in 1580 and in English in 1603, illustrate the critical potential of 'savages'.[81] In 'On cannibals', Montaigne argues: 'we are justified in calling [cannibals] barbarians by reference to the laws of reason, but not in comparison with ourselves, who surpass them in every kind of barbarity'.[82] Exemplary of 'positive' Orientalism, Montaigne says, 'I do not believe . . . that there is anything barbarous or savage about them, except that we all call barbarous anything that is contrary to our own habits.'[83] As Gong points out, this observation was lost on eighteenth-century international lawyers, who were prone to view European civilization as the only civilization that was truly 'civilized'.[84]

Montaigne specifically equates 'savages' with 'barbarians' in 'On cannibals'. However, we should note that even while Montaigne praises the natives of Brazil, he does so by representing them as markedly 'Other'. He says: 'there is a special savour and delicacy in some of the uncultivated fruits of those regions that is excellent even to our [corrupt] taste, and rivals our own'.[85] Montaigne represents 'cannibals' as noble savages, who are free from the corruption of decadent society. It is also interesting to note that Montaigne distinguishes the savages of America from the Scythians, the barbarians described in Herodotus, Pliny and Gibbon's *Decline and Fall of the Roman Empire*. Montaigne says that the cannibals do not eat the flesh of their enemies 'for nourishment as the ancient Scythians did, but as a measure of extreme vengeance'.[86] Consequently, we see the tension between the discourse of the noble savage and the Scythian barbarian, even at a time when the terms were used all but interchangeably. Further, Montaigne argues that the corporal punishments popular in France were *more* barbarous than the cannibals were. 'Savage' and 'barbaric' customs provide a ground from which to criticize contemporary French customs at which Montaigne was taking aim. This distinction between the 'savage' and the 'barbarian' illustrates the different limits of the *polis*. The savage can be displayed in exhibitions, educated to mimic the European manners. The savage is also represented as being closer to nature and as more morally pure than the decadent or corrupt 'civilized' man. The barbarians cannot be displayed or educated – they are irredeemable and dangerous. The barbarian represents the liberal project gone awry; the barbarian has been educated falsely and cannot be re-educated. These distinctions between savage and barbarian reaffirm Todorov's taxonomy of relations with the Other. The *trope* of the savage and barbarian differs along the axiological dimension of self/Other relations – the savage and barbarian are both 'bad', but the savage is redeemable (or indeed closer to nature) whereas the barbarian is beyond the pale. All 'Others' are not equal.

Montesquieu's *Persian Letters* (1721) is both a self-critique and a projection of Otherness. By voicing his critique of contemporary France in the letters of 'Persians', the author insulates himself from dangerous political retribution.[87] The *Persian Letters* is representative of the popularity of the 'East' and of the Oriental stereotypes which were to dominate the European imagination for centuries to come. Montesquieu sketches the different 'essences' of Europe and the 'East:' science v. religion, reason v. mysticism, restraint v. erotic, masculine v. feminine, industrious v. indolent.

Montesquieu illustrates the ambivalent relationship of the barbarian to Europe. The barbarian hordes at once encircle and threaten Europe; at the same time the invaders have long since been seen as a source of innovation, strength and vigour. He exhorts the Tartar who, he claims, 'truly dominates the universe . . . in every period of history it has proved its power across the earth, and in every age it has been the scourge of nations'.[88] The Turk, the barbarian, lurks outside the borders of Europe – the barbarians define Europe's borders and act both as a threat to, and a catalyst for, European civilization.[89] Descriptions of the 'barbarians' can be mobilized simultaneously to reify Europe's position as superior *and* criticize its values, mores and institutions as inferior. As Bhabha suggests, the *repetition* of the trope reaffirms the 'fixity' of European civilization.

Jean-Jacques Rousseau presents an important perspective in the praise of the 'noble savage'. He describes the life of the savage in *Émile*:

> Attached to no place, without prescribed task, obeying no one, with no other law than his will, [the savage] is forced to reason

in each action of his life. He does not make a movement, not a step, without having beforehand envisaged the consequences. Thus, the more his body is exercised, the more his mind is enlightened; his strength and his reason grow together and one is extended by the other.[90]

In fact, Rousseau's work on education can be seen as an 'antidote' to the decadence of French civilization.[91] Rousseau's *Discourse on the Origin of Language* reiterates this point.[92] In this essay, Rousseau also repeats the assumption that climate determines character, which becomes a staple of colonial rhetoric. In this section, it must suffice to indicate the wide range of scholarship on the topic.[93]

'Barbarians' are distinguished in a double move – not 'us', meaning European, and not 'them', meaning savages. Thus, the civilized/barbarian dichotomy is situated within a larger symbolic framework and European geopolitical imaginary. The division of humanity corresponds to the central themes in European identity: theology (Christianity v. monotheism/polytheism v. animism); judicial structures (rule of law v. presence v. absence); governance (democracy v. despotism v. familial); civility (European manners v. clothes v. nakedness); sexuality (restrained v. exotic v. animalistic). The table illustrates some dimensions upon which 'barbarians' are placed 'in-between' 'civilization' and 'savages'.

'Civilized'	'Barbarian'	'Savage'
Christian	Poly/monotheistic [abstract]	Animism
Rule of law	Presence of laws	Absence of rules
Democracy	Despotism	Familial
European manners	Clothes	Nakedness
Cooked food	Spicy food [raw]	Humans as food
Adult	Adolescent	Childish
Masculine	Feminine	Childlike
Restrained sexuality	Exotic sexuality	Animalistic sexuality
Sovereignty	Indirect rule	Direct colonial domination
High culture	Low culture	Nature

In making this division, I mean only to delineate my own discussion. The 'savage' – both 'noble' and 'ignoble' – has an important place in the political imaginary of Europe. In particular, the notion of a state of nature – a philosophical and anthropological 'first position' – has played a central role in European thought regarding property and property relations. Vittoria (1527), Hugo Grotius (1625) and John Locke (1690) all used the 'savages' of North America as examples of their theories of property.[94] Recent work by Edward Keene has examined the importance of property relations to International Relations.[95] However, as I have indicated, the discourse of 'barbarians' is somewhat different.

In this project, I will concentrate on 'imperial' or 'colonial' barbarians. Within the European imperial context, 'barbaric' societies were viewed as lacking the conditions of European civilization. 'Barbarians' were both feared and patronized. The presence of 'barbarians' legitimized the rhetoric of the 'civilizing mission'. However, because the barbarians were never fully civilized, imperial rhetoric had to struggle to reconcile the promise and the realities of colonial rule. Because civilization was often taken to mean a civility or restraint in social relations, the lack of restraint made the 'barbarian' both alluring and frightening. Generally, the term 'barbarians' has been applied in a negative way to individuals and societies whose actions and mores do not accord with Europe's. Postcolonial criticism, led by Edward Said, has indicated that even when the East is described positively in relation to the West, the Western source of this description reflects an inherent Orientalism.[96] Lisa Lowe's *Critical Terrains* provides an insightful and important analysis of the multiple, national Orientalisms.[97]

English School scholars provide the only major exploration within IR theory of the transition from a European to a global international society in which the civilized/barbarian discourse played a key role. Martin Wight, C.A.W. Manning and Hedley Bull were each interested in intercultural relations and mentioned barbarians specifically in their theories of world politics. Wight used 'barbarians' as an object of study in order to distinguish what he terms the three traditions of IR theory. Wight specifically described the centrality of 'barbarians' to all international societies: 'All other states-systems, including the Western in its earlier chapters, have expanded or had to defend themselves against alien pressures. Hence the designation of those outside of the states-systems as "barbarians".'[98] The identification of a states-system as 'civilized', for Wight, depends on the existence or construction of 'barbarians'. Within Anglo-Saxon realism Wight identifies positive and negative doctrines which justify imperialism, both of which are represented in popular culture: civilization has an absolute right to expand itself; barbarians have no rights.[99] The rationalist school of international theory usually sees barbarians as underdeveloped states and thus sees imperialism as part of the 'civilizing mission'.[100] The revolutionist school of international theory views the barbarians as beyond redemption. Wight makes specific reference to Kant and the limitations of perpetual peace.[101] This illustrates a dynamic within international theory and Western thought in general: dialectic between cosmopolitan and communitarian notions of community. Bull and Watson point to this tension in their introduction: 'In the European tradition ideas of a universal law of nations or law of nature were contested by doctrines of a fundamental division of humanity between Greeks and barbarians, Christians and infidels, Europeans and non-Europeans.'[102] Though the division between 'us' and 'them' remains 'common to all forms of human interactions', the status of the 'Other' is variable.[103] Cosmopolitan thinkers view the world as united in its humanity; communitarians view the world as divided naturally into groups. Cosmopolitans, therefore, believe that all can be educated to cosmopolitanism. The communitarian, however, may believe that the outsiders are often irredeemable. Thus, the distinction between 'savage' and 'barbarian' became important as to the degree of assimilation/integration/marginalization the colonial subjects could expect from their European masters.

The rhetoric of the 'civilizing mission' shows the result of this tension. On the one hand, the civilizing mission is to enlighten and lift up other peoples to the freedom, knowledge, wealth and security of Europeans. On the other hand, the barbarian was often represented as so beyond redemption that all efforts to improve his condition would be met with frustration, borne out by his inferior status and his resistance to European civilization. In both cases, acculturation was a major aspect of the transition. Whether acculturation made colonized subjects 'better' or merely 'controllable' does not affect the process of cultural imperialism, which accompanied the military expansion.

The site of the 'barbarian' in popular culture reveals intersections of cultural, political and ideological discursive structures. Barbarians are most often the locus of anxiety. The lack of restraint which they are represented as possessing in the sexual, political and military realms is assumed to endow them with more power than the restraint of the Europeans.[104] Whether or not the 'Other' of identity structures is viewed in benign terms, the 'barbarian' is never afforded the same rights as 'insiders'. Lewis and Wigen describe admirably how the geographical location of the 'East' or the 'Orient' has shifted over time.[105] The barbarian always marks the foreign, dangerous and threatening.

Because the term 'barbarian' is such a powerful image or trope, it is revealing to trace the changing groups which are described in popular and academic discourse as barbaric. In the nineteenth century, the term 'barbarian' was first applied to the 'East'.[106] However, as the Industrial Revolution created an underclass of disenfranchised, newly urbanized European peasants, the term was applied to them – reflecting the fears of the middle and upper classes.[107] The European individual also saw the 'barbarian' within, represented by Freud's description of the Id. The rhetoric of the barbarian was mobilized during both world wars, by all belligerents. The term also came to be used by anti-colonial writers to criticize Western imperial governance. The resurgence of the trope of the barbarian in contemporary discourse to describe Third World populations repeats this imperial mindset and indicates the direction from which the West perceives its chief threat. The civilized/barbarian discourse is a powerful rhetoric, and the use of this discourse in the post-Cold War era is particularly interesting. While it does highlight the continuity of the (post)colonial condition in contemporary politics, it is also being used as a tool of identity politics. The political implications of the 'naming' or presentation of 'barbarians' are seldom emancipatory. Whether looking at nineteenth-century forms of imperial warfare, twentieth-century genocides or international theories, the trope of the barbarian often represents an exclusion and dehumanization of the target group.

In sum, I use a definition of identity which represents a post-structural position: identity is taken to be constructed, contested and reified through practices of representation and performed in specific sociological, historical and political contexts. While primarily constituted by the self/Other dualism, the relationship between the self and the Other is not simply exclusion or inclusion, but involves a continual negotiation of difference and identity. This negotiation takes place at the boundaries of identity and within the sphere of culture. Following this definition, I take culture to represent the discursive field of representations in which dominant and minority discourses constitute, reify and contest identities. Using the concept of the 'popular international imaginary', I emphasize the popular over the elite culture in an attempt to redress a general neglect of the popular in the field's analysis. The remainder of this project reflects my exploration of the civilized/barbarian rhetoric. The civilized/barbarian discourse was first developed and circulated in the nineteenth century. This period of imperial expansion also corresponds to a change in both International Relations and the development of the 'modern' state.

3 Empire of Barbarians

In the nineteenth century, 'international relations' were understood as taking place either within the context of the European family of nations or between the civilized European states, 'barbaric' Others and savage lands. At times, the 'Other' was portrayed as exotic, alluring, superior to the West or even internal to the West. However, the category 'barbaric' has almost always been portrayed in negative ways and always defined in relation to, and as the absence of, 'civilization'. Even when represented positively, the figure of the barbarian implies disorder, threat, danger and the radical overthrowing of the social order. The threat of the barbarian justified European deviations from their own standard of 'civilization'. Because of the latent anxiety about the unrestrained barbarian, Europeans were loosened from the restraints of civilization in dealing with barbarians and imposing order upon them. By illustrating the unstable boundary of 'civilized' and 'barbaric' behaviour, we see the ambivalence within the discourse, and indeed within the identity, of the 'European'. It underscores the importance of the colonial scene in the nineteenth century.

The identity of Europe became tightly bound up with imperial ideologies, and the trope of the barbarian marked an intersection of several of these discourses. In part, the barbarian was represented as an external threat to European civilization. As such, it had the effect of shoring up European identity. The barbaric was also represented as an internal threat – the barbaric lower classes, minorities or inner demons of Europe. As Kiernan reports: 'There is a story of the Austrian representative saying to the Hungarian, when the Hapsburg empire was transformed into the Dual Monarchy in 1867, "You look after your barbarians, and we'll look after ours" – meaning Czechs, Serbs, and so on.'[1] The barbarian, whether in the darkest depths of Africa, the darkest depths of Central Europe or the darkest depths of London, was coded in terms of race, class and gender. The discourse of the barbarian complicates the domestic/international divide on which the glossing of imperialism rests and disrupts the order/anarchy description of these two realms.

Traditional narratives of the nineteenth century in International Relations characterize it as 'ninety-nine years of general peace in Europe after the Vienna settlements'.[2] There was a startling lack of Great Power war from the Congress of Vienna (1815) until the First World War. However, if violence committed in the periphery is taken into account, the century is not nearly as pacific as it has been portrayed. Another common theory is that violence in the imperial periphery allowed nineteenth-century European conflicts to take place elsewhere.[3]

The beginning of the nineteenth century saw the inauguration of several social and ideological trends that fundamentally changed the fabric of European international society. The French revolution spread the ideals of liberty, equality and fraternity. The industrial revolution gave rise to the globalization of capitalism, accompanied by a series of technological revolutions which made the world physically more accessible to Europeans.[4] European international society expanded its influence to encompass the globe. Traditional portrayals of this period in IR theory focus on the peace within Europe between 1814 and 1914, and the ability of the Concert of Europe to prevent the outbreak of Great Power war.[5] This is explained in classical terms, either as the triumph of balance of power dynamics or the growth of liberal interdependence. Hedley Bull and Adam Watson remind us that:

> Nor should it be overlooked that the European states, as they evolved this non-hegemonic system in their relations with one another, at the same time established a number of empires which, while they were rival and competing, taken together amounted to a European hegemony over the rest of the world, which in the nineteenth century became an immense periphery looking to a European centre.[6]

A global history, which accounts for European expansion outside of Europe, reflects a much less pacific century.[7] In the course of this expansion, Europe marked its boundaries in encounters with cultural and racial Others: civilized inside, barbarians outside. This boundary both defined and fortified European identity.[8] Gerrit Gong concurs: 'the standard of "civilization" helped define the internal identity and external boundaries of the nineteenth century's dominant international society'.[9] By looking at the barbarian as the marker of 'civilization' and Europe, I hope to introduce an additional, colonial perspective of the nineteenth century to International Relations, and illustrate the political utility of the barbarian discourse.

This chapter explores four prominent sites of the 'civilized/ barbarian' discourse. First, I will look at the connection between violence and imperial order, an important aspect of imperialism that is often overlooked in IR representations of this era. Second, I will trace the portrayal of the stereotype of the barbarian. Because the barbarian is described as dangerous, Europe attempted to impose a 'visual order' on their colonies. By 'visual order' I mean that the mode of governance was structured along lines of sight and according to a geometric systemization of power.[10] I will look at the visual order in the practices of imperialism and trace their path back to the imperial centre: specifically, the exhibitionary order and the theme of surveillance. Third, in conjunction with this visual order is a common appeal to demography and population. Fourth, I will look at the linkage made in the imperial order between race, class and gender.[11] Not only are these three discourses of race, class and gender interconnected in the nineteenth century, but the connections explain the distinctions and comparisons made between internal and external barbarians. This section focuses on popular media – notably, travelogues and the Great Exhibitions of the mid- to late nineteenth century. Popular culture was especially important because, in the nineteenth century, 'imperialism [became] a public phenomenon – which was not the case with expansion in the preceding centuries' – a move that was shored up by increasing literacy and state-sponsored education.[12] These representations of the barbarian international realm shaped the imaginary of European publics, which in turn supported imperial violence. The discourse of civilization/barbarians persists in the popular international imagination and its imperial roots are essential to the understanding of its later permutations.

PHILOSOPHERS OF BARBARISM

In the early nineteenth century, philosophers, anthropologists, biologists, geologists and other thinkers began to look at the non-European world as an object of study, not as a fantasy or a vehicle for self-criticism. The 'civilizing mission' was situated at the intersection of a number of discourses: racial theories, social Darwinist theories of evolution, economic understandings of imperialism, religious ideas about salvation and liberal theories of education. These ideas framed the 'civilizing mission', which was the central justification for imperialism. Ashis Nandy argues that, in fact, 'colonialism minus a civilizational mission is no colonialism at all'.[13] The 'civilizing mission' became the touchstone for much imperial activity, but how was it framed?

International lawyers, or publicans, had investigated the question of territory, property and sovereignty since the seventeenth century. Jean-Jacques Rousseau and John Locke both used colonial experiences of civilization and property to ground their theories of European society.[14] Others, from a Christian or cosmopolitan perspective, attempted to undermine imperial rhetoric.[15] A group of specifically anti-colonial or anti-imperial thinkers challenged the prevailing ideology. Karl Marx, J.A. Hobson, and V.I. Lenin attempted to undermine the imperial ideology on economic grounds.[16] Economic justifications of expansion had long been central to the imperial ideology. However, in the late eighteenth and nineteenth centuries, there was a move from independent trading companies with royal charters to state-sponsored colonialism. Economic advantage was also coupled with the 'civilizing mission'. As Kiernan argues, in the nineteenth century 'there was again a feeling that expansion ought to have some ideal purpose, a goal beyond sordid greed which came to be expressed in the phrase "civilizing mission". Backward lands would be given civilization, in return for the products wanted by Europe.'[17] While economic imperatives were certainly central to European expansion, I will focus in this project on the ideological/imaginary foundations of the project – the 'master dichotomy' of self/Other, civilized/barbarian that supported imperialism.

Hegel's lectures on world history and the geographical bases of history are essential to an understanding of nineteenth-century European ideas about the larger world. Hegel argues: 'The History of the World travels from East to West, for Europe is absolutely the end of History, Asia the beginning.'[18] A consequence of this geopolitical vision, which was adopted by the populace and elite alike, is that Africa is absent from History. Shiraz Dossa argues: 'in this grand design of European Reason, [history-less] nations have neither rights nor duties, in fact Hegel characterizes them as "*barbarian*" nations'.[19] Hegel speaks specifically about Africa: '*Africa* proper, as far as History goes back, has remained – for all purposes of connection with the rest of the World – shut up . . . – the land of childhood, which lying beyond the day of self-conscious history, [is] enveloped in the dark mantle of Night.'[20] These themes of light and darkness, progress and maturity, historical and history-less, resonated within imperialist ideology for the remainder of the century. Hegel's portrayal of peoples and nations devoid of history legitimated the 'civilizing mission' of the European countries whose superiority was transformed into duty. Hegel's deterministic connection between History and geography shaped the study of international relations in the nineteenth century. Dossa contends that Hegel's representations endure in the contemporary IR imaginary: 'the Third World was intellectually apprehended and appropriated as weak, chaotic, and primitive; it was assimilated into the European consciousness and practice as a cluster of inferior, exotic cultures right from the start'.[21]

Edward Said provides a cultural perspective to the study of imperialism, from which this study draws:

> We may thus consider imperialism as a process occurring as part of the metropolitan culture, which at times acknowledges, at other times obscures the sustained business of the empire itself. The important point is how the national British, French and American cultures maintained hegemony over the peripheries. How within them was consent gained and continuously consolidated for the distant rule of native peoples and territories.[22]

Edward Said's perspective on imperialism shifts our focus away from elite and Marxist perceptions of the economic expansion of proto-multinational corporations or the power balancing among the Great Powers, and towards popular support of imperial ideologies. Roxanne Lynn Doty grounds her important exploration of imperial encounters on the observation that 'the question of representation has historically been excluded from the academic study of international relations'.[23] She examines how the imperial power imbalance came to be represented and reinforced in popular discourse.[24] The 'popular international imaginary' shaped national responses to international stimuli.[25] The specific representation of the 'Other' as barbaric has specific political effects in the nineteenth century, which lay bare the knowledge/power dynamics of imperialism.

EGYPT

This section draws examples from English and French sources on Egypt, although other Anglo-French colonies will also be used.[26] Lucie Duff Gordon wrote in 1863: 'This country is a palimpsest, in which the Bible is written over Herodotus, and the Koran over that.'[27] Europe came to be written over that history. Egypt is also important because France and England, the two largest colonial powers of the period, both took considerable interest in Egypt, partly because of its geopolitical position but also because of its resources and economy.

Napoleon's invasion of 1798 is canonically accepted as the inaugural moment of Orientalism as an academic discipline and the beginning of the modern European fascination with the Orient. Said argues:

> Most historians [who] speak of empire speak of the 'age of empire' as formally beginning around 1878, with the 'scramble for Africa.' A close look at the cultural actuality reveals a much earlier, more deeply and stubbornly held view about overseas European hegemony; we can locate a coherent, fully mobilized system of ideas near the end of the eighteenth century, and there follows the set of integral developments such as the first great systematic conquests under Napoleon . . .[28]

Alice Conklin states: 'in Egypt . . . the mission was defined – in Napoleon's own words – as one of emancipation and "civilization". This idea was manifest in Napoleon's decision to set off from France not only with troops, but with all the scientific and cultural apparatus for which the expedition is deservedly famous – an apparatus that the French had not deemed necessary for any European state they had conquered.'[29]

As several critics have pointed out, Said represents Orientalism as a monolithic academic discourse, which is uncontested and homogeneous.[30] However, English and French experiences, and English and French Orientalisms, are not identical. The differences are the subject of an important work by Lisa Lowe.[31] She points out that Orientalist discourse changed over time and is better understood as a multiple discourse which participated in any number of ideological and material struggles.[32]

The extent to which Egypt entered the European imagination is also evident in the attention that Hegel devotes to it. In the *Philosophy of History* lectures of 1823, Hegel argued: 'The Empire of the solitary Nile is only present *beneath* the ground, in its speechless Dead . . . in their majestic habitations; – for what remains above ground is nothing else but splendid tombs.'[33] Africa is the continent without History; Asia the continent of History past. Europe is the end of History. Egypt is the fulcrum of the passage of History. Mindful of this notion, the Khedive Ismail announced at the opening of the Suez Canal, 'Egypt is henceforth part of Europe, not Africa.'[34] However, as with all colonial mimicry, it never quite succeeded in *passing* as a European state. Kiernan argues: 'Egypt was the theatre of a thorough-going experiment, the first in all the East, in Westernization by decree . . . There was much debate among foreigners, sharpened by rival interests, as to whether the new Egypt was a *bona fide* imitation of Europe, or a grotesque travesty of it.'[35] Huntington later refers to the tension of a Westernized elite and non-Western populace as a 'torn' country. This early Westernization may also give an insight into the post-independence dilemma of postcolonial states in the 1960s. Egypt's propinquity to Europe made it accessible, while remaining strange, exotic and Oriental. Napoleon's invasion was well documented and became a point of French pride. The British expedition effectively made Egypt an autonomous province of the Ottoman Empire. The opening of the Suez Canal in 1869 made Egypt the access point to India. The occupation in 1882 was coincident with British expansion in Africa. The Suez crisis of 1956 was a catalyst for the first peacekeeping mission of the United Nations. Even in light of the terrorist attacks in 1997 and 2001, Egypt remains present in Europe's imagination, outside and yet familiar; a 'land of ruins', which presages the future.[36] The concept of 'barbarian' grows to its maturity in Egypt. The European boundary in Egypt is written in racial, class-based, gendered, geographical and cultural terms – embodied in the image of the barbarian. The chief characteristic of the barbarian stereotype is *his* propensity for irrational violence, which the Europeans both feared and respected.

MAXIMS AND THE MAXIM GUN: VIOLENCE AND THE IMPERIAL ORDER

The violence inherent in the colonial project undermines traditional IR narratives of a pacific nineteenth century. Violence was not only present in the conquest of colonial territories, but also manifest in those already conquered territories. Political leaders have long been able to refer to palpable threats in the immediate international environment to justify violence in the domestic societies of Europe.[37] However, a different representation of threat was needed to legitimate war with one's own colonial subjects. There was a pressing need to explain the long-drawn-out resistance to the light of civilization, such as the British defeat in Sudan, the Boer War, the Indian Mutiny or the Algerian Civil War and unrest in Indochina. The extent to which imperialism was viewed as continual warfare, either expansive or defensive, is evidenced by the fact that the British government had a single department for the Colonies and War from 1794 to 1854.[38]

The barbarian stereotype was represented as not merely ignorant of civilization, but also as antagonistic and destructive towards it. One of the chief benefits of 'civilization' and imperial rule was the supposed elimination of violence in everyday society – which lies at the root of the discourse of civilization – the principle of civility.[39] Kiernan argues: 'To be bringing order out of such chaos could be regarded as justification enough for British conquest, if any were asked for; Order was from first to last the grand imperial watchword.'[40] In French colonies too, 'French imperial ideology consistently identified civilization with one principle more than any other: mastery. Master not of other peoples – although ironically this would become one of civilization's prerogatives in the age of democracy; rather, master of nature, including the human body, and master of what can be called "social behaviour".'[41] Civil peace, the hallmark of imperial rule, was continually contested by the oppressed and thus necessitated constant policing. It is this unstable balance which I want to highlight here. Within the discourse of imperialism, there is a tension between the violence that was necessary to justify imperial rule and the omnipresent threat of violence implicit in imperial governance.

The image of the barbarian clearly illustrates this tension. Barbarians were, by nature, violent and irrational. Imperial rule, though violent itself, was rational and justified by the 'civilizing mission'. Massacres committed by 'natives' were portrayed as barbaric; massacres committed by imperial rulers were portrayed as regrettable, but in the final account necessary. Novelists, among others in the nineteenth century, popularized the contrast between 'barbaric' violence and 'civilized' violence.[42] Joseph Conrad's *Heart of Darkness* shows the limit of this distinction: Kurtz, the pride of Europe, ends his report with the infamous command to 'Exterminate the brutes.'[43] The discourse of civilization represents an attempt to stabilize this tension, through representations of the barbarian. If the 'civilized' administrator and the barbarian were inherently different, then their violence could have different values.[44] Indeed, that tension was present from the beginning. Kiernan argues that while British and French armies began under the sign of 'civilization', the European also learned barbarism.[45] 'If conquest was doing something to civilize the outer world, it was also doing something to barbarize Europe . . . One sinister omen was a recrudescence in Europe of police torture, whose taproots in colonial warfare and repression can scarcely be missed.'[46] The ambivalence, uncertainty and insecurity were characteristic of the colonial experience. Homi Bhabha's postcolonial theory has usefully explored this ambivalence to provide a more nuanced, if dense, understanding of the material and psychic conditions of colonialism.[47]

The insecurity was expressed in terms of the stereotype of the barbarian: the threat of violence, indolence and sexual/racial mingling. The barbarian was seen as a threat not only to order, but also to the regimes of capitalism and race. Stoler details the regimens of hygiene and manners that were instigated to prevent English men and women from 'going native' in India.[48] In another study, she details how racial (im)purity became a barrier to Dutch citizenship, colonial government posts and inheritance.[49] The same point is made, through the literary portrayal of the social restrictions of colonial life, in Orwell's *Burmese Days*, E.M. Forster's *Passage to India* and Graham Greene's *Heart of the Matter*. Barbarism was also seen as a threat to the European, either as the administrator-gone-native or as the barbaric lower classes portrayed in racial terms. However, through policing, regulation and surveillance, the colonies were constructed as special, intermediate zones of controllable violence, where order could be imposed – however tenuously – by a more civilized culture. The traditional narrative of international theory and the realities of colonial rule seem to be at odds. At the very moment of a consolidation of a European identity, domesticated colonies were more violent than 'anarchic' European international space.

Even when the European rule in the colonies was 'secure', the threat of violence was omnipresent.[50] Ronald Hyam cites an anonymous writer in 1898: 'there was no power in the hands of those that governed India or Africa . . . to resist a general effort of the population to throw the white races out. In such a situation the only course was "to rule, as completely and with as little repentance, as if we were angels appointed to that task".'[51] This general fear of war, or the threat of war, necessitated constant preparedness.[52]

Traditional IR explanations of international anarchy map well onto descriptions of imperial rule. Citing Hobbes, Kenneth Waltz asserts that anarchy is not only the actual state of war between units, but 'with each state deciding for itself whether or not to use force, war may break out at any time'.[53] IR theory traditionally distinguishes between the anarchy of the international and the peace of the domestic. I would suggest that in the context of nineteenth-century Europe the divide between international anarchy and imperial 'peace' is even more problematic. The possibility of the 'good life' is repeatedly deferred in the colonial scene.

Between the Great Powers, there was little conflict between 1814 and 1914.[54] As a consequence, the balance of power system embodied in the Concert of Europe is hailed for keeping the peace.[55] This is not to deny that some European conflicts were violent or barbaric in themselves. It is only to argue that International Relations neglects to portray imperialism as a violent process or colonial governance as institutionalized violence. It also largely ignores the 'anarchical' condition of European rule in the colonies. While violence in the colonies was not incessant, there was certainly the continual threat of violence. Colonial rule was never absolute; imperial security was always uncertain. Imperial governments were always preparing for war against their native subjects, in addition to preparing for war against other European states. Of course, the threat of violence of the international realm and the threat of violence in the colonial realm are not identical, but certain parallels are compelling.

There are two relevant aspects to imperialist strategy in the nineteenth century: the acquisition of 'new' territory and the control of occupied territory. The acquisition of 'new' territory was seen as an entirely European game, regulated by European rules and played out in non-Western space. Gong argues:

> the practice of bothering at all to create international legal agreements with 'uncivilized' countries was justified as necessary to maintain law and order in the 'civilized' international society ... when a 'civilized' power makes a legal agreement concerning 'uncivilized' peoples, its title is an affair between the occupying European state and the rest of the 'civilized' states of the world.[56]

The Berlin Conference of 1884–85 is emblematic of this structure, though the Brussels Conference of 1889–90 and the League of Nations Mandate system continued it.[57] The European powers convened in Berlin to divide Africa in order to prevent conflict among themselves, which reversed nearly two centuries of viewing the space beyond Europe as entirely war-ridden.[58] Watson mistakenly infers a 'remarkable achievement' from a lack of European war to indicate of a lack of war generally in the nineteenth century.[59] In fact, Watson ignores colonial violence in what we now recognize as wars of a 'third kind'.[60] The 'remarkable achievement' of the reduction of intra-European war was predicated on the externalization of violence to the non-European world. With the inclusion of colonial wars, the record of the nineteenth century becomes far less peaceful.

BARBARIC WARFARE

The legal norms surrounding 'civilized' warfare did not apply in the barbarian, non-European world. The mobilization of the civilized/barbarian discourse makes the difference between European and colonial wars clear. Jürgen Osterhammel argues: 'colonial wars were viewed as wars to spread "civilization" to adversaries who were said to lack civilized rules of conduct ... Methods of warfare that in Europe were morally and legally barred were considered legitimate in the face of an enemy who did not seem to subscribe to the same cultural code.'[61] Kiernan concurs:

> Europe was fond of parading its concept of 'civilized warfare', but in contests overseas it was 'scientific warfare' that was being

talked of more and more . . . As conquest quickened, a book on it would introduce Africa as a continent delivered from native barbarism by breech-loaders, Maxims, etc. . . . and go on to hail any mass slaughter by the latest weapon as a 'deadly blow dealt at barbarism; a triumph gained for humanity and civilization'. Civilization drove forward in a mortuary cart.[62]

The notorious Maxim gun and dumdum bullet or the French *Coloniale* bomber, developed specifically for colonial use, were technologies considered too horrific to use against Europeans.[63] This, of course, was to prove a major aspect of the disillusionment brought about by the First World War. There are many examples of the 'uncivilized' behaviour of European troops in the colonies. Two notable incidents indicate the 'barbarity' of Europeans breaking their own codes of 'civilized' warfare in the colonies: the asphyxiation of over 500 Arab fugitive men, women and children by the French military commander Pélissier in the Dahna caves in 1845,[64] and the massacre, and subsequent desecration, by the English of the Sudanese Madhi and his forces, who had slaughtered General Gordon in Khartoum.

From both the colonized and colonizer points of view, the threat in the colonies was dispersed and continual: the colonized feared state and extra-governmental violence just as the colonizers feared uprising and rebellion. Michael Mann explores the extent to which militarism was a part of the civil society in the European colonies. In the colonies, there was not a 'governmental' monopoly on the legitimate use of force. He argues: 'most atrocities were committed in a series of irregular, decentralised waves organised in paramilitary forms by vigilante or volunteer units of the local [white] population itself, with states turning a blind eye or with its local agents complicit because they too belonged to "White" civil society'.[65] War in the colonies substituted the 'civilizing mission' for *raison d'état*, which liberated Europeans from the restraints of the rules of 'civilized' warfare.

The expansion of European society was not a uniform or uncontested process. The resistance of indigenous peoples to European domination continues to this day, and that uneven expansion determined the political culture of much of the globe.[66] This violent history, though it may have been legalistically domestic to each of the European empires, resonates in the international imaginary of the Third World.

The uncertain rule of the colonies made violence and the threat of violence an integral part of European imperial relations. However, the tenor of the rule of colonies that took place was different from European governance. The control of conquered territories was different, if only because the legitimacy that the European state had fostered domestically was uncertain in the colonies. In India, 'The British [saw] themselves as a garrison in a country which could still explode into disorder and revert to the civil war of the eighteenth century if their central power was removed.'[67] In Algeria, the French rarely achieved complete control of the territory they claimed. In Egypt, passports and model villages were used to attempt to monitor and control the colonial population.[68] Order was the goal of colonial rule, but constant policing was required because its application was so incomplete. The image of the barbarian helped resolve this paradox; the barbarian could be only partly tamed and educated, but racially he was still closer to the savage than the European. The colonizer was, then, constantly on his guard from insurrection and degradation. This siege mentality would persist until independence and led to methods of control, which were later exported back into the European metropolis.

The connection between order and violence is also seen in scientific and military operations in the empire. The projects of Orientalism as an academic discipline and imperialism as a political practice were intertwined; just as violence and order were intertwined. Some of the first descriptions of Egypt came from Napoleon's invasion and the Institut de Kaïre that he founded. Marc Ferro argues: 'Bonaparte's expedition to Egypt represents the change from one type of expansion to another. Bonaparte wanted to show that he was landing with an army which represented *civilization*.'[69] Vivant Denon published his *Travels in Upper and Lower Egypt* in 1803, which preceded the larger, 23-volume work of the Institute by several years (1809–23). The *Déscriptions de L'Egypte* heralded a new era of 'authenticity' about the East, rather than fantasy. However, it should be noted that the illustrations of Egyptian monuments are all but devoid of 'real' Egyptians and resemble empty theatrical stages waiting for European players.[70] The extent to which early writers were complicit in military and governmental structures is striking. In the preface, Denon writes how his position as observer was often forgotten in the heat of battle:

Being aware that the aim of my travels was to visit the monuments of Upper Egypt, [Napoleon] sent me with the division which was to achieve the conquest of that territory . . . In short, I made so truly a part of the battalion it formed, and within which I had in a manner taken up my abode, that I was frequently in the heat of action without recollecting myself, and without reflecting that war was foreign to my avocations.[71]

In fact, war was not foreign to the Orientalist. The British, in their expedition to liberate Egypt from the French, were quick to publish their own account of Egypt. Thomas Walsh snidely remarks on the relative security of his own position as observer in relation to Denon:

The work is accompanied by forty-one plates, including upwards of fifty subjects, most of them Drawings made by the Author with the utmost attention to correctness. Taken in perfect security, and with all the necessary deliberation; they are, at least, not the hasty sketches of a solitary traveler, who holds pencil with a trembling hand . . . [72]

Such fear for personal safety resonated for the duration of colonial occupation, as did the connection between Orientalism and colonial rule.

The threat of violence was also implicated in other realms of European colonial life: sexual threat, indolence, miscegenation and cultural contamination. The threat of disorder was also seen as the threat of cultural contamination, and consequently a threat to European identity. Insecurity and disorder were conditions of colonial rule. The relationship of order to disorder in the colonies is not a straightforward presence/absence dichotomy, but is similar to the IR formulation of anarchy as the threat of war. Disorder is not solely the absence of order, just as peace is not solely the absence of violence. Disorder is the state of being threatened with disrupted order. As such, order is not a transitory condition, but a structure that regulates expectations and behaviour. The imperial threat of violence and disorder was not the fear of specific instances, but that perpetual fear of uprising which stemmed from the colonizer's tenuous physical position.[73] Conklin argues that the 'civilizing mission' was instrumental in dealing with this problem:

Administrators – vastly outnumbered, and equipped with little more than their prejudices – relied upon the familiar categories of 'civilization' and its inevitable opposite, 'barbarism', to justify and maintain their hegemony overseas. These categories served to structure how officials thought about themselves as rulers and the people whom they ruled, with complex and often contradictory consequences for French colonial policy – and French republican identity – in the twentieth century.[74]

Disorder, like the threat of violence, was a condition of imperial rule.

I have suggested in this section that the problem of violence in the imperial order complicates the domestic/international divide, with its descriptions of order and anarchy, and that violence was implicit in Europe rule. In the next section, I will look at one of the primary ways in which French and English rulers in the empire attempted, never completely successfully, to maintain order through surveillance and the application of visual order to the barbarians, and eventually, to the civilized as well.

'I SPY WITH MY LITTLE EYE': VISUALITY AND THE IMPERIAL ORDER

Regimes of governance in the nineteenth century took a decidedly visual turn, by which I mean the structuring of space to enable visibility as a mode of control became a central motif of the nineteenth century. The application of visuality as a principle of colonial rule helps make clear the relationship between cultural practices and political power. The primary mechanism that England and France used to combat the uncertainty of colonial rule and the constant threat of violence was an economy of space structured around the principle of surveillance. This shift can be seen in three themes: surveillance, demography and exhibition.

The modern state developed in conjunction with, and was partly a function of, mechanisms of surveillance. A surveillance regime has as its goal the policing action of the state internalizing in the mind of the citizen. Crime is conceptually linked to punishment, and thus state governance becomes centred on deterrence rather than on punishment. Foucault charts this development:

When you have thus formed the chain of ideas in the heads of your citizens, you will then be able to pride yourselves on guiding them and being their masters . . . a true politician binds [his slaves] by the chain of their own ideas . . . on the soft fibers of the brain is founded the unshakable base of the soundest Empires.[75]

Surveillance entails the ordering of social space along the lines of authoritative sight, as seats bolted to face the teacher in a classroom.[76] Policing through a visual ordering of bodies on a Cartesian plane is illustrated in Foucault's exemplary institution the panopticon. Jeremy Bentham designed the panopticon to be the perfect mechanism for the control of bodies. The structure, which can be used in prisons, schools or factories, applies utilitarian principles of maximization of utility to lines of sight. The surveyed are arrayed in transparent cells, displayed before an obscured guard in an opaque tower. Bentham argues that the power of the panopticon is in the indeterminacy of the observer: if the observed never know when they are watched, they will assume that they are always watched. Thus, surveillance can be understood as an economy of power, the result of which is self-policing. Foucault states: 'the perfection of power should tend to render its actual exercise unnecessary . . . hence the major effect of the Panopticon: to induce in the inmate a sense of consciousness and permanent visibility that assures the automatic functioning of power'.[77] The panoptic principle was generalized to society, creating what Foucault terms the disciplinary society.[78] This metaphor has clear applications to the models of balance of power in international relations, wherein Great Power regulation becomes self-regulation in the context of international institutions and globalization. The concept of 'discipline' also supplements theories of deterrence which rely on intent and rationality.[79] For the moment, I will concentrate on the application of this surveillance regime to the colonies, and to European, imperial metropolises.

The genealogy of the panopticon is particularly interesting with respect to imperialism. It was Bentham's brother who first discovered a panoptic institution in the Ottoman Empire.[80] It is ironic that the architectural configuration, which epitomized European power for Foucault, was found in the Sultan's Palace of Justice, in Constantinople.[81] Further, panoptic institutions were most often constructed in the colonies. Colonial power used this economy of power through lines of sight and the ordering of space to make the natives police themselves. It was an extension of European modes of dealing with the poor, the insane, the perverse and the criminal to the colonial races.

The strangeness of the Orient was refracted through this prism of perspective and order. Part of what distinguished barbarous from civilized spheres was the visual disorder that presented itself to Europeans. This theme of visuality is reinforced by what Timothy Mitchell terms the 'exhibitionary order': the presentation of the world through pictures, artifacts, tours and world exhibitions in ways that naturalize structures of surveillance. Foucault himself did not trace this principle to the colonies,[82] but Mitchell has applied this framework to Egypt.[83] The disorder of the colonies was seen as further justification for imperial rule, and Europeans imposed a Cartesian order on colonial space. One of the other legalistic markers of the standard of civilization, in addition to the rule of law, was 'an organized bureaucracy with some efficiency in running state machinery . . .'[84] Visual disorder, or chaos, was seen as a marker of barbarism.

Denon, travelling with the French army, Walsh, who chronicled the British campaign, Lane in the 1830s, Gustave Flaubert and Richard Burton in the middle of the century, *all* describe approaching Cairo from the Nile in the same way – chaotic and unseeable, and consequently described as politically, culturally and racially unstable. An elevated perspective, either racial or spatial, was the only remedy to chaos:

> In our present position we saw numerous minarets surrounding Mount Katam, and proceeding from the gardens on the banks of the Nile, whilst Old Cairo, Bulac and Roda, appearing as part of the town gave it an appearance of verdure and freshness, and added to its magnificence. As we approached, however, the illusion vanished; every object returning as it were to its proper place, we only saw a heap of villages collected near an arid rock.[85]

> The streets are unpaved, and most of them are narrow and irregular . . . By a stranger who merely passed through the street Cairo would be regarded as a very close and crowded city, but that this is not the case is evident to a person who overlooks the town from the top of a lofty house or from the minaret of a mosque.[86]

> The numerous villages on both banks . . . have at a distance a

very pretty appearance; and the minarets of the mosques, with which they all abound, improve the prospect, from their light and airy structure. But, as you approach nearer, the beauty gradually disappears; and when you arrive opposite them, they offer nothing to the view but an assemblage of miserable half-ruined houses.[87]

Each detail reaches out to grip you; it pinches you; and the more you concentrate on it the less you grasp the whole. Then gradually all this becomes harmonious and the pieces fall into place themselves, in accordance with the laws of perspective.[88]

In the face of such disorder, Europeans sought to impose the visual order of Europe. At the same time that Georges Haussmann was constructing the boulevards of Paris, the Egyptians were doing the same in Cairo. It was a natural outgrowth of the visual nature of security that the British and French made the disorder of the colonies observable and thus controllable. Mitchell writes:

the disorder of Cairo and other cities had suddenly become visible. The urban space in which Egyptians moved had become a political matter, material to be organised by the construction of great thoroughfares radiating out from the geographical and political centre. At the same moment Egyptians themselves, as they moved through this space, became similarly material, their minds and bodies thought to need discipline and training. The space, the minds, and the bodies all materialised at the same moment, in a common economy of order and discipline.[89]

The visual chaos of the East obscured the inhabitants. Colonial space itself undermined European rule. The attempt to render the colonies and their inhabitants visible was, of course, incomplete.

The corollary implication of this visual order was the obsession with obscured bodies, people who could not be seen;[90] in Foucault's words, 'Visibility is a trap.'[91] The unsurveilled, the uncharted, the uncatalogued were not under the control of the empire, and were thus a source of disorder. The notion of barbarians being invisible accompanied this. Portrayed as wild and uncivilized, colonies were not safe if the barbarian could not be seen. The use of passports both to certify racial heritage and control movement illustrates the dangers of differences that could not be seen by

Europeans.[92] Stoler notes how a discourse of 'degeneracy' connected race and culture to citizenship.[93] It is interesting to note that by the middle of the nineteenth century, the passport had ceased to be used in Europe, but was resurrected in the colonies as a means of controlling the native population.[94] The passport as a marker of identity also made it unnecessary for the European administrator to differentiate between colonized individuals – which reaffirmed his own identity as a differentiated member of the white, ruling class.

A common comparison between the colour of the natives' skin and the earth invokes the danger of the unobserved or uncharted, and the hostility ascribed to nature itself. Flaubert observes: 'the colour of the earth is exactly that of the Nubian women I saw in the slave market'.[95] The use of the skin as racially marked is taken up by Fanon, Bhabha and other postcolonial theorists. Cartographic expeditions were an attempt to fix unknown spaces, taming the earth as quinine tamed nature.[96] Said argues: 'the geographical space of the Orient was penetrated, worked over, taken hold of. The cumulative effect of decades of . . . Western handling turned the Orient from alien into colonial space.'[97] Benedict Anderson links map-making to this larger discourse of order:

> European-style maps worked on the basis of a totalizing classification . . . the entire planet's curved surface had been subjected to a geometrical grid which squared off empty seas and unexplored regions in measured boxes. The task of 'filling in' the boxes was to be accomplished by explorers, surveyors, and military forces. They were on the march to put space under the same surveillance which the census-makers were trying to impose on persons.[98]

The imposition of geometric orders onto the towns, houses and institutions in the colonies was an effort to make the entire population visible. 'The legible order of the model village would overcome this kind of inaccessibility, this problem of a population and a way of life invisible to the observation of police.' As Foucault writes: 'in such ways the architecture of distribution and the art of policing can acquire a hold over individuals not simply by confining them but by opening up and inscribing what is hidden, unknown, and inaccessible'.[99] It was the condition of empire that this would always be incomplete.

The discourse of surveillance/obscurity had an interesting side-effect. By the middle of the century, Europeans had begun to perceive Lower Egypt as 'civilized' and thus inauthentic. The European in search of the 'authentic' experience took to disguising himself as 'Oriental' to get to the true Orient, hidden from the tourist eyes of the European. Ali Behdad calls this attitude 'sentimental' Orientalism, which despairs at the proliferation of tourists in favour of the 'true' Orient.[100] The European use of disguise has a tradition stemming from the first chroniclers of Egypt through to the present day: Burckhardt (1788), Lane (1834), Burton (1852) and even Kaplan (1994). Being unseen allowed Europeans freedom from civilized moral codes and enabled European travellers to revel in their Orientalist fantasies. These fantasies were markedly sexual for Flaubert[101] and cartological for Burton: '[I sought a place] which no vacation tourist has yet described, measured, sketched, and photographed.'[102] Flaubert elaborates the tension between his desire for authenticity and the desire for safety: 'We look quite the pair of Orientals [however] considerations of our safety limit our sartorial splurges: in Egypt the European is accorded greater respect than the native, so we won't dress up completely until we reach Syria.'[103] This ability to disguise oneself as the cultural and racial 'Other' is a function of the power relationship of European occupation. While Europeans could pass as natives, natives could never pass as Europeans.[104] Just as Egypt was not seen as a Western nation but rather a grotesque travesty of Europe, Europeanized Egyptians were considered objects of mimicry.[105] This was certainly true of Fanon's personal experience, and is described by Bhabha as 'almost the same, but not quite'.[106] Bhabha also explores the ambivalence of mockery and imitation as a practice of resistance to colonial rule.[107] Postcolonial theorists argue this power dynamic and consequent prejudice is present in contemporary race relations. The way in which world exhibitions were used to represent the colonies and the colonized to the metropolitan population provides further evidence of the power of this discourse.[108] The world exhibitions displayed the world for consumption by the metropolitan citizens, in terms of race, geography and capitalism.

EUROPEAN EXHIBITIONS

The extension of this visible, exhibitionary order is also apparent within metropolitan European culture. World exhibitions were displays of industry, culture and empire for the imperial population. The exhibitions were representations of the world on a grand scale, global in scope, nationalist in tone and pedagogical in intent. They reflected the mutually constituting ideologies of consumerism, nationalism and imperialism. The exhibitions were intended to educate the public in the products of the industrial revolution and imperial expansion, both of which had negative side-effects that needed to be obscured. Also, the exhibitions had a nation-building intent – to represent the nation to itself.[109] The civilizing mission was central to the display of cultures in hierarchical fashion, Europeans representing the end of progress and other races representing earlier evolutionary epochs.[110]

McClintock argues that this exhibitionary order displays peoples as evidence of a Hegelian progression of history. 'The axis of time was projected onto the axis of space and history became global. With social Darwinism, the taxonomic project, first applied to nature, was now applied to cultural history. Time became a geography of social power.'[111] And the metropolitan masses flocked to see the spectacle. Eric Hobsbawm marks a convergence between the expansion of tourism within European countries for the poor and to the Orient for the rich:

> The day trip for the masses . . . was the child of the 1850s – to be more precise of the Great Exhibition of 1851 . . . Thomas Cook himself, whose name was to become a by-word for organized tourism in the next twenty-five years, had begun his career arranging such outings and developed it into big business in 1851. The numerous International Expositions each brought its army of sightseers and the rebuilding of capital cities encouraged the provincials to sample their wonders.[112]

In this way, we see a parallel in the imperialist representation of colony to metropolis and the nationalist representation of rural to urban. The nationalist intent of these exhibitions connected to class- and race-based discourses. These strategies helped to describe the imperial project to its participants and its objects. Mitchell argues: 'The new apparatus of representation, particularly the world exhibitions, have a central place to the representation of the non-Western world, and several studies have pointed out the importance of this construction of otherness to the manufacture of national identity and imperial purpose.'[113] David Strang continues:

'imperial propaganda was directed at the colonial official and *the metropolitan population*, aiming to make the public resources of Western societies available for overseas adventure and administration'.[114] And Marilyn Wan argues more specifically: 'the colonial exhibit at the 1889 Exposition Universelle was useful in representing France as a formidable imperial power to its international rivals, it was also instrumental in convincing a skeptical domestic public of the benefits of colonialism'.[115] Burton Benedict expands on this international competition in the realm of prestige: 'Major powers [vied] with each other to present fairs . . . Among the tokens of rivalry were colonies and their peoples. World's fairs showed the power of the imperial nation and were meant to impress both foreigners and the home population.'[116] Exhibitions were designed with two audiences in mind: other countries with whom the hosts vied for prestige; and domestic populations in whom the organizers tried to instil a sense of national pride. Such pride was constructed, in part, through the description of its success in 'civilizing' barbarians – who were portrayed as opposite and inferior to nationals. There is an interesting split in how 'savages' and 'barbarians' were differently represented at these exhibitions. Savages were displayed in their 'natural habitat'. Their performance was merely living. However, 'barbarians' – Egyptians, Japanese, Turks – were displayed in interactive modes. One could not only observe the 'Other', but also buy goods, ride donkeys or pay for dancing girls. Thus, while Britain and France were defined, in part, by sexual restraint, education, Christianity and racial homogeneity, barbarians were displayed as either highly erotic, uneducated, anti-Christian and racially heterogeneous or as the product of a Western 'civilization', in which they approximated – though never attained – European ideals.

McClintock argues that the exhibition is an extension of the panoptic principle of surveillance. In this formulation, the national public becomes the surveyor of the whole world. 'Implicit in the [Great Exhibition of 1851] was the new experience of *imperial* progress consumed as a *national* spectacle. At the exhibition, white British workers could feel included in the imperial nation, the voyeuristic spectacle of racial "superiority" compensating them for their class subordination.'[117] Wan also illustrates how one aspect of the discourse of visuality, 'seeing as education', was a prominent theme in the planning of the Exposition and she details the way in which space was configured to represent the whole world to the masses.[118] Allan Pred combines this pedagogical aspect with the exhibition's spatial characteristics:

> As a public space designed to manufacture private desires; as a space suggesting an unlimited profusion of commodities; as a space where the commercial, the political, and the cultural were ideologically melted together; the space of such exhibitions was a precursor to the 'society of the spectacle' [and] the ultimate spectacle of an ordered reality.[119]

The colonies, and colonial peoples, were displayed as national products and as evidence of European superiority. The planned order of the exhibitions was in stark contrast to the contrived chaos of the colonial peoples inhabiting 'indigenous' buildings. In an illuminating juxtaposition of visual order and Oriental chaos, the *only* disorderly part of the Exposition Universelle in Paris was the Cairo exhibit:

> The Egyptian exhibit has been built by the French to represent a street in medieval Cairo, made of houses with overhanging upper stories and a mosque like that of Qaitbay. 'It was intended,' one of the Egyptians wrote, 'to resemble the old aspect of Cairo.' So carefully was this done, he noted, that 'even the paint on the buildings was made dirty.' The exhibit had also been made carefully chaotic. In contrast to the geometric layout of the rest of the exhibition, the imitation street was arranged in the haphazard manner of the bazaar.[120]

However, visitors could still pay for coffees in a café, pay for a ride on a Cairo donkey, buy a souvenir or watch a belly-dancer.

Imperial products, shows and natives on display were illustrative of three popular discourses. The display of goods inculcated the promise of the industrial revolution, in counterpoint to its detrimental societal effects. Global capitalism celebrated the production of consumer products as the return on investment overseas and the export potential of new markets. National pride in cultural traditions was embodied in displays of artwork, architecture and empire.

The scope of rule and the character of the rulers were presented as triumphs of administration as manliness. The cult of the explorer and the honour of public servants administering the empire entwined notions of masculinity in the colonizer and femininity in the colonized.[121] The display of actual barbarians gave a face to the stereotype and bolstered evidence of the success of the imperial civilizing mission. Walking through the exhibition, the upper, middle and lower classes walked through the world, viewing each other as well as the exhibits.[122]

> The universal expositions of the nineteenth century were intended as microcosms that would summarize the entire human experience . . . In their carefully articulated order, they also signified the dominant relations of power. Ordered and characterization ranked, rationalized, and objectified different societies. The resulting hierarchies portrayed a world where races, sexes, and nations occupied fixed places . . .[123]

This world claimed to be an authentic representation of the outside, but was in fact implicated in the legitimization of imperialism through capitalist, nationalist and imperialist ideologies. Just as popular culture identified external and internal barbarians (colonized peoples and the poor or the criminal), the exhibitions also reinforced European stereotypes. Public commitment to the imperial project wavered, especially during the crises of the Indian Mutiny and the Algerian Civil War, so these representations were political to the extent that they conveyed an image of the international imaginary that supported the imperial project.[124] What I want to emphasize is that these domestic representations functioned to construct an image of what international relations constituted. Because domestic support was necessary to support the imperial, civilizing mission, these political representations act as early propaganda and illustrate the importance of popular culture on world politics.

Faced with a continual threat of violence within the colonies, European administrators developed regimes of surveillance. Geometric spatial orders were a sign of 'civilization' which made barbarism visible and created the illusion of imperial security.[125] The colonized was a body to regulate, order and control – though always imperfectly. This panoptic visual order was applied equally in the colonies and in the imperial centre to observe and contain threatening populations, the criminal, the insane, children, the poor – the internal barbarians. This return of colonial governance mechanisms to the imperial centre helps complicate the civilized/barbarian dichotomy. Both global and domestic underclasses were feared, and mechanisms of control were used to control both internal and external barbarians.

DEMOGRAPHY: THE RISING TIDE OF NUMBERS

Foucault best describes the connection between this visual turn and the rise of demographics. He identifies a general shift in the pattern of European governance in the late eighteenth/early nineteenth centuries from a regime that claimed to protect a 'people' to a regime that aimed to control a 'population'.[126]

Demography – the study of populations – was a central part of the power/knowledge structure of the modern state. Demography was used to describe domestic and international populations. Thomas Malthus became popular at the end of the eighteenth and beginning of the nineteenth centuries. The anxieties expressed became popular currency throughout the period of imperial expansion. After briefly indicating how Malthus operated, I will chart some of the ways in which this anxiety was manifest.

Malthus wrote *An Essay on the Principle of Population* in 1798; it was re-issued in 1826. He argues that while food production technology grows at an arithmetic rate, population grows at a geometric rate.[127] However, there are several important social and political assumptions that make Malthus's analysis less objective than it first appears. First, he assumes that 'the poor' cannot improve their own condition and that their position cannot be improved from outside: 'the poor laws of England tend to depress the general condition of the poor in these two ways. Their first obvious tendency is to increase population without increasing the food for its support . . . Secondly, the quantity of provisions consumed in workhouses . . . diminishes the shares that would otherwise belong to more industrious, and more worthy members . . .'[128] Thus, the poor are not only responsible for their own condition, but are morally inferior, because their poverty is due to their lack of 'industriousness'. As Anderson argues in relation to the census, the representation of class changed over the course of the nineteenth century: 'the census categories became more visibly and exclusively racial.'[129]

Second, Malthus separates the degree of progress or civilization from its population 'carrying capacity'. This sets the stage for critics of imperialism to associate population growth in 'barbarian' colonies with a decline of European civilization. He argues that the proportionate rates of growth between food production and technology are most efficient in the colonies.[130] This sets the stage for the stereotype of the fecund barbarian in the face of a declining European population. Restraint characterized the difference between the barbarian and the European. The barbarian's sexuality – and thus fertility – was unrestrained, while the European's sexuality – and thus fertility – was restrained. Population imbalances remained constant throughout the nineteenth and twentieth centuries, but were invoked only during times of crisis and self-doubt. While migration to the colonies may reduce the metropolitan population, releasing some of the inherent pressure of a growing lower class, the colonies represent a much more productive site of lower-class population growth. Malthus argues that the basics of 'civilization' enable the fecundity of the colonies. Savage population growth is limited naturally by the trials of living without society.[131] Barbarians are described as 'naturally' more fertile, but their uncivilized condition limits the gross population. However, as the material, sanitary and developmental benefits of civilization lower the mortality rate of subject populations, the population in the colonies explodes as fertility is translated into numbers, with the restraining of 'natural' morbidity.

The chief point for this project of Malthus's work, and the science of demography which it spawned, is that the underclass – whether national or global – is more numerous, less industrious and less moral, and consequently a threat to the social order. Fear of the lower classes is translated by the turn of the nineteenth century into a fear of the colonized as a kind of global lower class.[132] Malthus represents the beginning of a souring of the 'civilizing mission'. From this point of view, the civilizing mission is perceived as having the effect of making the barbarians more populous, better educated, healthier – in sum, more dangerous. Demography is used throughout the nineteenth and twentieth centuries to shore up domestic civilizing missions and international imperialism.

Next I shall elaborate the connections between race, class, gender and empire that mobilize the notions of threat and surveillance within and without Europe.

WAITING FOR THE BARBARIANS

The rhetoric of civilized and barbarian was mobilized not only in imperial discourse, but was also applied to the internal 'Others' of European society. The lower classes, the criminal, the perverse and women were all labelled barbaric or described using exactly the same rhetoric.

Lowe argues: 'nineteenth-century orientalism provided a means of displacing, while obliquely figuring, both domestic instability *and* colonialist conflicts; orientalism supported a coherent notion of the "nation" – the "one" – while subsuming and veiling a variety of social differences in the figuration of the Orient as Other'.[133] In the face of other races, Europeans were all similar – despite religious, class or ethnic differences.[134] National identity must be constructed, and the representation of the nation to itself was instrumental in making national characteristics paramount over other characteristics.[135]

The sexual stereotype of the barbarian was coupled to the national identity figured in terms of race and class. McClintock makes this argument powerfully in *Imperial Leather*. Britain and France were figured as masculine nations, while the colonies were figured as feminine peoples. Women were regarded as a 'degenerate' race.[136] However, women were also held up as the virginal, ignorant, vulnerable, promise of civilization – as in 'the Intended' of Joseph Conrad's *Heart of Darkness*. The international was figured as a realm in which women were vulnerable, but also redeeming for both white colonialists (to save them from the sexual and moral dangers of 'going native') and the colonial subject (to save them through their good works and moral example). Kiernan notes how the popular headlines in the Boer War depicted women as the victims of barbarity.[137] Darby argues that gender relations often stand for colonial relations and makes an excellent analysis of this dynamic:

> Gender is a means of shaping and signifying relationships of power internationally as well as in the domestic sphere. It has thus played a major part in the construction and deconstruction of the relationship between ruler and ruled.[138]

There is a rich literature on colonialism and gender, to which I will only refer here. McClintock, Stoler and Spivak have canvassed the relationship between colonial discourse and gender/sexuality in particular. The stereotype of the barbarian is often cast in gendered/sexualized terms. However, as representations of gender within 'Western' culture are complex and unstable, so too are representations of the gendered barbarian. On the one hand, male barbarians are often characterized as hyper-masculine. This corresponds to the notion of the barbarian being creatively violent, sexually rapacious and unmannered – which, ironically, make him more powerful than the restrained European. On the other hand, female barbarians are characterized as hyper-feminine – most often as over-sexualized and undomestic. The gendering of the barbarian stereotype can be viewed as a mirror of gendering the European stereotype. The barbarian is represented in relation to the European stereotype of itself. These stereotypes are not stable within Europe or across the colonial scene. African males were often portrayed as masculine, whereas Asian and South Asian men were often portrayed in feminine terms. Amazonian women, 'Oriental' belly-dancers and bare-breasted women of the South Pacific were all staples of popular European culture.[139] These examples are provided to indicate how gender and sexuality are mobilized within the 'barbarian' stereotype and not to exhaust the subject. It must be noted that the description of the gendered/sexualized barbarian often reflects more on the identity of the European than it does on the 'Others'.

Imperial discourses did not merely mirror class and gender discourses of the nineteenth century, but were constitutive of them. Class relations were represented in terms of race relations: for example, the lower classes were portrayed on the scale of 'humanity' on which barbarians and savages were placed. Thus, the upper classes were depicted as more 'evolved' than the lower classes. The British and French were as superior in race as the aristocrats were in class. Anderson attributes empire with the 'shoring up' of class structure: 'if English lords were naturally superior to other Englishmen, no matter: these other Englishmen were no less superior to the subjected natives'.[140] These intertwining discourses, which connected race, class and gender, generated a series of dualities that were mapped on to imperial and metropolitan cultures alike. 'The regulatory mechanisms of the colonial state were directed not only at the colonized, but as forcefully at the "internal enemies" within the heterogeneous population that comprised the category of Europeans themselves.'[141]

Race relations were understood in terms of class relations: in Egypt, the ethnic division of labour was translated for European audiences into classes (farmers, bourgeois, aristocracy, etc.). Sexual and gender characteristics were portrayed in racial terms: racial characteristics were portrayed in terms of sexuality and gender.

These connections were not made explicitly by the framers of the discourse, as Foucault shows with respect to Victorian sexuality. R.J. Vincent shows this connection with respect to race.[142] To understand imperial relations, we need to understand how the discourse of civilization and barbarians was applied within Europe, as well as outside Europe.

McClintock argues that the discourses of race, gender and class were connected in the ideology of imperialism.[143] This relates the Victorian chain of being to the racialist theories which also propped up the imperial ideology. Vincent argues: 'in the popular mind the notion of racial superiority was woven into the pattern of European empire . . . and when the problem was not seen as one of ordering the lesser breeds, but of coping with the "rising tide of colour" that threatened to engulf the white world demographically and economically, then it was necessary to construct a white redoubt to preserve higher civilization'.[144] Thus, the 'civilizing mission' was coupled to racial threats. Stoler also argues that racial dynamics were central to popular nineteenth-century culture and European identity: 'race becomes the organizing grammar of an imperial order in which modernity, the civilizing mission and the "measure of man" were framed'.[145]

This externalization of class theory had the internal effect of racializing the classes of the metropolitan populations. Paralleling Stanley's In Darkest Africa, in 1890, William Booth, the founder of the Salvation Army, published In Darkest England (1890).[146] Kiernan argues: 'in the European mind the affinity between race and class is equally palpable. In innumerable ways his attitude to his own "lower orders" was identical to Europe's to the "lesser breeds" . . . Much of the talk about the barbarism or darkness of the outer world, which it was Europe's mission to route, was a transmuted fear of the masses at home.'[147]

Two excerpts from travelogues illustrate the conflation between Egyptian races, and classes.

> Lastly [of the races in Egypt] the Arab cultivator, the most civilized, the most corrupted, the most degraded, in consequence of the state of bondage in which he is held, and the most varied in person and character, as may be remarked in the heads of the sheiks, or chiefs of villages, in those of the fellahs or peasants, in those of the beggars, and finally, those of the artisans, who constitute the most abject class.[148]

Egypt is inhabited by several races of people, all differing greatly
in their manners, customs, religions . . . Besides these four classes
[Mamelukes, Bedoween, Arabs, Fellahs], which constitute the
chief population of the country, there are several others, as Turks,
Greeks, Jews, etc. that are settled in the towns, and follow different
employments.[149]

Because these two discourses were mutually constituting, the fact
that they evolved not only at the same time but using the same
vocabulary, class relations could be used to explain racial relations, and
vice versa. Thus, race and class were conflated in the colonies, where
colonial administrators tried to assign class positions to different races.

The imperial discourses of racial hierarchy and the capitalist
understandings of free trade and the subsequent class relations
were intertwined. Justifications of imperialism cannot be understood,
except with reference to internal tension in European societies.[150]
Also, the maintenance of colonial rule was informed by the class
experience. The 'creation' of ethnic categories, which paralleled
domestic classes, and the subsequent empowerment of collaborators
made for a complex social system. In addition to the colonial civil
service, the army was a main vehicle of acculturation in the colonies.
Kiernan notes that the use of native troops 'started as soon as white
men began to find their way overseas. In the course of their classes
in India the French and British pioneered the system of "sepoy
armies", from then on an indispensable part of Europe's ability to
go on conquering. Afro-Asia was taught to conquer itself for foreign
pay, most of it taken out of Afro-Asian pockets.'[151]

Thus, the stereotype of the barbarian was mobilized to marshal
forces against internal and external classes or races. The characteristics
of these barbarians were usually linked to ideas about capitalism,
order and sexuality. Barbarians, whether colonized or the poor,
were indolent, violent, licentious and, above all, dangerous.

Flaubert, Lane and Denon all point to the sexual fantasies which
dominated popular notions of the Orient. In addition to these
cultural stereotypes, the actual interaction between colonizers and
colonized is central to imperial and postcolonial culture. Fanon,
Said, McClintock and others would all study the sexual dynamics
in colonial rule.

Sex in any case formed an important area of contact between
societies. Impressions of foreign lands owed much to men's

impressions of their women, and vice versa, and also of the way their men and women behaved to each other.[152]

While it is difficult to fix the specific stereotype of the libidinous Oriental, textual sources point to how powerful the stereotype was. Denon's first impressions of Egyptian women illustrate the stereotype. While enamoured of their beauty, he states: 'I also deferred the pleasure of drawing the Egyptian women, until we should, by our influence over the manners of eastern nations, remove the veil by which they are covered.'[153] The Egyptian belly-dancer was to be a primary image of the Orient, representing its lasciviousness, accessibility and strangeness.[154] 'At the commencement of the dance [it] was voluptuous: it soon after became lascivious, and expressed, in the grossest and most indecent way, the giddy transports of passion.'[155] Lane authenticates his own writing by living in disguise in Cairo for five years. 'The women of Egypt have the character of being the most licentious in their feelings of all females who lay any claim to be considered as members of a civilized nation.'[156] Lane clearly marks a tension between licentiousness and civilization, suggesting later that

the libidinous character of the generality of the women of Egypt, and the licentious conduct of a great number of them, may be attributed to many causes – partly to the climate, and partly to their want of instruction and of innocent pastimes and employments, but it is more to be attributed to the conduct of husbands themselves.[157]

Geography and character are connected in a manner that echoes Hegel and Rousseau. Further, licentiousness is coupled with a lack of domesticity, which was understood as the racial purview of the colonizers.

Flaubert's travel notes and letters home are extremely frank about the sexual nature of his Oriental tour.[158] Bhedad argues that by the mid-eighteenth century the thrill of discovery had waned with the popularization of tourist package tours. As such, 'what brings the tourist to the Orient is not the "lordly" attempts of earlier orientalists to understand and "make sense" of the internal dynamics of Oriental culture and to gain "new" knowledge about them, but the desire to identify the already defined signs of exoticism as erotic.'[159] Europeans had been sufficiently imbued with representations of the Orient that 'anyone who is a little attentive *re*discovers here much more than he discovers'.[160] However, this does not stop Flaubert from discovering a great number of sexual delights. He writes: 'the oriental woman is a machine, and nothing more; she doesn't differentiate between one man and another. As for physical pleasure, it must be very slight since they cut off that famous button, the very place of it, quite early on. And for me, this is what renders this woman so poetic, that she becomes absolutely one with nature.'[161] Lowe admonishes postcolonial critics that the stereotype of the Oriental woman is not unidimensional or uncontested.[162] Stoler argues that the sexual policing in the colonies prefigured the policing of perversion in Europe that Foucault explores in his work on sexuality.[163] The stereotype represents the frightening lack of restraint – to which the white (male) administrator was susceptible. The (inevitable) products of the unions between white administrators and 'native' women were treated as a challenge to the racial order.

The discourse of Oriental sexuality was not unambiguous, but certainly reflected the power difference between colonizer and colonized. Burton, known as 'Dirty Dick',[164] is quite plain in his coupling of sexual and class relations in Europe and the Orient alike. 'How often is it our fate, in the West as in the East, to see in bright eyes and to hear from rosy lips an implied, if not an expressed, "Why don't you buy me?" or, worse still, "Why *can't* you buy me?"'[165] The anxiety of sexual liberty or racial degradation is transmuted into a consumer's anxiety of insufficient buying power and the consolation of the security of property relations.

Whether the difference was figured as titillating, threatening or incidental, the sexualized stereotypes of the colonized played a formative role in the representation of the colonial world. McClintock argues that specifically sexual metaphors were used to reify colonial relations.

> Women are the earth that is to be discovered, entered, named, inseminated, and, above all, owned . . . linked symbolically to the land, women are relegated to a realm beyond history and thus bear a particular vexed relation to narratives of historical change and political effect. Even more importantly, women are figured as property belonging to men and hence as lying, by definition, outside the male contests over land, money, and political power.[166]

This connection between Hegelian notions of African geography and female characteristics is important to the deconstruction of the rhetoric of empire. The threat of racial degradation is central to Stoler's application of Foucault into the colonial context. The constant allure of 'going native' or 'growing black' undermined the superiority of the colonizer.[167]

Contemporary critics and postcolonial scholars comment on this reliance on markers of race connected to the skin, the body and the sexual organs extensively. Hyam argues: 'Endless emphasis on the differences between "natives" and themselves was one of the necessary props of empire. They could have only ruled subject peoples, especially when hopelessly outnumbered, by honestly believing themselves to be racially superior, and the subject race to be *biologically* different.'[168] This illustrates Foucault's fascination with notions of 'bio-power'.[169] Burton continues this point:

> Phrenology and physiognomy, be it observed, disappoint you often amongst civilised people, the proper action of whose brain upon the features is impeded by the external pressure of education, accident, example, habit, and necessity. But they are tolerably safe guides when groping your way through the mind of man in his so-called natural state, a being of impulse, in that chrysalis condition of mental development which is rather instinct than reason.[170]

Stoler points out that this discourse of difference was mobilized not only between metropolis and colony, but also within classes and races in each community. She contrasts the myth of imperial unity to the actuality of class and racial division in the East Indies.[171]

Those 'Others' of mixed race or low status were seen as dangerous because they undermined the supposed unity of the colonizers. The relations between colonial rulers, almost universally men, and indigenous women lays bare an important vector of imperial power. Multiracial relations and their progeny, who often claimed colonizer status, complicated clear simple racial divisions. This effort reflects a change in public opinion regarding sexual morals in the colonies. At first, the colonies were seen as realms exempt from sexual mores. Hyam argues:

> The regulation of sexual relations with indigenous peoples was

inherently a central feature of the colonial relationship, and it was fundamental to the construction of racial perceptions and misperceptions. As race relations became less relaxed in the later nineteenth century, so missionaries and memsahibs insisted on tighter controls. Sexual contacts thus became more depersonalized, and prostitution was preferred as politically safer.[172]

This convergence of discourse is interesting. The formerly racially dangerous sexual consort becomes 'safe' once she is bought and incorporated into European structures of consumerism and the sexual politics of domesticity. The uncertainty of racial relations is reconfigured in terms of 'safe' class relations, similar to Burton's. This change in popular morality is seen to have had the effect of solidifying racial boundaries, which had previously been more fluid. Lloyd argues: 'It has been suggested that part of the reason why British attitudes to Indians became more hostile after the Mutiny was that British women came to India in larger numbers as the Suez route became less troublesome and were more concerned about keeping a due and proper distance between Indians and themselves than man had ever been.'[173]

This constellation of gendered, racial and class discourses illustrates the pervasiveness of imperialism as a way of understanding European imperial culture. Wandering through the exhibition grounds in Paris or London, the public was educated towards, and made complicit in, the national, consumerist and imperial project. Not only were the colonies, their products and peoples on view, but the nation was on view to itself. Anderson's constructivist account of nationalism defends the notion that the production of a seeming homogeneous nation from heterogeneous populations requires the representation of the people to themselves.[174] At the exhibition, classes viewed each other. Races were viewed and souvenirs were bought. Class and racial hierarchies were reaffirmed through spectacle. The chaos of the crowd contrasted the ordering of the architecture. The ordering of the races was coincident with the ordering of classes. The barbarians, both internal and external, were on display. The hyper-sexualized Orientals were tamed by their participation in consumer capitalism and by the architecture of spectacle. Masculine Europe was seen as the father of the family of man, paternalistic to the rest of the world through its civilizing mission. Race, class and gender rhetoric were used to stabilize the image of a national identity, despite the class, sexual and racial tension. The spectacle of the exhibition was an attempt to educate the metropolitan population of their similarity, in the face of lesser subject races, and their shared consumerism. The decline in the display of colonized peoples after the First World War is indicative of the wane of racism in Britain and France, the rising nationalism of the colonized peoples and the undermining of the justification for the civilizing mission. However, for the majority of the nineteenth century, racial, class and gender politics were all tied to the imperial project.

BARBARIANS IN THE COLONIAL SCENE

In traditional IR theories, imperialism is portrayed as a uniform process of power accumulation, distinctly international in scope, but domestic in nature. However, as this chapter has suggested, nineteenth-century imperialism complicates the domestic/ international divide. Further, certain prevailing cultural trends cannot be understood without reference to the colonial condition. Rather than isolating European and non-European politics as two separate realms of politics, I have suggested that the civilizing mission was central to European identity and integral to non-European culture. Europe defined its identity in part by what it was not – and it was not barbarous. The image of the barbarian implied continual threat and insecurity, descriptions that were also applied to dangerous domestic populations. Thus, the barbarian was implicated in the construction of the disciplinary society, the extension of surveillance to the general metropolitan and imperial populations. The continual state of war between colonizer and colonized resembles traditional definitions of anarchical international relations. Imperialism also involved extensive violence, which is traditionally downplayed in studies of war in the nineteenth century. European identity was constituted in reference to lesser races and the concomitant civilizing mission. The boundary of European identity was policed at cultural and racial levels, often using visible markers and authoritative texts such as the passport and the census.

The discursive formation constituting the image of the barbarian attempted to resolve a number of tensions with the ideology of imperialism. Violence against the barbarian was justified in almost every instance. The rules of 'civilized' warfare did not apply to barbarians, nor did the rule of civilized governance. To get a full picture of international relations, we must not only investigate both sides of the domestic/international divide, but also look at liminal cases, such as colonial rule, which were both domestic and international. The reality of colonized peoples is, of course, far more varied. Indeed, Nandy and Césaire argue that Europe was far more negatively affected by colonialism than the colonies were.[175] However, since the Orientalist stereotype of the barbarian reached its peak in the nineteenth century, a brief mapping of the ideological terrain upon which he stands is useful.

The barbarian is irrational, uneducated and violent. He is libidinous and indolent. She is libidinous and undomestic. His subjugation must be violent because he cannot understand the benefits of civilization. Once conquered, he must be continually under surveillance because he is always planning sedition or revolt. The barbarian's only hope of redemption is through a European education and acculturation. The barbarian proves his inferiority through his evident underdevelopment, and any reluctance he may show to the imperial project. The barbarian proves the colonizers' superiority at the same time. As Said argues about the stereotype of the Oriental: 'The Oriental is irrational, depraved, child-like, different, thus the European is rational, mature, virtuous, "normal".'[176] European identity was thus deeply implicated in the colonial project and the image of the barbarian specifically. 'Conscious of this [barbarian] world at his elbow, the Western felt his identity by contrast to it: it was his shadow, his antithesis, or himself in dreams.'[177]

At the close of the nineteenth century, the discourse of civilization collapsed under its own weight. In bringing the light of civilization, Europe had darkened itself. The First World War, in addition to being fostered by the atmosphere of competition for imperial prestige, revealed that Europeans were just as barbaric as any other civilization. The use of colonial troops within the boundaries of Europe marked a change, which led in turn to the growth of the nationalist movement. The Second World War saw the barbarizing of Europe and the glorification of violence and barbarism, after which the rhetoric of civilization took a profoundly pessimistic turn. Decolonization was the result of a number of these forces. The discourse of civilization and barbarians brings all of these discourses to the fore.

4 A Civilized/Barbaric Europe

Like the travel writers, novelists and statesmen of the nineteenth century, philosophers and politicians of the twentieth found the rhetoric of civilization and barbarian useful in their attempts to understand and describe international – that is, imperial and intra-European – relations. The philosophers and intellectuals of the turn of the century – Arthur de Gobineau, Friedrich Nietzsche, Oswald Spengler and Sigmund Freud in particular – redefined the terms civilization and barbarian as they re-evaluated the ideological principles which had justified inter- and extra-European relations in the nineteenth century's period of rapid expansion. The work of these intellectuals became part of popular political culture, albeit in polarized and simplified terms.

This chapter examines the more serious critical attempts to understand the world order at the turn of the century through the civilization/barbarian distinction. I will touch on three illustrative intersections of the 'civilized/barbarian' discourse and the popular international imaginary: four important philosophers and thinkers of the period, the use of imperial troops and strategy, and indicate some interesting points in the development of International Relations. The chapter will also evaluate the extent to which the then new discipline of International Relations affected and was effected by the circulation of the trope civilization/barbarian during this period.

PHILOSOPHERS OF BARBARISM II: de GOBINEAU, NIETZSCHE, FREUD AND SPENGLER

To understand fully the cultural mood at the turn of the century, we must first touch on the intellectuals of this period. Of these, de Gobineau, Nietzsche, Freud and Spengler are the most important to the general cultural mood of pessimism from which the inversion of the civilized/barbarian trope develops. While they may not have been widely read in the original, 'many of [Nietzsche's, Freud's and Heidegger's] ideas were conveyed in popular phrases and political clichés', and their ideas became common currency in political discourse.[1] These intellectuals investigated the valuations of 'civilized' and 'barbarian' critically – treating them as constructed, contentious terms of judgement. I will also look briefly at the racialist theorists who began to circulate and gain public adherents, referring chiefly to de Gobineau and Chamberlain. None of these thinkers left the discourse of civilization/barbarian unaffected by their analysis and their work had an impact on the popular imaginary of Europe.

de GOBINEAU, RACE AND CONFLICT

Racial competition held a central place in the international imaginary of the period.[2] If the international system is perceived as a realm of constant racial competition, the civilizing mission could be interpreted variously as the white man's burden or as giving aid to the enemy. Anxieties about the rising power of the colonized populations were especially prevalent in the pre-First World War and interwar periods. The first Oxford professor of International Relations, Alfred Zimmern, described the defeat of the Russians by the Japanese as 'the most important historical event in our lifetime; the victory of a non-white people over a white people'.[3] Politicians and theorists began to discuss the impending 'race war'.[4] Whether cloaked in scientific or imperial discourse, racial inequality was a pillar of the popular international imaginary of the nineteenth and early twentieth centuries.[5] Of these, de Gobineau is the most popular and egregious.[6] He argues in 'Essay on the Inequality of the Races' that racial 'mixing' is responsible for the general cultural deterioration in Europe and the world. Written in 1855, its first English translation during the First World War made a significant impact on the popular imagination.[7]

Another figure, Houston Stewart Chamberlain, connected fears of racial decline with fears of cultural decline. 'Chamberlain played upon all the diverse anxieties then afflicting Europe's industrial powers – militarism, anticlericalism, "pan-isms", the degeneration of political life, the rise of technological and managerial society – in an effort to create an integrated theory of race.'[8] Racialist theories can be seen as an extension of the *Kultur* v. *Zivilisation* debate then prominent in Germany. Hugh Tinker described the Second World War as a war that was explicitly 'racial' from the Nazi perspective, but not perceived as such from the Western perspective.[9]

Race is often neglected as a concept in International Relations. Frank Füredi argues that racial anxiety was fuelled in large part by 'perceptions that the white race was under pressure from more fertile others'.[10] Michael Teitelbaum and Jay Winter have shown that while demographic trends have not changed significantly since Malthus's time, the rhetoric of racial conflict based on population emerges only during periods of political tension.[11] The stereotype of the barbarian is often mobilized concurrently and complicity with this demographic rhetoric – in part because the barbarian has always been portrayed as fecund, over-sexual, racially threatening and dangerous. However, at the turn of the twentieth century, rather than represent a significant change in the population of the 'Others', European anxiety reflected its own self-doubts.

NIETZSCHE: THE NEW BARBARIAN COMES

Nietzsche is one of the most complex and challenging figures of the nineteenth century. His ideas became popular throughout the Western world in the twentieth century and, as Arthur Herman notes, 'in the realm of the written word, terms such as "übermensch", "will to power", "master–slave morality", "transvaluation of all values", and "blond beast" became standard parts of the vocabulary of intellectuals and political writers'.[12] His popularity was such that, during the First World War, *Thus Spoke Zarathustra* was one of two books in a German soldier's knapsack (the other being the Bible).[13] Nietzsche's popularity in Germany in turn caused him to be vilified in England and America as the 'apostle of German ruthlessness and barbarism'.[14] Because Nietzsche's writings set out a philosophy of culture in which he praised, rather than condemned, the barbarian, he is central to this project. Consequently, I will focus on two aspects of Nietzsche's considerable corpus: his praise of the barbarian and his writings as a philosopher of culture and a prophet of pessimism.

Nietzsche's praise of barbarism is related to two of his central concepts: the death of God and the will to power. I will look at these in turn to explicate the pessimistic cultural mood that Nietzsche diagnosed and popularized. Nietzsche relates the parable of the madman in *The Gay Science* and offers this infamous dialogue: '"Whither is God?" he cried; "I will tell you. *We have killed him* – you and I. All of us are his murderers . . . God is dead."'[15] While Nietzsche indeed criticizes Christianity on a host of charges,[16] he intends a deeper indictment of European thought. God represents an anchor in philosophical – or theological – certainty, which by definition must lie outside the sphere of uncertain human affairs.[17] Nietzsche believes this foundation has come undone, and has been shown to be an ephemeral psychological convenience. His genealogy of moral valuations – and the attempted revaluation of all morals – traces the 'all-too-human' origins of moral codes.[18] 'Nietzsche's fear was that in a secular age men would replace God by their own man-made divinities.'[19] Morals, language and reason itself are shown to be the inventions of fallible individuals. 'Against positivism, which halts at phenomena – These are only *facts* and nothing more – I would say: No, facts are precisely what there are not, only interpretations. We cannot establish any fact "in itself" . . . It is our needs that interpret the world . . .'[20] Against reason and causality, Nietzsche argues: 'Not "to know" but to schematize – to impose upon chaos as much regularity and form as our practical needs require. In the formation of reason, logic, and the categories, it was *need* that was authoritative: the need, not "to know" but to subsume, to schematize, for the purpose of intelligibility and calculation.'[21] Thus, all the ideals of the Enlightenment, reason, logic and progress, are various aspects of the human need for order and thus not consistent with an objective reality or within themselves. They represent a belief system that invents the foundation that it requires. This questioning of the very foundation of reason, language and logic turns on its head the notion of progress and truth:

> *Progress* – let us not be deceived! Time marches forward; we'd like to believe that everything that is in it also marches forward – that the development is one that moves forward. The most levelheaded are led astray by this illusion . . . 'Mankind' does

not advance . . . The overall aspect is that of a tremendous experimental laboratory in which a few successes are scored, scattered through the ages, while there are untold failures, and all order, logic, union, and obligingness is lacking.[22]

'Truth': this, according to my way of thinking, does not necessarily denote the antithesis of error, but in most fundamental cases only the posture of various errors in relation to one another. Perhaps one is older, more profound than another . . . What is truth. Inertia: that hypothesis which brings satisfaction, the smallest expenditure of spiritual force.[23]

This condemnation of reason, progress and truth – in short all the ideas of Enlightenment culture – found a surprisingly receptive audience. The lack of an objective foundation for reason, calculation and history meant that individuals created meaning for themselves. The lack of foundations induced despair on the one hand, but on the other liberation. The individual is free to create his own truth. Meaning did not come from the Church or state (Nietzsche was a notorious enemy of nationalism[24]), but from within – the will to power. Power created meaning. 'You say that it is the good cause that hallows even war? I say unto you: it is that good war that hallows any cause. War and courage have accomplished more things than love of the neighbour.'[25]

Nietzsche argues that the belief in the ideals that acted as the pillars of modern European civilization were corrupt. And, as such, Europe itself is corrupt and in decline: 'For some time now, our whole European culture has been moving us toward a catastrophe, with a tortured tension that is growing from decade to decade: restlessly, violently . . .'[26] This decline can be halted only by the affirmation of the 'noble virtues' through a 'will to power'. Nietzsche contends that the values of weakness, piety, sickness, humility – the so-called 'slave morality' – have been valued higher than the 'noble' values of strength, will, responsibility.[27] The 'solution' to decadence Nietzsche prescribes is the 'will to power': it was the imposition of one's strength, one's will, on the world. For Nietzsche, the slave ethic centred on 'restraint'. The will to power is portrayed as the actualization of instinct, the unshackling of the individual from restraint. In short, the barbarian is represented as the solution to the decadence of European civilization at the end of the nineteenth century.[28] Nietzsche exhorts his readers: 'Where are the *barbarians* of the twentieth century? They will be the elements capable of the greatest severity towards themselves, and able to guarantee the most enduring will.'[29] Coupled with his remarks elsewhere, we see that 'barbarians' are not simply not-decadent, not-civilized beings, but rather are individuals with a vital energy that will regenerate European culture, through the disregard of moral inhibitions. The barbarian is Nietzsche's *Übermensch*, or 'overman'. This interpretation is at odds with Kaufmann's assertion that 'Nietzsche thinks of qualitative degrees of power as corresponding to various forms of behaviour and of culture; and the saint I considered the most powerful man. The barbarian, who is uncultured, is the least powerful.'[30] As a testament to Nietzsche's opaque style, Kaufmann provides a tortuous, gymnastic explanation of one aphorism from 'The Dawn' on which he bases his wholesale repudiation of the barbarian. Kaufmann mistakenly makes a distinction between 'barbarians' and 'new barbarians'; he concedes that the 'new barbarians' mentioned in *The Will to Power* are seen not as a descent into bestiality, but an ascent beyond morals to naturalness. Kaufmann argues that the 'new barbarians' are not very barbarous.[31] Nietzsche does not distinguish between the man and his behaviour and so this explanation is strained. The simpler analysis, that Nietzsche does indeed value the barbarian as an individual of strength and will, not only accounts for Kaufmann's misreading, but also corresponds more precisely to Nietzsche's praise of the barbarian both new and old. The *Übermensch* is also the most evolved man, the supreme product of civilization (if not *Zivilization*). He overcomes morality and restraint to impose his will to power on the world, creating his own truth and re-investing barbaric characteristics with moral value.

Part of Nietzsche's criticism of the 'slave ethics' concerns the self/Other dynamic, of which anti-Semitism is a particularly virulent variety. He argues: 'Slave ethics . . . begins by saying *no* to an "outside", an "other", a non-self . . . Slave ethics requires for its inception a sphere different and hostile to its own. Physiologically speaking it requires an outside stimulus in order to act at all; all its action is reaction.'[32] In short, Nietzsche is suggesting that the modern conception of identity – that identity requires difference – suffers from an internal weakness. The self depends upon the 'Other' for recognition, which immediately complicates the difference. This critique prefigures much current critical thinking on identity.[33]

The only solution Nietzsche foresaw was a revaluation of these characteristics and the rise of a new man. He describes the barbarian as one 'who comes from the heights: a species of conquering and ruling natures', who has the power and lack of restraint necessary to obey his natural instincts, and who gives vital energy back to European society.[34] While Nietzsche's work proposes a radical change in the terms by which European civilization was to value itself, he shares with his nineteenth-century predecessors an interest in seeing Europe as the centre for the dissemination of these (new) values and of power. This perhaps accounts for his popularity and the extent to which his cry of decadence and appeal to power were disseminated in European popular culture through literature, music and philosophy.

Nietzsche was not anti-Semitic. His dense style lends itself to misinterpretation. He cites Jewish theology as responsible for the inversion of values: 'It was the Jew who, with frightening consistency, dared to invert the aristocratic value equations good/noble/ powerful/beautiful/happy/favoured-of-the-gods and maintain with furious hatred of the underprivileged and impotent that "only the poor, the powerless, are good; only the suffering, sick and ugly truly, blessed" . . . it was the Jews who started the slave revolt in morals . . .'[35] However, distinct from Nietzsche's criticism of the 'slave ethic', he is vociferously against anti-Semitism. He writes in a letter, 'It is a matter of honour to me to be absolutely clear and unequivocal regarding anti-Semitism, namely *opposed*, as I am in my writings.'[36]

Ironically, this explicit repudiation of anti-Semitism was directed at his sister – Elizabeth Forster-Nietzsche – who was an ardent anti-Semite and shameless promoter of her brother's work.[37] After his death, Forster-Nietzsche, Wagner and Houston Stewart Chamberlain marshalled Nietzsche in support their beliefs. Nietzsche was also adopted as a patron saint of Nazism. However, as Kaufmann argues, 'Nietzsche could be quoted in support of Nazism only when passages were torn from their context.'[38] It should be noted that anti-Semitism was rife throughout Europe during this time.[39]

Nietzsche represents a powerful critique of the Enlightenment values, which had been predominant in European culture during the nineteenth century. As part of this critique, he inverts the value ascribed to the civilized/barbarian dichotomy. Nietzsche argues that the barbarian is the saviour of a decadent European civilization. This theme was to be popularized by Spengler, among others.

SPENGLER: DECLINE OF THE WEST

Oswald Spengler represents the anti-Enlightenment, Romantic theme of European thought. Spengler is one of the prime proponents of valuing *Kultur* over *Zivilisation*. Seeing himself as the heir to Nietzsche's prophecy, he came to the German public's attention only when Elizabeth Forster-Nietzsche awarded him the 'Nietzsche Prize'.[40] Eventually, however, his influence stretched from Arnold Toynbee to Hitler. His historical epic, *The Decline of the West*, popularized two ideas that were to become central to interwar German, and European, culture. Spengler is a prophet of decline and describes all cultures as organic forms. He elaborates the distinction between *Kultur* and *Zivilisation*, which described 'culture' as the healthy, strong spirit of a people and 'civilization' as the decadent, baroque, decay of the spirit.[41]

Spengler also popularized the pluralization of civilizations which could be studied comparatively.[42] This is part of a larger discourse that is sceptical of 'civilization' and praises the strengths (lack of restraint) of the 'barbarian'. One finds this distinction in Nietzsche, but Nietzsche projects culture as the unrestrained actualization of the spirit of a people and civilization as the restraint of instincts. He argues: 'the great moments of culture were always, morally speaking, times of corruption [of the slave ethics]; and conversely, the periods when the taming of the human animal ("civilization") was desired and enforced were times of intolerance against the boldest and most spiritual natures.'[43] For both thinkers, civilization in itself is decadent. The restraint of a culture's spirit marks its decline and inevitable collapse. It is interesting to note that Freud, who considered himself cosmopolitan, rejects the distinction between culture and civilization – seeing restraint of the barbaric as a necessary evil.[44]

Spengler associated civilization with a decline in the quality of high culture and a baroque emphasis on style over substance. Significantly, he also associated civilization with imperialism. 'Civilizations are the most *external* and *artificial* states of which a species of developed humanity is capable. They are a conclusion, a thing-become succeeding a thing-becoming, death following life, rigidity following expansion . . . '[45] Imperialism, in this view, was taken to be not only the external direction of both individuals and resources, but of the 'spirit' of the nation. He argues that the civilizing mission has the effect of looking outward rather than inward. The national spirit was engaged in 'civilizing' others, rather than developing one's own national character further. The material expansion of European society depends upon the spiritual calcification of European culture. In sum, he says, 'The energy of culture-man is directed inwards, that of civilization-man outwards' towards empire.[46]

This rejection of the civilizing mission challenged contemporary justifications of imperialism. In opposition to the altruism of late nineteenth-century imperialist ideology, expansion was seen to be the imposition of a people's collective will to power – not just an expression of their moral superiority. Spengler did not see imperialism as Progress; it was only territorial and economic expansion. This questioning of the civilizing mission was to have a profound effect on Germany after the First World War and the loss of its colonies.[47]

The second idea that Spengler helped legitimize, which was certainly circulating among the Front generation, was that of a 'Fifth Column' responsible for Germany's defeat in the First World War. German soldiers at the Front felt that they had been stabbed in the back by the General Staff's surrender in 1918. 'Spengler blamed Germany's defeat on the presence of an *innere England*, the defection of a class that had been contaminated by liberal ideas, a group of which welcomed the defeat as a chance to introduce Western parliamentarianism into German political life.'[48] I will return to this theme in later chapters.

With Nietzsche and Spengler, the primitive, instinctual, will-to-power is set up in opposition to decadent civilization. The barbarian culture of expansion and domination is lauded as the remedy for the restraints of civilization. Both are influenced by the racialist views of Joseph de Gobineau. However, it is worth noting that neither of these writers was anti-Semitic. Their work was, however, to be appropriated by Hitler and the Third Reich in the 1930s and 1940s to such ends that barbarism would never again have positive connotations. Thus, while 'noble' savages could be lauded until the present day for being more natural, spiritual or environmentally conscious, barbarians come to have a uniformly negative connotation.[49]

FREUD: THE BARBARIAN WITHIN

Sigmund Freud is one of the most important thinkers of the

twentieth century and the impact of his work is felt in diverse academic fields. In addition to being the 'father' of psychoanalysis, he was a cultural critic and it is in this capacity that he speaks to the civilization/barbarian discourse. Freud felt himself to be the heir of the best of the European tradition. He also felt a certain intellectual kinship with Nietzsche. Freud acknowledges his debt to Nietzsche obliquely: 'Nietzsche, whose guesses and intuitions often agree in the most astonishing way with the laborious findings of psychoanalysis, was for a long time avoided by me on that very account . . .'[50] Nietzsche's description of the processes of repression and sublimation in *The Genealogy of Morals* bears an uncanny resemblance to Freud's work.[51] Freud, like Nietzsche and Spengler, was sceptical of the supposed progress of European civilization. He considered himself a cultured cosmopolitan and was horrified at the rhetoric of nationalism stirred up by the First World War and even more horrified at the carnage that ensued.[52]

Freud's psychoanalytic and anthropological work reflects an ambiguous attitude towards civilization and barbarism, taking the view that both are inevitable forces in the history of humanity. Freud spoke directly to both aspects of the civilization/barbarian discourse. I will look at his treatment of civilization and the barbarian within, concentrating on *Civilization and Its Discontents* and *Thoughts for the Times on War and Death*.

Freud made several attempts at anthropological writing, in which he deduced primeval group structures and contemporary moral prohibitions from psychoanalytic and therapeutic evidence. From his evidence of an 'Oedipus complex', in which the developing (male) child wishes to occupy the (authorial and sexual) place of the father in the family, Freud speculates that early society was formed from a similar desire.[53] The desire to take the place of the father led to patricide as the first fraternal, community-forming act. The violent act at the core of a society is sublimated in guilt. However, the 'barbaric' impulse that fuelled the initial patricide remains deep in the structure of society.[54] Thus, for Freud, 'civilization has been attained through the renunciation of instinctual satisfaction, and it demands the same renunciation from each newcomer in turn. Throughout an individual's life there is a constant replacement of external by internal compulsion.'[55] Civilization is a veneer of restraint over primordial instincts. For Freud, and many Europeans, the First World War showed how fragile that veneer was.[56] He views civilization as a precarious 'struggle between Eros and Death', in which civilized values demand the repression of instinct and in which those values are internalized as the voice of conscience.[57]

Freud, like Spengler and Nietzsche, focused on European culture. Unlike Nietzsche, he felt that European civilization remained a productive project. He saw himself as a citizen of the 'wider fatherland' – of Europe – whose work was a part of a pantheon of European accomplishments. Freud's cosmopolitanism led him to condemn war and its concomitant nationalism and parochialism, as well as the states system of which it was a fundamental institution. He argues that states have ignored the moral code that they require of individuals – and have thus unleashed the restraints of civilization leading to a barbaric war. This leads to an interesting psychoanalytic interpretation of the domestic/international sphere. He argues against realist notions of self-interest as aggression: 'It should not be objected that the state cannot refrain from wrong-doing, since that would place it at a disadvantage. It is no less disadvantageous, as a general rule, for the individual man to conform to the standards of morality and refrain from brutal and arbitrary conduct.'[58] Freud's mix of idealism and pragmatism provides a thoughtful counterpoint to parsimonious views of human nature.[59] In fact, this statement of Freud's emergent theory of International Relations resembles E.H. Carr's combination of idealism and realism.

> The attempt to replace actual force by the force of ideas seems at present to be doomed to failure. We shall be making a false calculation if we disregard the fact that law was originally brute violence and that even to-day it cannot do without the support of violence. There is no use in trying to get rid of men's aggressive inclinations . . . It is enough to try and divert them to such an extent that they need not find expression in war.[60]

For Freud, civilization is a process of continual restraint and negotiation between instincts and rationality, not of decay or decline. Barbarism is not external to Europe, but internal to Europeans. The barbarian-Other is not a type of human or a 'race', but an indelible aspect of our unconscious. The barbarity of every civilized individual – which is unrestrained in wartime – levels the distinction between colonial-barbarian and European imperialist. The implicit universalism of psychoanalysis implies a uniformity of 'barbarity' within all individuals, which civilization restrains by degrees. Freud, like Nietzsche, argues that the civilized states may feel that 'barbarous' means of warfare are necessary in barbarous times.[61] But he also admits that this involves the constant attempt to restrain barbarian instincts within the state and within the individual. Freud firmly believes that cosmopolitanism and civilization work towards peace.[62] While Freud sees psychoanalysis as a tool for the resolution of the tension between instincts and the restraint of civilization, his discourse fits into the wider fear of (racial, sexual and civilizational) degeneration, which was an anxiety endemic to the colonial scene.[63] The constant danger to society thus becomes 'the return of the repressed' instincts, a term that has recently found its way back into International Relations with the end of the Cold War. The (re-)emergence of ethnic conflict after the supposed peace of the Cold War has been likened to Freud's 'return of the repressed'.[64] This is evident in the US-sponsored *mujahadeen* turning into the US-targeted Taliban.

Freud also has some interesting insights into the process of identification and group psychology. Since Matthew Arnold's *Culture and Anarchy* (1869), crowds had been identified as a novel and frightening social phenomenon. Scholarly treatises on the study of crowds began appearing in 1895 with Gustav LeBon's *Psychologie des foules*. Freud investigated the crowd and mass psychology in 1922, by which time the crowd had become a fixture in the imaginary of Europe. Indeed, Coker argues that the crowd 'dominated the imagination of twentieth-century Europe'.[65] This has special relevance as a diagnosis of the spirit of the First World War, which was epitomized by the mass rallies of support when war was declared.[66] Freud argues: 'by the mere fact that he forms part of an organized group, a man descends several rungs in the ladder of civilization. Isolated, he may be a cultivated individual; in a crowd, he is a barbarian – that is, a creature acting by instinct.'[67] The crowd is represented as an individual psyche writ large (with the attendant fears, wishes, instincts, fetishes, neuroses) – the fear of the crowds was the fear of one's own instincts. The 'barbaric' crowd is an indication of how close to the psychic surface the barbaric instincts lie.

This analysis of crowd psychology as barbaric is reminiscent of Nietzsche's condemnation of the 'herd instinct'. However, Nietzsche believes that noble and slave mentalities lead to powerful or weak instincts, rather than sheer numbers. Freud and Nietzsche disagree in this respect: whereas Nietzsche sees the natural instincts of the barbarian as 'noble', Freud considers unrestrained 'instincts' destructive to society. Psychoanalytic therapy is, in some aspects, the process of reconciling the necessary repression of society with one's instinctual drives. The traumatic experience of war by the individual lays this process bare and psychoanalysis became a popular therapy to treat war neuroses during the First World War.[68] Like Nietzsche, Freud is extremely critical of nationalism and of German nationalism in particular. However, Nietzsche views struggle as a far more positive process for spiritual growth than does Freud.

'WHAT DOES NOT KILL ME MAKES ME STRONGER'[69]

These prominent thinkers cultivated an attitude of cultural pessimism in Europe. This widespread nihilistic disposition took two popular forms: first, the belief that all civilizational values were transient and a matter of politics; and, second, that barbarism was a vital part of the human will-to-power. Nietzsche and Freud insisted that not only was the world unknowable, but 'we remain necessarily strangers to ourselves, we don't understand our own substance'.[70] Barbarians were not 'them', but 'us'. The barbaric was an integral – if repressed – component of every European's psyche. This led either to a fear of degradation or to repression and subsequent psychoanalysis. The killing zone of the Western Front in the First World War seemed to legitimize this view. European culture was itself racialized, as it had racialized its subjects in the colonies. Imperial methods of rule and imperial methods of killing were transplanted to the metropolitan centre. The drive to expand one's culture was internalized within Europe. The rhetoric of the civilizing mission began to sound hollow.

THE FIRST WORLD WAR: EUROPE'S FIRST BARBARIC WAR

The First World War marks a cultural break between the nineteenth and twentieth centuries. It was a war of mass mobilizations in which industrialized, mechanized, depersonalized death became familiar to civilians and soldiers alike. Nationalist propaganda was utilized, transforming the popular perception of conflict from a Newtonian 'balance of power' to an existential war of cultures and races. In fundamental ways, the First World War was, in part, a continuation of the nineteenth century.[71] The imperialist, paternalist rhetoric of civilization and barbarism was mobilized to shore up domestic identity and vilify the enemy on both sides of the conflict. The discourse of culture and race was used to mobilize popular opinion. Imperial competition was central to a nation's self-image as a world power; and nationalism was a chief determining factor in world politics. By the war's end some of the foundations for the twentieth century were also laid: the birth of modernism[72] as doubting authority and the power of representation, the eroding belief in rationalism and reason and the growing belief in irrational forces and vitalism, the birth of total war and the subsequent mobilization of entire societies in war, the centrality of technology in war, the rise of democracy, the beginnings of colonial independence movements, and, finally, the beginning of the decline of Europe as the centre of international society.

The discourse of 'civilization/barbarian' illustrates both the continuous and discontinuous aspects of the nineteenth and twentieth centuries. Daniel Pick argues:

> It would be difficult to overestimate the centrality of the notion of 'civilisation' in the language of the First World War. A broad distinction between 'civilisation' and 'barbarism' was used to distinguish the European imperial powers from their colonies; at other times to differentiate sections of the domestic population within a specific state; alternatively, 'civilisation' was deployed to contrast the behaviour and genealogy of one European nation with another.[73]

The persistence of the discourse and its power in the popular imagination illustrate the endurance of imperialist worldviews in International Relations. However, the First World War also saw the inversion of the civilization/barbarian discourse. For the first time, Europeans described each other, and even themselves, as barbaric.[74] By tracing the shift in the rhetoric of civilization/barbarian, we see how popular culture shapes identity, and how identity is politicized, especially in the event of war, to shore political support. The simultaneous inversion of the imperialist civilized/barbarian trope also illuminates the inherent ambivalence and instability within discourse, culture and European identity.

THE FIRST WORLD WAR AS A MASS PHENOMENON

Two of the most enduring popular photographs of the First World

War are the massive crowds that gathered to celebrate the outbreak of war (with a jubilant Hitler among the sea of faces) and the exotic portrait of Lawrence of Arabia in native dress. The heroic spy is the antithesis of the crowd, but both speak to the First World War as a mass phenomenon. Other wars have, of course, been hotly debated or loomed large in the public imagination – the American Civil War, and the Russo-Japanese and Franco-Prussian Wars clearly shaped the public's conception of war. However, the First World War required mass mobilization and subsequently mass support in a manner not required of previous conflicts. In this section, I will look at crowds, propaganda and war itself to illustrate the shift from a nineteenth- to a twentieth-century culture.

One of the important modes of governance that evolves from the colonial context and finds its way back to the imperial metropolis is that of *surveillance*. The twin concern with seeing and the unseen leads to the geometric, panoptic layout of colonial barracks, schools, prisons and even, in the case of Haussmann's boulevards, cities themselves. The opening of spaces, for the circulation of both people and commerce, has the effect of creating public spaces in which large numbers could gather. The first significant, pan-European moment of this mass 'euphoria, even ecstasy' is the outbreak of the First World War.[75] Eksteins argues that 'the crowds, in fact, seized the political initiative in Germany'.[76] The young and aimless Hitler claims to have found his purpose in the crowd at Munich celebrating the outbreak of war.[77] Freud is also caught up in this initial excitement for the Great War: 'For the first time in 30 years, I find myself to be an Austrian', he writes to a friend.[78] But, there is a double meaning to these discoveries of national sentiment. Only in the face of an existential struggle with a powerful enemy could either feel a part of the national community. Hitler feels German for the first time, instead of the provincial Austrian he was. Freud feels Austrian, despite the extent to which he had hitherto been excluded because of his Jewish heritage. The crowd gives a sense of identity and purpose to the nations at war, in large part, by defining an absolute enemy. The crowd is, in essence, a microcosm of the state and a product of the popular international imaginary.

The use of propaganda to create a national readership is a specific example of the wider pattern Benedict Anderson puts forward in *Imagined Communities*.[79] In creating a common national geography of enmity and friendship, 'internal differences were screened out of the representation [of the nation]; the lines of conflict were treated as purely external'.[80] Thus, the representation of a common enemy – or 'Other' – has the effect of reifying the nation – the 'self'. Hitler's provincialism, Freud's Jewishness, class antagonisms, political divisions are all subsumed under the grander, more important, national unity against the enemy – be they British, French, or German. Cate Haste argues: 'the essence of propaganda is simplification. In wartime, the intricate patterns of politics are refined into simple and crude messages of right and wrong.'[81] While this characterization of propaganda is a good starting point, we must recognize that propaganda is not simply the statements of a government, but is 'itself an active and often unsettled, a continuing and sometimes uneasy attempt to grasp and define national character'.[82]

Propaganda can be understood as politicized popular culture and international identity made explicitly part of political discourse. Rather than viewing it as a product, Philip Taylor suggests that we view propaganda as 'a *process* for the sowing, germination, and cultivation of ideas'.[83] As such, propaganda is understood as situated within a field of contested meanings and ambiguous identities. Propaganda makes an effort to portray political conflict in moralistic tones. The 'self' is virtuous; the 'Other' – the enemy – is evil incarnate.[84] This is not to say that propagandistic discourse goes uncontested. Peace groups in particular often provide a dissenting view. However, the ways in which propaganda constructs a threat helps to delegitimize other discourses. In short, propaganda is a critical intersection of national identity and popular culture.

National identity in the context of the First World War was overdetermined, not merely as the result of the propaganda ministry's statements, but that a whole network of institutions and cultural fields reified the same message. Narratives of empire, capitalism, liberalism and International Relations all circulated in the international imaginary.[85] The masculine, imperialist, righteous British were united against godless, Prussian militaristic, barbaric Huns and Germany. The masculine, cultured Germans were united against 'Asiatic barbarism and Latin indifference'.[86] The use of the barbarian stereotype to portray the Germans to the British and the British to the Germans deserves specific attention because of its effect on the attitudes and the actions of those engaged in waging the First and Second World Wars.

In many ways, Europe was primed for the First World War. From the end of the Franco-Prussian War, there had been a popular fascination for invasion stories in Britain, France and Germany. These popular novels, often serialized in magazines, described the nation's imminent war with its traditional enemy. I.F. Clarke argues that the protagonists of these invasion stories display 'a shift in both attitudes and expectations which would come to dominate all future-war fiction from 1871 onwards. Monarchs and their dynasties vanish from these dramas. The whole nation – soldiers, sailors, volunteers, and citizens – become the principal actors in the battle-to-come.'[87] These stories played a major role in shaping the pre-war imaginary in Britain, France and Germany.

Specifically, 'William Le Queux's *The Invasion of 1910* fill[ed] the public mind with the fear of invasion by a stereotyped enemy, "The Hun".'[88] Other stories shaped the technological expectations for the next war, including fictional treatises on submarine warfare, aerial warfare, and even the dangers of the Channel Tunnel. These stories filled the popular imagination with prophecies of defeat and decline, and projected the cultural decadence of Europe into the national and military spheres. The crowds of Europe expected, even anticipated, a war with which they had already become familiar in contemporary fiction.

The crowd sees two chief threats to its identity: the external, knowable enemy and the internal, seditious enemy. In some cases, the mobilization against this unseen enemy may take more extreme forms than those against the external enemy. In the nineteenth century, European civilization constructed its 'Other' in the form of the domestic underclass and the global colonized. This pattern of 'internal' and 'external 'others' was repeated during the First World War. The new 'internal Other' was racialized and ascribed many of the characteristics used to portray colonial 'barbarians'. The *'innere England'* or 'Hun under the bed', became the prime internal Other – which had the effect of both exaggerating and minimizing racial, class and gender differences within the national community.

This image of the power of the 'spy' and his invisibility can be seen as an extension of the fetish for dressing in native costume in the nineteenth century. Hannah Arendt argues that the secret agent is central to colonial governance, dressing up to rule rather than just explore.[89] However, what makes the place of the secret agent in the colonies secure is the fiction of the ability of the white to appear non-white, and the inability of the non-white to appear white. This visibility function makes the white, intra-European spy so dangerous in comparison. The German spy does not have the visible marker of colour to distinguish him/herself from the 'safe' English citizen. As such, spy paranoia was heightened by the earlier popular images of the Burtonesque imperial traveller. A manic attempt to locate 'actual' national markings ensued. 'Letters poured in telling authors and editors [of newspapers] of suspicious behaviour by German waiters, barbers, and tourists which presented an almost exact mirror image of Le Queux's book.'[90] The suggested reprisals against German nationals in Britain were strikingly totalitarian. It is surprising that the methods used to alienate the Jewish population from Germany were first suggested by the British to be used against the Germans in England.

> Horatio Bottomley [in May 1915] called for more colourful reprisals against Germans. All German property should be confiscated and all Germans locked up. Naturalized Germans should wear a distinctive badge and not be allowed out after dark. Their children should not be allowed to attend schools.[91]

Without the external signifier of race, the internal, European 'Other' is more seditious and thus demands other signs of racial Otherness.

The use of the barbarian trope in propaganda illustrates exactly the awareness of external and internal 'Otherness'. Barbarians, who had heretofore been confined to the non-European world or the lower classes, were suddenly 'found' inside Europe's bourgeois populace. The citizen of Britain, for example, became convinced that the citizen of Germany was visibly marked – if not by his/her skin colour, then by his/her unmaskable barbarous behaviour. The appeal to the civilized/barbarian rhetoric started almost immediately:

> On the 8th of August 1914, The London *Evening Standard*, shouted 'Civilization at Issue', and the theme reverberated ever after. 'Guerre contre les barbares' was simultaneously declared in France, while in Germany, the defence and nurture of *Kultur* became the duty and privilege of all good Germans.[92]

The barbarian stereotype immediately calls to mind 'danger'. Stereotypes are powerful because they simplify, and in doing so minimize ambiguity. They are most readily effective when they agree with previously held opinions.[93] Bhabha elaborates: 'the stereotype is [colonialism's] major discursive strategy, as a form of knowledge and identification that vacillates between what is already "in place", already known, and something that must be anxiously repeated . . . as if the essential duplicity of the Asiatic or the bestial sexual licence of the African that needs no proof, can never really, in discourse be proved. It is this process of *ambivalence*, [which is] central to the stereotype.'[94] Kiernan argues:

> In one sphere the colonialists, Britain in the lead, were far better equipped for the propaganda struggle which has been so essential a part of twentieth century warfare. They were well versed in the art of denigrating opponents, in order to justify their own less laudable acts and obviate fault-finding at home or abroad . . . in 1914–18, passion and prejudice long worked up against other races were diverted against a new target, with Germans in the roles of the 'Huns'. Once again civilization confronted barbarism.[95]

The stereotype of the barbarian called forth not only the passionate, irrational, oversexed 'coloured' man from the tropics, but also the atrocities of Attila the Hun and the Asiatic hordes which decimated Europe. Both British and Germans used this rhetoric of the barbarian to identify their enemy. The British reported, and invented, atrocity stories – crimes against women, children, the rule of law, cultural and historic sites – all symbols which represented civilization itself. The British nurse Edith Cavell, who was captured and shot by the Germans in Belgium, was a spy. Her capture and execution, however, were portrayed by the British press as an unprovoked assault on a defenceless woman, lending to the reification of the barbarian stereotype.[96] Again, propagandists linked national identity to other discourses – such as gender and class. The Germans portrayed the Russians as the direct descendants of the Mongols bent on ravaging European culture, and portrayed the English as perpetrating 'a kind of treacherous miscegenation, forging an alliance with black and yellow-skinned people . . . blurring the lines of division between European and non-European, or between superior and inferior Europeans'.[97] Both sides of the conflict saw themselves in an existential struggle for European culture, and each side saw itself as its protector of European culture. However, in naming other Europeans as barbaric, the imperialist ideology that was in part based on the palpable differences between civilized Europeans and barbaric non-Europeans began to unravel.

BARBARIC WARFARE

Another enduring image in the popular imaginary of Europe is the apocalyptic landscape of First World War battlefields and the faceless silhouettes of troops going 'over the top' into oblivion. First World War warfare was destructive on a scale previously unimagined.[98] It should be recalled, however, that the Spanish 'flu epidemic of 1919 caused more death than the First World War. Three notable facets of the new, modern type of warfare were specifically considered barbaric: barbaric weapons, barbaric tactics and barbaric troops.

It has been argued that the strategists of the First World War should have foreseen the prospects for a prolonged, costly war in the examples of the American Civil, Crimean and Russo-Japanese Wars.[99] In the American Civil War, we see the precursors of modern warfare: the first use of railways for mass mobilization, trench warfare, aerial balloons for surveillance, the destruction of civilian property as a military strategy and shell shock.[100] The Crimean War saw the first photographer, the use of colonial troops and widespread peace movements in Britain. The Russo-Japanese war saw a majority of casualties occurring from artillery, rather than from sickness or face-to-face combat. The First World War saw the first use of general submarine warfare, toxic gas, the machine gun and tactical air bombing. The codes of 'civilized' warfare were being overturned by technology.

Submarine attacks and bombing raids did not discriminate between civilians and combatants, and thus complicated one of the primary customs of warfare. The submarine was incredibly effective when submerged and when sinking other ships outright, but ineffective when acting as a small warship. International law attempted to restrict the indiscriminate killing of civilians and neutrals by proscribing rules of submarine warfare which neutralized all of the submarine's advantages – giving fair warning, capturing the ship with a prize crew rather than sinking it, and so on. 'Submarine commanders openly refused to act in accordance with this "absolute duty" pleading military necessity . . . The only alternative was not to use submarines at all, or to use them ineffectively.'[101] Whereas in the nineteenth century the use of technology was viewed as positive in the advancement of civilization, new technologies at war were considered to be barbaric. Technology had outpaced moral ideology.

Aerial bombing was first conducted in a colonial context, but was quickly adapted to the First World War:

> In October 1911, during the Italian-Turkish War, they bombed Turkish troops and Arab tribesmen in Libya . . . A year later the French Air Force used terror bombing to put down an anticolonial rebellion in Morocco. Targets included villages, markets, flocks of sheep, and fields of grain . . . Only a few thousand tons of bombs were dropped on strategic targets in World War I, an amount soon matched in various colonial bombing campaigns by France and Britain. The French even developed a fighter-bomber for just such a role, *Type Coloniale*, while the British initiated in parts of the empire a system of air rule called 'Control without Occupation'.[102]

Although a conference was convened, the international agreement on the use of aeroplanes in warfare was never signed. While both Allies and Axis powers denounced these tactics as 'barbaric', within the logic of deterrence they could not afford to forgo them.

The machine gun, which had pacified Africa and Asia, truly consumed a generation on the Western Front. Machine guns made killing an industrial process: 'While the infantry remained under cover, the effect of much of this fire was wasted; but when they rose to advance in attack, [a machine gun] might destroy a battalion of a thousand men in a few minutes.'[103] 'Maxim, the inventor of the first machine-gun, believed that "only a barbarian general would send his men to certain death against the concentrated power of his new gun".'[104] Outdated military tactics fed poorly trained recruits into the maw of the Western Front in orderly lines.

The imperial origin of the machine gun and strategic bombing is not insignificant. 'The only difference between the battle of the Somme (1916) and that of Omdurman (1898), the last of the great colonial battles, was that both sides in the European war had the same technology.'[105] It was not the use of these weapons in particular that was considered barbaric, but it was the use of these indiscriminate weapons against other whites.

Part of the objection to some weapon technology used in the First World War was the lack of discrimination between civilians and soldiers. Illustrative is Germany's 'shelling of the peaceful coastal resorts of Scarborough and Hartlepool . . . killing 137 people and injuring 592, including a party of schoolchildren . . . '[106] Also, '"strategic" [air] attacks far behind the lines such as German airships and Gotha bombers carried out against English cities from 1915 onwards, and the Royal Naval Air Service against the Rhur and Rhineland cities' were clearly not *military* targets.[107] The destruction of the library at Louvain, the 'scratching' of Nôtre Dame and the destruction of Rheims Cathedral were all described by France as 'the destruction of buildings consecrated to Religion, Art, Science and Charity, [a] treacherous method of warfare'.[108] Germany too had a list of complaints against Britain and France, including 'the use of dumdum bullets, unlawful and inhumane methods of conducting war, a method of waging war contrary to all international law, the bombardment of towns and villages from aeroplanes'.[109]

In the beginning of First World War, the military adhered to the 'cult of the offensive', which favoured movement and decisive victories – epitomized by the Schliffen Plan. However, the predominance of defensive weapons over offensive weapons in the First World War led to a static war of attrition. Attrition as a strategy was intended to 'bleed the enemy white', the pouring of troops into the battlefield until the opponent could no longer provide sufficient manpower to defend. Attrition was a battle of competing death; the winner being the country which could die more. 'Battles had become an industrial operation in reverse, in which rates of destruction at the Front matched the rates of production in the industries at home.'[110] Not only were individuals expendable, but the living conditions in the trenches, where heat, food and safety were scarce, made 'each man a savage'.[111] This shovelling of men unto death was barbaric by any standard and drained the meaning from the expectation of a short, glorious war. Disillusion was the prevailing mood of the 'Front Generation', those veterans who had witnessed the carnage even if they could not express it.[112]

One group that suffered even greater disregard by the high command, on the side of the Allies, were the 'coloured' troops employed in the First World War.[113] One of the most serious indictments by the Germans of the Allied war effort was 'the employment of barbarous and warlike tribes in a European war'.[114] The First World War was the 'first time in history that "coloured" troops were used in warfare on the continent of Europe', and it shocked the European world.[115] However, the colonial troops fought alongside 'whites' with little distinction. Indeed, they were considered so loyal as to be used to quell French mutinies in 1917.[116] The use of colonial troops against other whites violated the racial hierarchy that is central to the ideology of imperialism. The right of Europeans to rule over colonial subjects was based on a strict racial and national hierarchy. The willingness of colonial subjects to die patriotically for the European undid this hierarchy. The propaganda of the First World War made sacrifice in the Great War the greatest patriotic duty of the British or French citizen. If colonial *subjects* could die just as well as Englishmen and Frenchmen, it was unclear what the essential difference was.[117]

The use of colonial troops in a European conflict was not unforeseen. Hobson predicted the use of colonial troops in *Imperialism* in 1902.[118] France's fear of declining birth rates and the dynamic growth of Germany led Colonel Mangin to propose *La Force noire*, made up of Africans, which could defend the homeland.[119] Colonial troops suffered higher casualty rates in battle than their European counterparts did.[120] On the one hand, using native troops was in keeping with the racialist conception of colonial subjects as bodies, for attrition if not surveillance. However, the valour attached to the wartime deaths of white Europeans – who in the colonies would be their rulers, but whose death on the battlefield was no different, no less valorous, no less national, from theirs – complicated the imperial rhetoric. Colonial subjects were disposed of like bodies, but ironically in death were valorized like national citizens. This tension could not help but spill over into the political imaginary of the colonies when veterans returned.[121]

There is an interesting convergence of rhetoric with the use of 'barbaric' troops against the 'barbaric' Germans. The Germans, while depicting themselves as the defenders of civilization against the barbarians of the East, found themselves facing the 'barbarians' of the South – the Senegalese, Indian and West African units of the Anglo-French armies. The Germans 'were told that Gurkha and Sikh troops crept across no man's land at night, slipped into German trenches, slit German throats, and then drank the blood of their victims, and that Senegalese fighting with the French were cannibals'.[122] The Germans, for their part, dropped propaganda on South African compounds which read: 'In this war I hate black people the most. I do not know what they want in this European war. Where I find them, I will smash them.'[123]

Interestingly, the French camps in which both English and

French colonial troops were housed used the same plans as model villages in the colonies. Whereas in the colonies surveillance was designed to prevent insurrection, 'the self-contained nature of the camps and the degree of internal security possible there also minimized that which the French authorities were most anxious to avoid – contact between the African troops and the French populace'.[124] European colonizers clearly anticipated the disruption in the imperial discourse if contact were to occur. Given that the British strategy was attrition, and that Senegalese or Indians died just as well as their British or French rulers, the 'essential' difference in evolution was difficult to see. As Kiernan wryly comments: 'Britain wanted to think its native troops good enough to help win the war, but not good enough to be able to break away from the empire.'[125]

So shocking was the war's impact on European culture and European identity that the 1920s can be seen as a manic expression of relief at the war's end. The civilized/barbarian discourse had been used extensively in propaganda by both sides in the conflict. As such, the stereotype was in the forefront of the European imaginary. However, the war's barbarity – by Europe's own standards – had left many Europeans with doubts. After describing fellow Europeans as barbarians, it was problematic to return to the simplistic imperialistic dichotomy of civilized colonizer and barbarian colonized. This was especially true when 'civilized' Europeans had behaved barbarically towards one another, and when 'barbarian' natives had acted with valor in war.

The self/Other dichotomy, which proved so powerful, was mobilized against both internal, European 'Others' and colonial 'Others'. While these different groups were often described in the same way – relying on the discourse of civilization/barbarian – the national 'self' was strengthened by these threats. National identity was solidified in the face of threats within the nation, from other European nations, and from the colonized.

INTERWAR YEARS: THE GREAT DISILLUSION

The primary intergovernmental institution of the interwar period was the League of Nations, the Covenant of which is steeped in the discourse of 'civilization'. Article 22, which deals with the Mandate System, refers specifically to the 'sacred trust of civilization'.[126] Those people who could not govern themselves were to be 'tutored' by 'advanced' nations, until such time as they could participate meaningfully in international society. The different categories of trust ('A', 'B' and 'C') correspond to 'savage' and barbarian' hierarchy – redeemable or irredeemable in the eyes of Europe. The League of Nations retained some of nineteenth-century Europe's definition of itself as the civilized ruler of barbarian colonies, which were unable to rule themselves. Gong has traced this specific development in his seminal book, while Bull and Watson have traced the general shift from a European to a global international society.[127]

Two trends are visible. On the one hand, there was a popular panic over the 'rising tide of colour', which predicted the overthrow of European/Western culture by the barbarous savages. A rising anxiety about racial struggle began to emerge during the interwar period. On the other hand, imperialism had begun to come under attack as a form of European self-aggrandizement, rather than as the pursuit of altruistic or concrete interests.[128] Hobson's critique of imperialism on economic grounds had been bolstered by Lenin's polemic. As such, the new 'civilizing mission' was explicitly justified by its emphasis on more practical economic and governmental matters, as opposed to European nations' previously stated goal of spiritual enlightenment.[129]

Outside Western Europe, Wilson's rhetoric of self-determination was equally hard-pressed to distinguish between nations deserving of statehood and colonies unfit for self-rule.[130] Though independence movements were not widely successful, the idea of self-rule had entered into the political imaginary of Europe and its colonies.[131] In sum, the civilization/barbarian opposition was present in the international imaginary, but had lost some of its former rigidity. Europe was suspect as 'civilization', although the League of Nations Mandate System was still explicitly based on the distinction.

Within this uneasy interwar period, International Relations emerged as a political and academic discipline struggling with the competing images of European civilization and barbarism that appeared in popular and political discourse. Two important intersections between the civilization/barbarian discourse and the discipline of International Relations are the study of propaganda, and the characterizations of Hitler.

International Relations developed quickly between the world wars, though its roots can be traced before the First World War. As a product of the initial postwar optimistic worldview, it quickly reflected the change in cultural mood and politics signified by the fall of the League of Nations system and the rise of fascist power in Italy and Germany. It is interesting to note how briefly the 'idealist' turn of IR theory lasted, and the degree to which the early idealists felt themselves to be 'realistic'.[132] It is also interesting that the 'realist' mood of interwar International Relations integrated its idealist predecessor, rather than rejecting it outright. Alfred Zimmern, Arnold Toynbee and E.H. Carr are prime examples of this fusion. Carr argues in *The Twenty Years' Crisis* for a balanced approach to IR theory. He warns: 'it is as fatal in politics to ignore power as it is to ignore morality'.[133] There is more theoretical and methodological depth to these early realists than has usually been acknowledged.[134] Though I would argue that interwar realism is more nuanced than the traditional narrative allows, there is no doubt that idealism was denounced by these realist scholars. Again, to recall Carr: 'From [the Manchurian crisis] onwards, a rapid succession of events forced upon all serious thinkers a reconsideration of [idealist] premises which were becoming more and more flagrantly divorced from reality.'[135] The pessimistic turn of the 1930s can be represented by the shift in the *primus inter pares* of statesmen in the international imaginary: Wilsonian optimism is replaced by Hitler's *realpolitik*. Whereas Wilson shaped the discourse of an international society in the optimistic postwar years, Hitler shaped the trope of the barbarian in the imaginary of the pre-Second World War IR community.[136] In failing to respond adequately to Hitler, the discipline consequently adopted Hitler as their paradigm for the worst-case scenario – a rational actor with irrational aims. Hitler's foreign policy between 1933 and 1941 was the epitome of realist, power-maximization – however irrational his justifications or aims. Whereas the idealist view of international morality held that 'an obligation to our fellow-men seems implicit in our conception of civilisation', Hitler's power politics successes quickly prompted a realist correction.[137] Hitler's successes on both diplomatic and military stages shaped powerfully the imagination of the 1930–45 generation of IR scholars. Although the realist mode of international theory has been traced through Rousseau, Hobbes, Machiavelli and Thucydides, the post-Second World War discipline can be seen as guarding itself from Hitler's example. After the failure of the Wilsonian League system, the discipline adopted a theoretical stance that could expect Hitler-like foreign policy in the future. After Hitler, international behaviour is assumed to be barbarian before it is assumed to be civilized.

EUROPE'S UN-CIVIL WAR

European citizens had considered themselves 'civilized', both in absolute and comparative terms in the nineteenth century. The pessimistic mood that overcame Europe in the first 40 years of the twentieth century set the ideational basis to question this identity. Nietzsche, Freud and Spengler re-examined this discourse of 'civilization' and 'barbarians', with different conclusions. These intellectuals popularized ideas – such as will to power, the decline of the West, return of the repressed – which were to become central terms in early twentieth-century political discourse. The ideals of Nietzsche, Spengler and Freud placed a different, less pejorative, emphasis on barbarism. They also described 'civilization' as far more precarious than was previously imagined. These ideas were to resonate with ambiguity within the identity of many Europeans as 'civilized Europeans' in the early twentieth century.

Hitler's successes in the realm of International Relations led to his adoption by the IR community as its worst-case scenario – a lunatic against whom they had to protect themselves. Hitler's philosophy of struggle, violence and brutality became the touchstone of postwar theorists. Just as Napoleon had caused a conservative reaction in European society, so too did Hitler elicit a defence of the Westphalian system, with its values of balance, statehood and sovereignty.

This chapter has focused almost exclusively on the discourse of civilization and barbarians, and the relevance of culture and identity to International Relations. In chapter 5, I will look at the collapse of the imperial system. This trend was initiated by the sacrifice of native troops to defend their colonial masters, and in the rising awareness of Europe's own political values. The moral foundation for decolonization can be found in the Nazi use of colonial tactics to perpetrate the 'Final Solution'. Wight argues that 'the deepest reason why the West was shocked by Hitler was his introducing colonial methods of power politics, their own colonial methods, into international relations'.[138] Chapter 5 tackles the discrediting of the civilizing mission and the decline of imperialism in International Relations.

5 New Barbarians

THE LOSS OF EUROPE'S 'CIVILIZED' STATUS

In chapter 4, I argued that the discourse of 'civilized/barbarian' unravelled during the First and Second World Wars. For the first time, Europeans described themselves as barbaric and doubted their capacity for civilization. The Nazi invasion of Russia, and its attendant *Generalplan Ost*, provided the most shocking evidence of Europe's 'progress'. Immediately after the Second World War, the discourse of 'civilized/barbarian' was again undermined. In this chapter, the change from Idealist to Realist paradigms within International Relations is explored, looking specifically at the role of Adolf Hitler in this transformation. The anti-colonial movement prompted 'colonized' thinkers to decry Europe as barbaric and European civilization as bankrupt. Thinkers such as Aimé Césaire and Frantz Fanon showed that imperial governance was barbaric in itself, and debunked the rhetoric of the 'civilizing mission'. The 'civilized/barbarian' discourse was inverted to serve the ideological needs of decolonization and to shore up anti- and postcolonial identity.

BARBARIAN FOREIGN POLICY: THEORIZING AGAINST HITLER

The change from Idealist to Realist consensus in International Relations has much to do with the emergence of Hitler and the Nazi Party on the world stage.[1] Hitler is one of the most challenging figures in modern history, especially because of the initial successes of his foreign policy and his popularity in Germany, despite the violent and barbaric tenure of the Nazis. The scale of his crimes against humanity can barely be tallied, and the underlying banality of his personality fundamentally altered our understanding of evil in the twentieth century.[2] I would argue that Hitler's success in the face of academic Idealism led to the entrenchment of Realism in the discipline of International Relations at this time. Hitler, a barbarian statesman, is adopted as the primary role model in International Relations.[3]

Two trends in the IR community can be traced directly to Hitler's arrival on the international scene. Before Hitler, the default assumption of the 1920s seemed to be that statesmen and nations would act honourably and according to Christian morals, at least within the European family of nations. After the success of Hitler's aggression, individuals and nations were assumed to be 'imperialist', narrowly understood as seeking power.[4] After the revelation of Nazi atrocities in Germany and the East, the Enlightenment and Wilsonian assumptions that nations would usually act rationally and morally were completely discredited. These two changes, the barbarism of international affairs and the potential barbarism of all nations, shaped the postwar IR imaginary. After tracing Hitler's theory of International Relations, I will look at the contention that post-1933 IR adopted Hitler as a dangerous statesman. When considering Hitler's impact on International Relations, it is important to remember Bull's point that, initially, the Second World War started as a war to prevent German hegemony over Europe.[5] Without the evidence of the death camps, the impetus to war on the Allied side was primarily the reassertion of a balance of power in Continental Europe.

One might argue that American Realism had started the 'Realist' turn coincident to, but not because of, the rise of Hitler.[6] Frederick Schuman writes in the preface to his 1933 text *International Politics*:

> The analysis of international politics attempted in the following pages does not postulate the inevitability of sweetness and light or support the illusion that the law of the jungle in the international anarchy has, by some late magic, been superseded by the morality of the millennium. The approach is rather that of *Realpolitik*, characterized by Machiavellian detachment and

an earnest effort to delve beneath the phraseology to underlying realities.[7]

The United States' isolationist mood kept it insulated, in some regard, from the immediacy of Hitler's actions. However, it is certainly true that postwar International Relations in the United States was shaped by Hitler in two specific respects. First, Hans J. Morgenthau's personal experience as a refugee influenced his perception of international relations, statesmen and morality. Second, Hitler was taken as a model for Stalin's behaviour.

Hitler himself is remarkably clear in expressing his theory of international politics: 'I am concerned with power politics – that is to say, I make use of all means that seem to me to be of service, without the slightest concern for the proprieties or for codes of honour.'[8] While this frank statement of realist principles has not been incorporated explicitly into International Relations as a discipline, I would argue it has been accepted as the assumed viewpoint of postwar statesmen. There are two aspects of his thought, however, which have been totally discredited. First, it must be noted that Hitler's worldview was dominated by a racialist ideology, which Hannah Arendt has argued is similar to the imperialist ideology of the nineteenth century.[9] As he states in Mein Kampf, 'all who are not of good race in this world are chaff'.[10] The racialist aspects of Hitler's view have been rejected by IR scholars, to the extent that race is rarely considered a legitimate object of study in the discipline.[11] Second, Hitler's theory of International Relations is based on a pseudo-Nietzschean, social-Darwinist idea that in the realm of world politics the strongest, hardest and most brutal survive. This goes beyond notions of 'self-defence' and argues that aggression is the only way to guarantee security.[12] In this sense, Arendt argues, 'the struggle for total domination of the total population of the earth, the elimination of every competing non-totalitarian reality, is inherent in the totalitarian regimes themselves; if they do not pursue global rule as their ultimate goal they are only too likely to lose whatever power they have already seized'.[13] It can also be argued that Germany's Nazi identity was stable only in 'defence' against the enemies of the Volkgemeinshaft (national community).[14] Following this, both Hitler's declarations of war cited self-defence as the primary cause of his aggression.[15] However, separate from Hitler's public declarations, his private speech reveals his obsession with aggression and attack.

On the eve of the invasion of the Low Countries, Hitler told the German High Command, 'Basically, I did not organize the Armed Forces in order not to strike. The decision to strike was always in me . . . Without attack the war cannot be ended victoriously.'[16] Even earlier, Hitler had stated in *Mein Kampf*: 'Mankind has grown great in eternal struggle, and only in eternal peace does it perish.'[17] Written in prison when Hitler was far from power, he summarizes his view of foreign policy: 'The essential, fundamental and guiding principle, which we must always bear in mind judging this question, is that foreign policy is only a means to an end, and that the end is solely the promotion of our own nationality.'[18] In this statement we see the core of his international theory: naked self-interest, which subordinates all other consideration to the good of the nation. It must be said that this was not in conflict with the prevailing view of international politics. By the time of the Locarno Treaty, Germany had been reintegrated into the European family of nations, and it was widely accepted that Germany had been politically and psychologically prostrated in the Versailles settlement.[19] As such, the predisposition of European states was to appease Hitler, atoning for the unjust terms of the peace treaty. Hitler's claim to *Lebensraum* ('living space') on demographic terms was even treated in the popular press as if it were valid.[20] But the architects of appeasement ignored Hitler's earlier repudiation of a diplomatic solution to Germany's problems – and ignored the violence and brutality in the Nazi regime itself, which could not help but spill over its borders. Hitler, as part of a larger ideology that praised violence, scorned attempts to make international relations peaceful.[21] 'We must clearly recognize the fact that the recovery of lost territories is not won through solemn appeals to the Lord or through pious hopes in a League of Nations, but only by **a force of arms**.'[22]

In a revealing tirade, Hitler presents the view to which all postwar International Relations is a reaction:

> It was the Peace of Westphalia which was the foundation of the permanent weakness of modern Germany. I have always said to my supporters: 'It is not the Treaty of Versailles we must destroy, but the Treaty of Westphalia.'[23]

Hitler wanted to undermine the very notions of order and balance, which the Westphalia settlements and the institution of state sovereignty represented. He wanted an international system that was unipolar instead of multipolar, and was based on struggle rather than stability. The reaction of the IR community was to reassert the Westphalian system as its model.[24] The parallel that scholars drew between Napoleon and Hitler is revealing. Both are revolutionary and Realist, in Wight's sense of the terms, desiring to overthrow the international order.[25] And both provoked a conservative reaction in the international imagination. Carr argues: 'Hitler, like Napoleon, has performed the perhaps indispensable function of sweeping away the litter of the old idealist order. A new order must be built by other hands and by other methods.'[26] With Machiavelli as his intellectual patron and Napoleon as his historical example (along with Frederick the Great), IR scholars took these figures as paradigms and structured their expectations around them.

During the Idealist turn, the good of the nation was seen to be in 'harmony' with peace in the international system.[27] This Idealism was based on nineteenth-century philosophers such as Jeremy Bentham and John Stuart Mill.[28] The failure of idealist theories, international law and international institutions to prevent, deter or limit Hitler's foreign policy gave support to the realist camp. In short, Hitler was the most disruptive possible statesman, and International Relations after him took him to be their worst-case scenario. He was intelligent, a skilful diplomat, aggressive and imperialist.[29] After Hitler, IR scholars assumed no statesman was necessarily moral or could be swayed by moral condemnation without the resort to force.

There is more than a general correlation between Hitler's philosophy of International Relations and the realist conception of world affairs. The early realists in Britain described Hitler as barbaric and Nazism a threat to civilization. The coincidence in terminology resonates in popular culture and IR theory throughout the war, and after. Hitler himself saw the Third Reich as the celebration of barbarism. It was natural that his foreign policy reflects this: 'The German is always restrained by moral scruples, which mean nothing to the British; to the latter such an attitude is merely a sign of weakness and stupidity. In the past we have readjusted the balance only by resorting in the most ruthless and barbarous manner.'[30] Many international theorists agreed.

Three prominent members of the interwar and Second World War IR community in Britain were E.H. Carr, Arnold Toynbee and

Alfred Zimmern. Toynbee wrote the *Survey of International Affairs* under the auspices of the Royal Institute of International Affairs (Chatham House). They were familiar with each other's work, and committed to the ideals of Chatham House: 'systematic analysis of international affairs and public education'.[31] The use of the same 'civilized/barbarian' rhetoric to describe Hitler and Nazism by all of these scholars is striking.

At first, they reflected the view promulgated by Freud and Spengler, that barbarism was the necessary obverse of European civilization. Zimmern had stated in his inaugural lecture at Oxford that 'Our choice is not between a civilized life in a [*polis*] of our own and admitting the barbarian within our walls. He dwells there already.'[32] Toynbee, Zimmern's student, describes barbarism as an integral component of European civilization:

> The relation of the Nazi regime of 1933 in Germany to the rest of the World can be seen as a unity – and also, perhaps, seen in the clearest light – if it is regarded as one phase of the secular relation between the spirit of Western Christendom and the spirit of a European barbarism which Christianity had sometimes cowed and sometimes charmed, and had thereby partly tamed, but never wholly excised.[33]

As early as 1933, Toynbee had identified Nazism as a threat to Western civilization and Hitler as barbaric.[34] In a fashion that would become familiar in his postwar epic, *The Study of History* (also published under the auspices of Chatham House, between 1934 and 1954), Toynbee traces the ascendancy of the Nazi Party to the secular philosophy of Machiavelli. The realist invocation of Machiavelli is a rhetorical move.[35] The totalitarian state becomes a moral end in and of itself. Machiavelli's non-moral state is realized in the Nazi regime. Hitler is portrayed as the modern incarnation of Machiavelli.[36] At the same time, early realists identified morality as an important component for statecraft, which allowed them to distinguish Hitler from themselves. This is the dilemma of European identity after Nazism and Hitler. There is no *a priori* way to distinguish the Nazi strain of European culture from the democratic strain – both are heirs of the Enlightenment.[37] This was to raise questions about Europe's identity as civilized in the minds of both Europeans and non-Europeans.[38]

Toynbee argues that the Nazi regime is shown to be barbaric by the way it treats its minorities and dissenters.[39] Toynbee had met Hitler in 1936 and came away from the meeting impressed.[40] Like Carr, he initially supported the policy of appeasement.[41] On reflection, however, he ascribes Hitler 'barbaric' characteristics in a number of texts. Zimmern makes the analogy between Hitler and Attila the Hun in the first Oxford Pamphlet on World Affairs: 'The present rulers of Germany have been responsible for causing more human suffering than has ever been inflicted before by any body men in power. Attila's record is spotless compared with theirs.'[42] In *A Study of History*, Hitler is used as an example of the dangers of disarmament:

> Hitler perceived that, in a world whose peoples were all now miserably war-weary and war-shy, world-domination might be the easy prize of any nation that could still be coaxed, duped, doped, or flogged by an audacious demagogue or despot into being one degree less unwarlike than its neighbours.[43]

The realism of Hitler's policy was coloured by the manic nihilism of his ideology, making Hitler the epitome of *realpolitik* gone wrong.[44] Hitler is portrayed as the worst possible natural product of European political culture. He personalizes the stereotype of the barbarian for international theorists, and International Relations reacts to him as such. This connection between Hitler's barbarism and colonial methods of rule will be elaborated in the following chapter. Toynbee and Carr described a realist view of world politics, which pits Nazi barbarism against Western civilization.

BARBARIC BY ANY MEASURE: NAZISM, THE *GENERALPLAN OST* AND THE HOLOCAUST

The civilized/barbarian distinction, which Europeans made between themselves and their colonial subjects, and which had suffered in the First World War as a culturally self-authenticating device, collapsed after the Second World War. There are several aspects of this discursive shift which have serious implications for the development of the discipline of International Relations and the international imaginary. The Second World War marks a transition from an imperially-based barbarian – viewed from the European perspective – to an ideologically-based barbarian – viewed from the American perspective. Nazi Germany provides a clear example of the evolution of the barbarian stereotype and how it came to be applied to Europeans. Internally and externally, Nazi Germany's rule was barbaric, by its own standards and by the standards of the international community. The most striking examples of this barbarity are related: Hitler's attempt to socially engineer the German nation and the attempt to colonize the East. *Operation Barbarossa*, the German code-name for the invasion of the Soviet Union, and the *Generalplan Ost*, the plan for the Occupied Eastern Territories, developed by Heinrich Himmler and Hitler, were the extension of the European imperialist ideology to Europeans themselves. *Operation Barbarossa* and the *Generalplan Ost* can be characterized as imperialism without the rhetoric of a 'civilizing mission' – those that were not already civilized would be destroyed.

Hitler also applied this rationale to his own population through the euthanasia programme, social and economic policies which promoted a *Volkgemeinshaft* (pure racial/national community) and the Holocaust. The Holocaust and its attendant programmes were not thinkable without the imperialist modes of governance and imperialist theories of race.[45] The bureaucratic mechanisms that enabled the Holocaust were also dependent on apparatuses of the 'modern' state, which had developed, in part, to cope with the administration of the colonies. The German sociologist Max Weber argues that these characteristics of the modern state were specifically Western.[46] He also suggests that the development of 'rationality' makes Western civilization uniquely capable of imperial expansion.[47] Modern education, public health institutions, statistics, demography and 'rational' bureaucracies were valued as the epitome of European progress, but were also indispensable to the Holocaust.[48]

The logical limit of the process of dehumanization of the 'Other' is genocide.[49] Within the imperialist ideology, non-European colonial subjects were viewed as possessing varying degrees of humanity. Non-European cultures were considered, for the most part, inferior to European civilization. The most extreme point of imperialist ideology – which remains true to the logic of the discourse – is the extermination of non-European cultures and peoples. American and Canadian governments practised eugenic, race-based sterilization programmes until the middle of the twentieth century.[50] The British politician Horatio Bottomley suggested labelling dangerous immigrants during the First World War and excluding German immigrants from schools, professions and public spaces. The British first used concentration camps during the Boer War.[51] This is not to make a *post hoc, ergo propter hoc* argument – that because imperialism preceded Nazi genocide, imperialism is necessary to the Holocaust. I only wish to indicate that all the precursors to the Nazi atrocities had been present in European culture prior to the Second World War.

The Holocaust depended on the discursive practice of 'othering'. In the colonial scene, colonial subjects were represented as inferior to Europeans and as less-than-human. In the Nazi case, Jews, Sinti and Roma, homosexuals, Poles, communists, etc., were represented as inferior and less than human. Whereas European colonizers were restrained by the rhetoric of the 'civilizing mission', there was no such restraint in the Nazi discourse. Many of the mechanisms, structures and institutions that were used in the Holocaust, in fact, have their origins in the colonial context. However, the Nazis' unique application of European institutions to these barbaric ends undermined European confidence in itself.

The question of how a modern, civilized state like Germany could descend into wholesale barbarism is an essential part of the narrative of the civilized/barbarian discourse in European culture. This is not to say that the Japanese, Russian or others did not act barbarically in the Second World War, only that it was the stated ideal of Nazi Germany to become self-consciously barbaric.[52] What makes the horror of the Holocaust all the more profound is that it was conducted as a 'rational, scientific, bureaucratic' policy.[53] The Holocaust – as much as Hiroshima – shaped the post-Second World War international imaginary, destroying the supposed moral supremacy of Europe and European 'civilization'. The Second World War saw the institutionalization of barbarism, both as an ideology and as a mode of governance. The internal and external dimensions of Nazi ideology are, of course, two sides of the same coin. In the next section I will look at Hitler's attempt to overcome internal 'racial-hygienic' enemies, the attempt to colonize the Eastern territories of the Reich, and the connection between the Final Solution and *Operation Barbarossa.*

BARBAROUS UTOPIA: NAZI IDEOLOGY AND THE *VOLKGEMEINSHAFT*

Just as European identity was constructed around the dichotomy of external and internal barbarians from the imperial world, German identity in the Second World War was constructed around internal and external barbarians. However, the nihilist philosophy of Nazism negated any possibility of a civilizing mission. 'Racially unhygienic' barbarians who were uncultured and uncivilized had been left behind by history. They would be destroyed or left to die off. The most disturbing aspect of the 'euthanasia' programme and the 'Final Solution' was not that they were aberrant within European culture, but that they were the application of aspects of colonial strategies against other Europeans. Hitler and the Nazis imported the discourse of civilized/barbarian in order to shore up a fragmented, post-First World War identity and justify their attempts to destroy the 'enemies' of the Reich.

Germany's rise in international stature is not separate from its domestic regeneration after the rise of the Nazi Party. Germany had been formally reintegrated into international society with the Locarno treaties.[54] Between then and the outbreak of the Second World War, Germany's claims to colonies, lost territories and economic security were all treated as equal to the other powers of Europe.[55] As such, Hedley Bull reminds us that the Western Front of the Second World War was primarily fought to restore the balance of power within Europe, not to destroy fascism *per se*. 'The revelation of 1945 of the full extent of Nazi atrocities . . . made the war seem in retrospect to have been more of a struggle for human rights than in fact it had been.'[56] Although it must be remembered that a great deal of rhetoric portrayed the conflict in these Manichean terms. Churchill was particularly vociferous in his denunciation of Hitler and the 'Huns'.[57] However, Germany's meteoric rise from vanquished nation to Great Power was due primarily to the policies of the Nazi government. While the Nazis were notorious for their violent tendencies and xenophobic, incendiary rhetoric, they also instituted a large number of 'progressive' policies.[58] The Nazi government instituted many modern, 'social welfare' programmes, helped reduce unemployment and rejuvenated German identity through a revisionist foreign policy. The only way to understand these contradictory impulses of modernization in social and economic policy and primitivism in politics is to examine the Nazi ideology. Michael Burleigh and Wolfgang Wippermann suggest that Nazism constituted both 'a simultaneous regression and progression into barbarism'[59] and that progressive and regressive are not different impulses within the Nazi ideology but different aspects of the same 'racial-hygienic' worldview. The 'progressive' measures were taken to create a

Volkgemeinshaft, or pure racial/national community. The 'regressive' measures were taken against those enemies of the *Volkgemeinshaft*. The first campaign of the Nazi government was against 'racially unhygienic' internal enemies – individuals believed to undermine the 'health' of the nation. Initially, the unfit, handicapped and terminally ill were targeted, along with Jews, Sinti, Roma and homosexuals. However, soon these 'obvious' racial enemies came to include 'asocial' and 'lazy' individuals – in short, any and all enemies of Nazi ideology.[60] Coker draws the parallel between the Nazi 'internal colonization'[61] – the attempt to purify the German race – and Anglo-French external colonization. He argues that the Nazis

> set out with the same colonial zeal as the British and French
> ... The Germans had moved from redeeming Africa to redeeming
> Europe by subjugating the Jews, the gypsies, the Slavs and any
> other subspecies of mankind considered to be 'primitive',
> 'ritualistic', 'superstitious' or 'alien'.[62]

In a bastardization of Nietzschean principles of cultural rejuvenation, Nazi ideology sought the stewardship of German culture through racial-hygienic means. Nietzsche seemed to prefigure this: 'I know my destiny. Some day my name will be associated with the memory of something monstrous.'[63] As argued above, while Nietzsche was not anti-Semitic, his Nazi followers used the scapegoat of the 'Jew' to shore up post-First World War Germany. Zygmunt Bauman argues: 'Inside every nation, they were the "enemy inside".'[64] Nazis argued that the mythical Aryan alone could preserve true German *Kultur*: 'In this world, human culture and civilization are inseparably bound up with the existence of the Aryan. His dying off or his decline would again lower upon this earth the dark veils of a time without culture.'[65]

Anti-Semitism was inscribed in German legislation almost immediately after the Nazis seized power: the Law for the Restoration of the Professional Civil Service, which prohibited Jewish state employees, was followed by legislation against Jewish physicians, teachers and students, all in April 1933.[66] These laws were followed by further legislation against 'alien races'. The use of academic and bureaucratic institutions to identify physical characteristics of racial genealogy is evidence of the continuing complicity of academe in imperial projects and shows the extent to which racial ideology was accepted as normal within European culture up to this point.[67] These methods used to preserve German culture, and thus European civilization, were shockingly modern. Arendt argues that such totalitarian modes of governance are an extension of imperial modes into the metropolitan population.[68] Following on the emphasis of 'surveillance' as a mode of imperial governance in chapter 3, Burleigh and Wippermann argue specifically that 'the employment of modern data-gathering and demoscopic techniques to encompass and control the whole population [facilitated] the "eradication" of the "alien" and "less valuable"'.[69] The apotheosis of this 'demoscopic' technique is the wearing of the 'Jewish Star', made compulsory on 1 September 1941. It 'enabled "national comrades" to tell at a glance who was a Jew', a matter difficult to establish with other criteria. The introduction of this visible stigma also marked the formal transition from defamation and economic ruination to the total exclusion of Jews from the 'national community'.[70] The ideational distinction between Germans and Jews was *prior* to their physical separation and subsequent extermination.[71] This distinction, which became central to Nazi German identity, was made in popular culture through methods that originated in the imperialist practices of the nineteenth century. As Bauman argues:

> The truth is that every 'ingredient' of the Holocaust – all those many things that rendered it possible – were normal . . . in the sense of being in keeping with everything we know about our civilization, its guiding spirit, its priorities, its immanent vision of the world.[72]

Modern bureaucracy was used extensively in the lead-up to the Holocaust. Burleigh and Wippermann detail the way that racial policies were institutionalized. Marriage loans (which could be repaid by having children) were refused to individuals who were 'racially suspect'. 'Hereditary Health Courts' could order 'euthanasia' based on information from a network of bureaucratic offices and institutes which provided 'genetic' information; institutes and academic departments were established to parse the Nazi racial theories.[73] They conclude: 'the card indexes, charts, diagrams, maps, books, articles, and statistics [these academics] produced were partly responsible for the clinically comprehensive and devastatingly effective manner in which Nazi racist policies were carried out'.[74]

Daniel Goldhagen has traced how Jews, the mentally ill and Slavs were figured in a hierarchy similar to the imperialist model which accorded different status to savages and barbarians.[75] State education, which had been used to foster nationalist sentiment, included instruction in racialist doctrine after 1933.[76] The end-point of all of these measures was the Holocaust. The marginalization of Jews, Sinti, Roma and other 'racial aliens' started in 1933 and progressed throughout the Nazi regime.

There are many important scholarly works on the Holocaust, which track the exclusion of Jews from the beginnings of the Nazi Party through to the Final Solution.[77] For the purposes of this project, I will limit myself to discussing the implication of the racial ideology of the Nazi Party in popular culture. The measures by which 'racial aliens' and the 'socially unvaluable' were isolated, excluded and finally exterminated indicate that popular culture and identity are essential to understanding domestic and international politics.

The Nazi regime was dedicated to propaganda – to the forging of a Nazi consciousness through popular culture. George Mosse argues that the Third Reich controlled national popular and elite culture specifically in order to promulgate its ideology.[78] The most coherent sections of *Mein Kampf* are those that deal with propaganda, and the most effective arm of the Nazi Party was Joseph Goebbels' Ministry of Public Enlightenment Propaganda.[79] In order that *German* citizens (Jews, Sinti, Roma and homosexuals, etc.) could be exterminated, a process of alienation was necessary. 'True' Germans had to be distinguished from 'racial aliens'. 'Racial aliens' were excluded from the national community and made the source of evil. This had the effect of strengthening the identity of the national community and making it the 'true' nation, and thus the source of good.[80] 'The Jews were defined, and hence excluded, as the embodiments of general evils. Old legends and prejudices were revived and combined with the more up-to-date conspiracy theories like the falsified "Protocols of the Elders of Zion".'[81] In addition to elaborating stereotypes of Jews and 'Gypsies' as unclean, parasitic, lecherous, disease-ridden, and so on, there were political measures designed to accompany the ideational separation. The Reich Citizenship Law limited political rights to 'German citizens' and made Jews 'subjects' of the German Reich.[82] By excluding Jews and other 'racial aliens' from the *Volkgemeinshaft*, first professionally to make them 'socially dead', then economically and finally spatially, they became perceived and treated as internal enemies to the German nation.[83] What is most disturbing about this trend of exclusion is that 'modern' – and imperial – modes of governance, such as surveillance, demography, anthropology and public health organizations, were all implicated in the exclusion and subsequent extermination of the internal enemies of the German racial community. *Operation Barbarossa* and the subsequent *Generalplan Ost* make the connection to imperialism clearer.

EXTERNAL COLONIZATION: A BARBARIC EMPIRE AND THE UNCIVILIZING MISSION

The imperialist ideology treated colonial subjects with varying degrees of humanity. As Goldhagen elaborates, Jews, the mentally ill and Slavs were accorded less and less 'humanity' in comparison with Germans.[84] The Slavs and Jews were irredeemable in racial terms and subsequently were treated as slaves for labour or 'cancerous' bodies for extermination. Hitler's effort to colonize the Eastern occupied territories was a logical extension of imperialist ideology. In both *Mein Kampf* and *Tabletalk*, Hitler stresses his admiration for England and promises that Eastern Europe will be 'Germany's India'.[85] However, Hitler rejects the civilizing mission. Those people without culture – *Untermenschen*, a term that came into use after the launch of *Operation Barbarossa* – were to be destroyed or become slaves to German colonists.[86] Omer Bartov argues that because the *Untermenschen* were treated as subjects without humanity, these colonial conflicts 'quickly developed much stronger genocidal tendencies' than those free of such ideas.[87] The connection of the ideology of *Untermenschen* and imperialism is not accidental. Hitler's *Generalplan Ost* was the first application of an imperialist ideology to European peoples. The Asiatic barbarians were racially and culturally designated Others, considered as different from the Aryan, white Europeans.

Hitler viewed the Western Front as a war between European powers that could be settled through traditional diplomatic, power-balancing means. The Eastern Front, however, was a *Vernichtungskrieg* (a war of annihilation), a war between Asiatic barbarian hordes and the cultured and Europe-defending Germans.[88] The image of the barbarian thus moves from England, which projects it onto the German Huns, to Germany, which projects the stereotype onto the Slavs.

Hitler's search for a *Lebensraum* ('living space') for the German people, specifically in the East, was based on the British Empire's legacy of imperialism. Hitler's claim to *Lebensraum* initially appeared demographically sound. Population data, growth rates and agricultural statistics were all marshalled to make a case for more land for Germany. But, as Kuczynski showed in an Oxford Pamphlet on World Affairs (No. 8), this was merely a rhetorical mask for Hitler's Eastern ambition.[89] Both Salter and Kuczynski admit that Hitler's *prima facie* case for 'living space' is legitimate. They argue that Germany's demographic and economic situation require more space than Germany possesses. Salter argues that, if by *Lebensraum* Germany means 'a place in the sun', extra-European colonies, then it cannot be accommodated.[90] Thus, Hitler and his followers began to look eastward.

Hitler's plan for German colonies within the geographical boundaries of Europe is based on a consideration of the balance of power with Great Britain[91] and on the model of British rule in India.[92] Many scholars have studied Hitler's foreign policy. Eberhard Jäckel's outline of Hitler's foreign policy is compelling, tracing the choice Hitler perceived between a British alliance and continental hegemony, or a Soviet alliance and an attendant colonial policy.[93] No scholar has yet plotted Hitler's fascination with British rule in India and his plans for rule in the Eastern territories. This aspect of Hitler's foreign policy is illustrative of the power of imperialism in the international imaginary up until the Second World War and also shows the persistence of the civilized/barbarian discourse. Although Hitler's barbarians are Asiatic/Slavic or Jewish/Bolshevik, his programme for colonization uses the rhetoric of civilization and barbarian. It is telling that Hitler turned to Britain's empire for his notions of imperial governance. In some aspects, Hitler wanted to imitate Britain. Because this has not been explored, it is worth quoting at length:

> What India was for England, the territories of Russia will be for us. If only I could make the German people understand what this space means for our future.[94]

> Let's learn from the English, who, with two hundred and fifty thousand men in all, including fifty thousand soldiers, govern four hundred million Indians. This space in Russia must always be dominated by Germans.[95]

If the English were to be driven out of India, India would perish. Our role in Russia will be analogous to that of England in Russia . . . The Russian space is our India. Like the English, we shall rule this empire with a handful of men.[96]

To exploit the Ukraine properly – that new Indian Empire – I need only peace in the West. The frontier police will be enough to ensure us the quiet conditions necessary for the exploitation of the conquered territories.[97]

[The New German] will come to feel that nothing is impossible and, as the young Briton of today serves his apprenticeship in India, the young German will learn his lessons, looking round the most easterly territories of the Reich . . .[98]

Let us hope that our Ministry for Eastern Territories will not . . . introduce [in the East] our laws against contraception. In this respect the British are our superiors. They, too, are the most frightful bureaucrats; but at least they have the sense not to exercise their bureaucracy in occupied territory to the advantage of the local inhabitant and the detriment of their own country. They have a genius for keeping others at a distance and in winning and preserving respect. Here, perhaps, we have the worst possible example of our methods – de-lousing infuriates the local inhabitants, as does our fanatical desire to civilise them. The net result is that they say to themselves: 'These people aren't really our superiors – it's only the way they're made.'[99]

The *üntermenschen* Slavs are not worth de-lousing or civilizing, according to Hitler. This last quotation traces explicitly the affinity he felt for the British and his repudiation of the civilizing mission. In fact, even in the instances in which Hitler criticizes British rule in India, his policy was still formulated with the British experience as a touchstone. Hitler wants to construct a German India in Eastern Europe without the civilizing mission.

the local [Eastern] population must be given no facilities for higher education. A failure on our part in this respect would simply plant the seeds of future opposition to our rule. Schools, of course, they must have . . . but there is no need to teach them much more than, say, the meaning of the various road-signs.[100]

Anyone who talks about cherishing the local inhabitant and civilizing him goes straight off to the concentration camp.[101]

It's an imperative obligation for the white man, in the colonies, to keep the native at a distance.[102]

Read together, all of Hitler's prescriptions for the East are either taken from British examples or are in direct contradiction to British attempt to 'civilize' their subjects. Yet this ideational connection between British and German imperialism for the most part has been ignored. However, anti-colonial thinkers were adamant about the connection, pointing out repeatedly that imperialism and the Holocaust were different only in terms of degree. I will visit this response later in the chapter.

OPERATION BARBAROSSA AND THE FINAL SOLUTION

The connection between *Operation Barbarossa* and the Final Solution is important. Hitler saw the Eastern Front as an existential struggle, a part of the struggle against Jews. Jewry and Bolshevism were, for Hitler, two aspects of the same ideology. The struggle for *Lebensraum* in the East was 'inextricably intertwined with the extermination of Bolshevism and Jewry'.[103] It is also important that the 'Final Solution to the Jewish Question in Europe' did not commence until the invasion of the Soviet Union. Bartov has commented extensively on the 'barbarization of warfare' on the Eastern Front.[104] He traces the cause of this barbarization to the material conditions of *Barbarossa*, the harsh military struggle against the Soviet army and the ideological propaganda directed at the soldiers.[105] After looking at the propaganda that enabled the barbarization of the *Ostheer* (Eastern Army), I will briefly trace the connection between *Barbarossa* and the Final Solution.

The *Wehrmacht* was broken on the Eastern Front, and the greatest military atrocities of the European war are to be found in the conduct of *Operation Barbarossa*. It was the arena in which the trope of the barbarian was most prevalent. The propagandistic description of the Red Army as barbarous so saturated the Germany army that it conducted its own war with unparalleled barbarity, and assisted the *Einsatzgruppen* (Action Groups) behind front lines. The barbarian image was so powerful that the Germans broke all rules of warfare, assisted in the prosecution of the Final Solution and then destroyed

Germany themselves in order to deprive the Red Army of the opportunity.

The representations of the enemy on the Eastern Front seemed to precede, and even supersede, the actual experience of the individual soldier. Rather than test the Nazi stereotypes of the Jew or the Asiatic-Bolshevik, the Nazi worldview was so powerful as seemingly to prevent self-reflection.[106] The indoctrination of soldiers 'provided the soldiers with an image of the enemy which so profoundly distorted their perception that once confronted with reality they invariably experienced it as a confirmation of what they had come to expect'.[107] The barbaric stereotype of the Bolshevik-Jew was reinforced by Hitler's 'Commissar Decree' of 3 March 1941, in which he exempted German soldiers from international law and from the standard of civilized warfare: 'Any German soldier who breaks international law will be pardoned.'[108] The Asiatic barbarians were considered 'beyond the pale', beyond culture and therefore beyond the protection of international law. A barbaric enemy justified barbaric warfare – just as in the colonial scene. (It was not until 18 October 1942 that the corresponding Commando Order on the Western Front was to be issued, on separate grounds.) The image of the barbarous Asiatic horde led the *Wehrmacht* to conduct a campaign of shocking brutality against the population as they advanced into the Soviet Union.

In addition to the death camps, the *Einsatzgruppen*, formed from SS troops, ranged behind the front lines. These 'task-forces' were directed by orders, like the Commissar Decree, which ordered soldiers to commit massive reprisals for partisan activity, plunder the population for supplies Germany could not transport and make exploitative use of native labour. The reinstitution of slave labour by the German bureaucracy echoes imperial practice. German work camps using Russian prisoners of war had a shocking death rate.[109] Himmler's connection of slave labour to *Kultur* is germane:

> What happens to a Russian or to a Czech, does not interest me in the slightest . . . Whether nations live in prosperity or starve to death interests me only in so far as we need them as slaves for our *Kultur*: otherwise, it is of no interest to me. Whether ten thousand Russian females fall down from exhaustion while digging an anti-tank ditch interests me only in so far as the anti-tank ditch for Germany is finished.[110]

The *Einsatzgruppen* were responsible for mass shootings and gassings in the occupied territories. In addition to the national enemies, which they had exterminated in Germany, they also shot enemies of the Reich who endangered Nazi rule of the East – the Polish intelligentsia and Soviet bureaucrats.[111] The propagandistic image of the Slavic *Üntermenschen* so permeated the Eastern Front that even regular troops, not subject to the ideological training of the SS, were complicit in the massacres carried out by the *Einsatzgruppen*.[112]

A final testament to the strength of the barbarian discourse on the Eastern Front is found at the end of the war, both in the scorched earth policy followed by the *Wehrmacht* on its retreat to Berlin and the final negotiations of surrender. The German Army was merciless in its destruction. Bartov argues that 'the *Wehrmacht*'s barbarous policies [provided] a vivid and frightening model of what Germany itself could expect in defeat'.[113] By now, the Allies had issued their joint demand of unconditional surrender. Caught between the Slavic barbarians and an uncompromising West, the army felt it had no choice but to fight. As one general said: 'the demand for unconditional surrender gave us no hope from the West, while the men fighting on the Russian Front were well aware of the horrible fate which would befall eastern Germany if the Red hordes broke into our country'.[114] The rhetoric of barbarism returned to ravage the German imagination.

Racist propaganda came back to terrorize its authors. As the Red Army regained territory, the policies of retribution and massacres which the *Wehrmacht* had perpetrated against the Soviets now became crimes for which they would stand trial. In his last order of the day, on 16 April 1945, Hitler said:

> The hordes of our Judeo-Bolshevist foe have rallied for the last assault. They want to destroy Germany and extinguish our people. You, soldiers of the east, have seen with your own eyes what fate awaits German women and children: the aged, the men, the infants are murdered, the German women and girls are defiled and made into barrack whores. The rest are marched off to Siberia.[115]

While Hitler may have intended to describe the barbaric practices of the Soviets, he undoubtedly also described the practices of the German troops on the Eastern Front – a *double entendre* not lost on the soldiers defending Germany from the oncoming army. Hitler had persuaded the German people that he was forced to fight the Soviet Union in defence of European civilization from the Asiatic hordes. In the declaration of war, the Nazis told the German public that the Soviet Union 'is about to attack Germany from the rear, in its struggle for life. The Führer has therefore ordered the German armed forces to oppose this threat with all the means at their disposal.'[116] The Germans consequently believed that the barbarians were at the gates. A policy of national suicide was then undertaken. Hitler had often said that if Germany did not win the war for him, then he would destroy it: 'If the war should be lost, then the nation, too, will be lost. That would be the nation's unalterable fate . . . it is better ourselves to destroy things, for this nation will have proven itself weaker . . . Those who remain after the battles are over are in any case only inferior persons, since the best have fallen.'[117] With the advance of the Red Army, Hitler tried to fulfil that promise. 'Goebbels declared, "Germany must be made more desolate than the Sahara." Nothing could be left which the Allied – and in particular the dreaded "Bolsheviks" – could plunder.'[118] The Nazis set out to destroy not only any useful infrastructure, but also the records, documents, national treasures so that nothing, not even the artifacts of the German nation, would remain.

> [Hitler's] scorched earth policy in November 1944 was far more ruthless than the Soviet Union's own policy had been in 1941 – for Hitler was determined to destroy no less than the collective memory of the German nation. He gave orders for the destruction of every ration card and historical record, every birth certificate and bank account number, every church and museum, everything that made up the German identity in the imagination not only of the Germans but the world as well.[119]

Hitler's nihilistic *Götterdämmerung* was the end of his belief that he was the personification of Germany and his belief, which he promulgated to the German nation at large, that the barbarians of the East would destroy them given the chance. The degree to which Germans self-immolated is a testament to the power of Nazi propaganda and the image of the barbarian.

The use of slave labour, demoscopic surveillance techniques and modern bureaucracy to prosecute the Holocaust and the Eastern Front violated all standards of international law and international custom. While the West was shocked, the method was familiar to anti-colonial writers even if the degree was severe. Europe lost its status of 'civilized' in its own eyes. Postwar artistic movements, like abstract expressionism, testify to the malaise of European culture. While artists and thinkers within the West were 'deconstructing representation', their counterparts in the colonized world were writing the scripts of decolonization.

THE EMPIRE STRIKES BACK

The discourse of 'civilization' and 'barbarians' was invoked less often after the Second World War. Georg Schwarzenberger claims the distinction was broken down by the rise of legal positivism in international law.[120] However, there was also a decline in usage in popular culture, as well as with international jurists. There are two chief causes of the decline of this distinction in popular culture, which I will examine here. With the prosecution of the Nazi Eastern Front and its attendant Holocaust, Europe began to see itself as barbaric. Coincident with this turn was a rise in anti- or postcolonial nationalisms. Ali Mazrui argues: 'Because the term "civilized nations" was used to justify European imperialism, it began to decline in public usage with the rise of nationalism in Asia and Africa. The new assertiveness of the colonized peoples and their sense of dignity gradually discouraged Europeans from talking about them as "barbarians" and "heathens".'[121]

Aimé Césaire and Frantz Fanon argue that the Holocaust and Nazi rule removed any moral authority that Europeans might have. Europe's 'civilizing mission' was in crisis if Europe itself was barbaric. Both writers agree that the methods used by the Nazis were *colonial* methods, perpetrated for the first time on Europeans instead of 'natives'.

Césaire describes Nazism as

> the supreme barbarism, the crowning barbarism that sums up all the daily barbarisms . . . but before they were its victims, [Europeans] were its accomplices; they tolerated that Nazism before it was inflicted on them, they absolved it, shut their eyes to it, legitimized it, because, until then, it had been applied only to non-European peoples.[122]

Fanon argues: 'Nazism transformed the whole of Europe into a veritable colony.'[123] In comparing imperialism to the Nazi regime, Césaire and Fanon attempt to discredit the civilizing mission on its own terms. Europe is described as barbaric, precisely because of the way it attempted its 'civilizing mission'. Echoing the experience of occupation that was fresh in the metropolitan French imagination, Fanon draws a powerful contrast: 'A colonized people is not simply a dominated people. Under the German occupation the French remained men.'[124] Under colonial rule, the colonial subjects were not considered or treated as men. There are only 'relations of domination and submission . . . which turn the indigenous man into an instrument of production'.[125] Fanon argues that in addition to political exclusion from the metropolitan power and economic domination, the colonized suffer from cultural imperialism as well.

> It is apparent to me that the effective disalienation of the black man entails an immediate recognition of the social and economic realities. If there is an inferiority complex, it is the outcome of a double process: primarily economic; subsequently, the internalization – or, better, the epidermalization – of this inferiority.[126]

This is precisely the relationship that International Relations has forgotten: that coincident with politico-economic oppression, imperialism institutionalized a social oppression. While dependency theorists, and later Third World studies, focused on the politico-economic aspect of the imperial international structure, the social dimension of imperialism is almost completely neglected.

Rather than reinscribing the image of the native as victim, Fanon and Césaire attempt to paint the European colonizer as a victim. Building on the psychoanalytic method alluded to in chapter 4, both authors attempt to draw a precise picture of the relationship.

> Colonization, I repeat, dehumanizes even the most civilized man; that colonial activity . . . which is based on contempt for the native and justified by that contempt, inevitably tends to change him who undertakes it; that the colonizer, who in order to ease his conscience gets into the habit of seeing the other man *as an animal* . . . tends objectively to transform *himself*

into an animal. It is this result, this boomerang effect of colonization that I wanted to point out.[127]

Imperialism reveals the inner barbarism of the European. Fanon also writes about this 'boomerang effect' in *Wretched of the Earth*. He uses psychoanalytic evidence, through the retelling of case studies, to show that the colonizer who is accustomed to violence comes to practise it on everyone – not just the colonized, but even himself.[128]

Césaire and Fanon are key figures in an intellectual movement that helped discredit the rhetoric of the civilizing mission – by the comparison of Nazi and imperial rule, and by the description of the particulars of the colonizer/colonized relationship. Europe is represented as barbaric with evidence that is hard to refute. International Relations' concern with parsimony and power largely missed this important point.

CONCLUSION

The Second World War was represented as a caesura, a break, in the course of Western history. The Holocaust in particular was viewed as an aberration, rather than a natural part of Western culture. This chapter argues that, at least in part, the Holocaust was the extension of imperial rhetoric and modern bureaucratic institutions. The Holocaust and the prosecution of the war on the Eastern Front can be understood as imperialism without a civilizing mission. While Europe was slow to grasp this parallel, those anti-colonial intellectuals who had been subject to colonial regimes were certain of the similarity.

This chapter has concentrated on the popular dimension of the discourse of 'civilized/barbarian' during the Second World War and the years immediately afterwards. In chapter 6, I will look at the disciplinary response to decolonization. International Relations continues to be influenced by imperialist rhetoric and colonial ideas, even when struggling to come to terms with the new geopolitical facts of the Cold War and decolonization.

6 Decolonizing the Discipline: Forgetting the Imperial Past and the Imperial Present

The rhetoric of imperialism does not fade with the decline of the use of juridical status. I will argue that the discipline of International Relations, to the extent that it dealt with imperialism after the Second World War, can be seen as viewing imperialism and decolonization in terms of the civilized/barbarian trope. I will argue further that imperialist stereotypes are embedded in the discipline's analysis of the nature and role of the Third World and postcolonial states. The treatment of colonialism in extremely abstract terms also proves problematic. Postwar realists, such as Frederick Schuman and Hans J. Morgenthau, remove imperialism from its historical context, characterizing it as the generic pursuit of power.

Importantly, all the theorists examined here are concerned with decolonization and recognize its importance to International Relations, without developing sufficient tools to provide a nuanced analysis of the effects of colonization in International Relations. The Third World was largely ignored during the Cold War, except as an extraterritorial battlefield for the superpowers.

SCHUMAN AND MORGENTHAU

A certain sleight of hand is involved in treating the work of these two prominent realists together. Each realist comes from a distinct context and each realism differs from the other. However, both perform the same theoretical move in their treatment of imperialism; all elide historically specific imperialisms into one universal practice of power accumulation. This has the effect of removing imperialism from the realist view of International Relations. Imperialism is defined, and becomes accepted as, the standard operating procedure of powerful states.

Schuman and Morgenthau have another factor in common. When discussing the concept of imperialism after 1919, each must account for the so-called 'communist' view of imperialism, which was initiated by Lenin and became a rhetorical staple until the fall of the Soviet Union. Lenin's polemic described imperialism as the 'latest' – not highest – stage of capitalism, the natural extension of market capitalism into the non-European world in search of markets and resources.[1] However, later communists used the term rhetorically to mean any expansion of the Western powers or any policy to which the USSR objected.[2] Anti-colonial writers were also actively critical of imperialism. Whether or not the definition was precise or consistent, both theorists had to define imperialism amongst these contending, and politically motivated, definitions.

Following the more subtle theories of the interwar period, which generally combined elements of idealism and realism, Schuman provides the most expansive definition of imperialism in the 1933 first edition of *International Politics*. Schuman's definition accounts for the 'political, economic and cultural ramifications [of] a phase of the competitive struggle for power between the sovereign units of the Western State System'.[3] However, we also see in his explanation of imperialism the elision of cultural or ideological factors from considerations of power, which sets the stage for later realists to look at imperialism solely in terms of power accumulation. 'Values and purposes', in Schuman's view, are inconsequential to the success or failure of specific imperial enterprises: imperialism is successful only to the extent that states are 'technologically' capable.[4] Schuman argues that civilizational contests, determined by technological advantage, directly undermine the notion of Western superiority, which underpins the nineteenth-century rhetoric of the 'civilizing mission'. This argument rewrites Western dominance as the result of 'objective' technological sophistication, rather than 'subjective' ideas.[5] This rhetorical move also makes the success of European expansion seem accidental, suggesting that if any other civilization had achieved the technological sophistication of Europe, it too would have expanded.[6] As we see in Chinese and Arab imperialism, however, non-Western imperialisms did not match the scale or success of Western expansion.[7] Obscuring the ideational aspect of imperialism follows the realist bias towards the study of overt power politics, but neglects the more subtle power of ideas that proved so influential in the colonized world.

Following a more general trend in interwar society, Schuman's attitude towards imperialism is somewhat ambivalent. Although he recognizes the material benefits of imperialism, he cautions that 'the path of empire is red with the blood of its victims'.[8] He specifically debunks the myth of the 'civilizing mission':

> the argument that colonies are acquired for the purpose of civilizing and converting the naked pagan savages and of conferring upon them the blessings of western culture is undeserving of serious consideration in any effort to evaluate imperialism in the international politics of the Western State System . . . The 'white man's burden' rests heavily upon the shoulders of the black men and brown men and yellow men who have been subjugated. The benefits received by the victims have been entirely incidental and they have, moreover, been negligible in quantity, doubtful in quality, and bitterly resented because of their source and the methods employed in conferring them.[9]

While he disdains the ideological justifications of imperialism, Schuman argues that imperialism is supported by several ideological discourses.[10] The civilizing mission is predicated on notions of European superiority, racial hierarchies and geographic determinism, among others. He also makes the valuable but often forgotten point that Western imperialism was an uneven, sporadic, chaotic process – not a monolithic programme of expansion.[11] In the final analysis, Schuman contends that 'imperialism is intelligible as a factor in international politics only in terms of the imposition by military means of the power of the western nation-states upon the non-European parts of the world . . . the enhancement of power . . . is the alpha and omega of the quest for empire'.[12] Schuman represents the theoretical link between interwar idealist thinking on imperialism and interwar realist thinking on imperialism. Turning away from ideational factors, he concludes that power is the central motive and machine of imperialism, but his work attends to the historical specificity of the expansion of Europe.

Morgenthau's *Politics among Nations* is central to the evolution of classical realism in postwar IR theory. He defines imperialism simply as the 'foreign policy [which] aims at acquiring more power than it actually has, through a reversal of existing power relations – whose foreign policy, in other words, seeks a favorable change in power status'.[13] Unlike Schuman's, Morgenthau's definition obscures the historical and cultural specificity of imperialism. Morgenthau limits all possible foreign policy aims to three options: 'to keep power, increase power, or to demonstrate power'.[14] In his view, any country that seeks a reversal of power relations is an imperialist nation. Morgenthau hopes that this 'concrete' definition will clarify the current conceptual muddiness. However, in the process, he dilutes the term beyond utility. Imperialism becomes the default action of any powerful state that is not pursuing a status quo policy.[15] By removing imperialism from its historical roots in European expansion, that expansion drops from the view of study. Realists generally seek parallels across historical periods. I would argue that obscuring this particular expansion hides imperialism from the view of International Relations and precludes analysis of the impact of imperialism as a specific political practice on the contemporary states system.[16] The discipline in general adopts this theoretical move and imperialism remains out of sight until the introduction of dependency theory to the discipline in the 1970s.

Morgenthau follows the realist predisposition against investigating ideas and other such intangible forces. Like Schuman, he argues against the rhetoric of the 'civilizing mission'. 'Colonial imperialism, in particular, has frequently been disguised by ideological slogans such as the "blessings of Western civilization" which it was the mission of the conqueror to bring to the colored races of the earth.'[17] While he admits the power of 'cultural imperialism', Morgenthau argues that 'in modern times it is subsidiary to the other methods. It softens up the enemy, it prepares the ground for military conquest or economic penetration.'[18] This analysis downplays the fact that the three types of imperialism (military, economic and cultural) were used in concert in the colonized world. Cultural imperialism normalized the military and economic domination of the colonized peoples by the European powers. By discounting the power of cultural imperialism, realists are unable to evaluate the influence of cultural politics on postcolonial societies. Ironically, Morgenthau himself seems to anticipate this criticism. In a chapter titled 'the New Balance of Power', Morgenthau argues:

the colonial revolution sprang from a moral challenge to the world as it was . . . It is carried forward under the banner of two moral principles: national self-determination and social justice. It is these principles that Asia today hurls against the West condemning and revolting against Western political and economic policies in the name of the West's own moral standards.[19]

Even though Morgenthau admits that the trend towards decolonization was as much ideational as physical, he fails to analyse this cultural dynamic fully. Culture is a prime concern of politics in the postcolonial world. International Relations' inattention to the postcolonial world stems in part from this blind spot to the function of culture.

International Relations as a discipline is influenced by the political context in which it situated itself. International Relations sees itself as speaking to contemporary world politics – and this determined that the prime focus of American research in the postwar period was dominated by the Cold War.[20] The Cold War had a large effect on the theorizing of world politics in the postwar era, especially in the American academy. Morgenthau responds to the Russians' rhetorical use of imperialism to describe policies to which they were opposed. What's more, he turns the charge against its authors. 'The other outstanding example of cultural imperialism in our time, antedating and surviving the Nazi fifth column, is the Communist International.'[21]

However, culture and identity are subsumed into the state as a generic unit of analysis. This tendency to perceive colonial and postcolonial states as a single category reduces the ability of IR theorists to observe some fundamental differences between the two. Postcolonial critics argue there is an ingrained Orientalism within the discipline. This manifests itself in the tendency to regard postcolonial states as underdeveloped European states, as Doty argues.[22] The elision of all postcolonial states into a single category was fomented by the predominant politico-military conflict of the latter half of the twentieth century – the Cold War.[23]

The Third World was described primarily as a site of the East–West conflict. Throughout the period of decolonization, postcolonial states were never treated autonomously within mainstream IR theory. They were seen as having moved from the control of European states to that of the US or the USSR. The stance of non-alignment presented an attempt at independent foreign policy, about which many Cold War theorists were sceptical. While realist scholars praised the bipolar nature of the Cold War for bringing 'peace' to the latter half of the twentieth century, Acharya argues that, in fact, the Cold War exacerbated a large number of Third World conflicts.[24] These postwar theorists represent an important core of mainstream IR theory in the 1950s and 1960s. The use of imperialism to describe any grab for power that upsets the international balance has the effect of removing European imperialism from special consideration. This elision of all imperialisms leads to a miscalculation of how postcolonial states will (inter)act in the post-independence system.

THE HINTERLANDS OF WESTERN CIVILIZATION: DECOLONIZATION AND THE DISCIPLINE

This section traces some of the discipline's responses to decolonization through an evaluation of four important textbooks. Schuman's *International Politics* (6th edition, 1958) and Schwarzenberger's *Power Politics* (3rd edition, 1964) will be treated in some depth, while less extensive analyses will be made of Holsti's *International Politics* and Organski's *World Politics*. It will also look at some other important voices in the discipline at this time, notably Cecil Crabb and Ali Mazrui, who speak to these new states and International Relations. What is striking about these authors, despite later characterizations,[25] is that they do attempt to take decolonization seriously. Whether or not they are successful depends on the degree to which they can leave behind nineteenth century ideas of the colonized and colonial societies.

SCHUMAN AND SCHWARZENBERGER

Schuman and Schwarzenberger's textbooks were central in the field of International Relations during the 1950s and 1960s, and are taken here to be representatives of the mainstream response of the discipline. In both texts, I have looked specifically for new writing on the (post)colonial world, and sections on imperialism or decolonization. In presenting the ways in which Schuman and Schwarzenberger are concerned with imperialism and decolonization, and the extent to which they rely on imperialist tropes and stereotypes, I hope to present a balanced analysis of the discipline's response.

It is revealing to revisit Schuman's *International Politics: The Western State System and the World Community* in its sixth edition, published in 1958, in the midst of decolonization. Schuman is sensitive to the importance of decolonization and the rise of the new postcolonial states in world politics. However, he remains indebted to the imperialist stereotypes elaborated in the first edition of his work in 1933. For example, he argues that the Third World 'may well prove more decisive for the shape of things to come in the World Community than any amount of violence or bargaining between Washington and Moscow'.[26] However, in granting postcolonial societies a sort of agency in world politics, Schuman relies on colonial tropes of barbarism, describing the inhabitants of (post)colonial states as 'dark and impoverished multitudes'.[27] He continues:

> Thanks to the impact of the West upon 'backward peoples,' most of the human race in our time has been brought to the point of a vast and complex revolution against the *status quo*. This 'revolution' may be depicted in sundry ways, none of them adequately descriptive of the groping efforts of the 'lesser breeds without the law' to attain a better life.[28]

Schuman's use of Rudyard Kipling to describe postcolonial societies reflects a larger trend in *International Politics*, and the discipline in general, to rely on colonial ideas of the colonized to describe their new condition. This is not to argue that, empirically, there were few 'impoverished' Africans and Asians and that their efforts at self-government were universally unsuccessful. However, I do want to emphasize that the language and ideas used to describe newly independent peoples were neither objective nor entirely novel. Theorists such as Schuman and Schwarzenberger relied without reflection on their previous conceptions of the colonized to describe the conditions of new states. This is further evidenced by Schuman's final description of African states as 'The Terrorists'.

Schuman defines three possibilities for Africa in the face of the Cold War: first, acquiescence to one of the Great Powers; second, 'terrorism and violent rebellion against white "colonialism"'; or third, 'passive, watching, waiting, and hoping'.[29] This tripartite description of the colonized response to Europe is directly descended from the Orientalist stereotypes of the nineteenth century. 'Barbarians' may be assimilated, violent or passive. Schuman describes contemporary Africa in the same terms as Conrad uses to describe Africa in 1900 – barbaric.

To quote Schuman again: 'the world's disinherited [are] now resolved to recover their place in the sun'.[30] This reference to colonial rhetoric is not accidental: Schuman uses it again later to indicate that Western ideas, such as 'self-determination' and 'place in the sun', were adopted and appropriated by their colonial subjects to reject colonialism.[31] To use the specific phrase which inaugurated a period of rapid expansion into Africa to describe the desire of postcolonial societies to assert their independence seems to misunderstand the explicit aim of postcolonial nationalist elites to do so in a specifically non-Western way.[32] The attempt to figure non-Western states in terms of Western history is not only fallacious, but also intellectually imperialist.

The ways in which Schuman portrays postcolonial societies is also distinctly colonial. He makes repeated references to 'dark multitudes' and 'teeming hordes', stock rhetorical phrases in demographic predictions of 'white decline' in the early twentieth century. Schuman follows a common Orientalist trope in representing the societies themselves as backward, tribal and underdeveloped.[33] Following the trope of tribalism and absence of 'civilization', he states:

> we encounter something approaching a vacuum in most of the colonial lands. For here in the absence of industry, finance, and commerce, there is no equivalent of the 'middle class' . . . The nearest approach to this stratum consists of native merchants and a small but unhappy 'intelligentsia,' consisting chiefly of Western-educated sons of aristocrats, easily attracted to extreme nationalism.[34]

The same imperial stereotypes are used after independence, which has the effect of reifying imperial identities and eventually imperial politics. By reinscribing these colonial ideas, the cause of postcolonial underdevelopment is represented as the inherent nature of the colonized's society, rather than a dynamic of imperial (mis)rule and politico-economic factors.

Nonalignment, as the most popular foreign policy of postcolonial states, is seen as intensified passivity, framed by violent domestic repression. Crabb makes the criticism that independence-minded, or non-alignment-oriented, foreign policy is viewed as aberrant or extreme by Western IR scholars. While Schuman attempts to come to terms with a palpable shift in power from the West to the non-West, his persistent use of colonial tropes, embedded in the discourse of civilized/barbarian, simultaneously undermines that agency by representing postcolonial societies in colonial terms.

Schwarzenberger also presents a view of the postcolonial world as the 'hinterlands of Western civilisation' in his third edition of *Power Politics: A Study of World Society*.[35] Despite this initial characterization of postcolonial societies, Schwarzenberger offers an analysis of the decolonizing world that raises some important questions. First, it must be noted that Schwarzenberger presages Gerrit Gong's analysis of the legal standard of 'civilization'.[36] He observes that 'in the post-1919 period, the Powers jettisoned even the standard of civilisation as a test of international personality. Whether a State was civilised or barbarian ceased to be relevant.'[37] However, as I have argued against Gong, this analysis concentrates solely on the legal, juridical standard of civilization and does not take into account the popular persistence of the trope. Second, Schwarzenberger notes what will later be termed the 'weakness' of postcolonial states.

> All of these Afro-Asian states have three vital features in common: *first*, compared with the needs of their rapidly increasing populations, their economies are retrograde; *secondly* . . . the indigenous elites are too thin to allow for the rapid replacement made necessary by sheer exhaustion, internecine feuds and endemic corruption; *thirdly*, most of these States are saved from open bankruptcy only by continuous aid from outside.[38]

The relatively objective terms in which he frames the weakness of postcolonial states are interesting. Unlike Schuman, Schwarzenberger argues that this weakness is due, in some sense, to the anti-Western nationalism of post-colonial societies.[39] Many theorists were impressed with the anti-Western, anti-white rhetoric of postcolonial nationalist movements. However, Schwarzenberger connects the racialist rhetoric of independence propaganda to the Nazi discourse examined in chapter 5. He says, '[Pan-African, Asian, American ideas] have an unmistakable racial, and anti-white, undertone. The racialist nationalism of the Third Reich has shown the nihilism inseparable from this form of relapse into barbarism.'[40]

The connection between barbarism and anti-colonial nationalism is made explicit. Schwarzenberger also refers to this anti-colonialism/Nazi barbarity later in the work, citing the Belgian Congo, the repression of Kurds in Iraq and the Tamils as illustrations of racial struggles.[41]

Race and colour, which faded from view in the discipline after the horror of the Holocaust, were discussed briefly during this period. In addition to linking postcolonial nationalism to racialism and anti-white sentiments, Schwarzenberger argues: 'the rebirth of the Afro-Asian States . . . has brought to the surface a basic fact *hidden in the past by white world supremacy*: the minority of the white race in world society'.[42] Schuman points out earlier that 'two-thirds of mankind is "coloured", not "white"'.[43] However, it is only with the rise of the political viability of anti-colonial movements such as *Negritude* and Pan-Africanism that this racial divide assumes importance for International Relations. The concepts of race and colour are present in the 'civilized/barbarian' discourse, and inevitably in the discourse of decolonization and postcolonialism. Their presence in International Relations has not yet been fully explored, but shows some interesting avenues for research.[44]

Traditional IR theory tends to view the postcolonial world chiefly as a 'safe' terrain for proxy conflicts between the superpowers. Schwarzenberger makes the argument that from the weakness of the new states there is 'constant danger of the Balkanisation of the areas in question and their transformation into fields of fierce competition and shadow-fighting, if nothing worse, between the world camps'.[45] However, the emphasis on the postcolonial world as a passive site of the Cold War struggle does not prevent Schwarzenberger from mobilizing colonial tropes. 'These teeming millions', he argues, 'are ideal recruits for a primitive and fanatical hate-propaganda of social revolution which is likely to shake to their foundations or tear apart the bamboo structures of the new states involved'.[46] Postcolonial elites and their populations are viewed as irrational and easily swayed by more 'powerful' states. The stereotype of the individual colonial subject is applied to the new postcolonial state.

Many other mainstream scholars also under- or misrepresented the postcolonial world. The 'Third World' is repeatedly portrayed as the site of superpower proxy struggles during the 1950s and 1960s. Two brief examples of popular texts will suffice to show that scholars continue to misjudge the specific properties of the postcolonial state. I will cite Holsti and Organski to show that even as the (post)colonial world was being investigated, colonial tropes are reified.

Holsti's *International Politics: A Framework for Analysis* was first published in 1967, and has since gone through seven editions. In his introduction, Holsti himself diagnoses a Cold War bias in the majority of contemporary theoretical writing in International Relations 'to view almost all political problems in terms of [Soviet-American] rivalry'.[47] His solution is the use of concepts which are objective, and can be observed in great, middle and small powers. 'Objectives, capabilities, threats, punishments, and rewards' are universal characteristics of states, and can thus mitigate any ideological predisposition in the theorist.[48] This move assumes that all states have these characteristics or will act in predictable ways under the same conditions as Western states, given the pattern of European behaviour throughout the history of the Westphalian system. It is unclear if this assumption is warranted, as Holsti himself later points out.[49]

However, if Holsti is sensitive to the material differences in postcolonial states, he does not link these deficiencies to the process of imperialism.[50] He also seems to gesture towards what is of great concern to later postcolonial theorists: the search for identity in postcolonial states. Figured in terms of status and prestige, Holsti also mentions the predisposition of newly independent states to favour a foreign policy of non-alignment.[51] Thus, the Third World is treated in *International Politics* as a subsystem of the Cold War, and postcolonial states as a variant of the traditional Western states system, albeit with unique characteristics.

Organski presents another popular text to the discipline: *World Politics*, which provides an excellent example of the same argument. Organski situates his textbook using nearly the exact phraseology of Holsti: '[what] those who approach world politics need most is a framework within which to organize their data'.[52] First, Organski recognizes that colonialism is an important area of interest for International Relations. He then follows in the vein of Schwarzenberger and Schuman, using a definition of colonialism that removes it from the specific European experience.[53] By equating Greek, Roman, Indian, Chinese, Arabic, Turkic and European colonialism, imperialism is seen to be a recurrent, generic historical pattern.[54] This removes consideration of the specificity of European rule in the nineteenth and twentieth centuries, which has, in some part, determined the terrain of contemporary world politics. What is particularly interesting about Organski's analysis of European colonialism is his reliance on geographical determinism: the belief that climate determines character.[55] He claims: 'whether Europeans have settled in a particular colony or exploited it from a distance has been determined largely by climate, for Europeans on the whole have not adapted themselves to living permanently in the tropics'.[56] This notion of temperate climates producing a superior European civilization and the intemperate tropics producing inferior barbarians has a long pedigree, through the discourse of colonialism to Rousseau's 'Essay on the Origin of Languages'.[57] The trope of climate as character was mobilized extensively throughout the history of European imperialism, and its resurgence in Organski illustrates his reliance on colonial stereotypes.[58]

Second, Organski argues that the Cold War struggle over the Third World can be best understood in terms of colonialism.[59] This claim clearly follows from his definition of colonialism as any relationship between strong and weak powers. Third World countries are defined here, as in Schuman, as weak and malleable. First World powers are defined as rational and forceful. Organski's description of superpower contest as 'colonialist' over the 'dependencies' of the world is too general and too dependent on subjective colonialist rhetoric to account for the subtleties of interstate relations in the Cold War period he examines.

Organski remains indebted to imperialist discourses, treating postcolonial countries as new colonies of a different sort; economic as opposed to political.[60] Newly independent states are described as 'the spoils' of the Cold War.[61]

To conclude, Organski's focus on colonialism seems admirable at first glance. In addition to describing the 'civilizing mission' as a vital piece of imperialist policy, he describes how European colonialism sows the seeds of its own destruction.[62] The parallel between historical and modern colonialism seems also to hold promise. However, his reliance on the realist, universalized definition of imperialism dilutes any analytical power this comparison might have, as does his ideological use of the term. Organski describes the entire postcolonial realm of International Relations as a subset (the spoils) of the Cold War and fails to accord the underdeveloped countries any agency or particularity whatsoever.

This mixture of attention and neglect of (post)colonial states seems representative of the discipline as a whole in the 1950s and

1960s – using traditional tools to analyse the politics of postcolonial states. This leads to two results: the diminution of the particularity of the postcolonial state and the use of traditional models, images and stereotypes to characterize these states. While the discourse of civilized/barbarian, which had been prominent in previous writing, all but disappears during the period of decolonization, these examples show that the enduring stereotypes, which constitute the discourse, were still very much in circulation. While Schuman, Schwarzenberger and Organski do not mention barbarians specifically in relation to postcolonial societies, the stereotypes of the barbarian resonates in their characterization of the Third World.

Postcolonial states are assumed in much contemporary International Relations writing to be under-evolved European states.[63] While their material conditions differ, theorists such as Huntington, Holsti and Organski represent their juridical status as a single analytical category. Mazrui argues that the postcolonial state is unique in several important respects. Primarily, he argues that African nationalism developed in the colonial setting and thus was chiefly negative nationalism. African nationalism developed largely in opposition to imperial rule and European conceptions of the self and other.[64] I have argued that discourse and culture have material, political effects within the identity of Europe. Mazrui argues here that African identity was determined, in large part, by the European characterization of Africans in colonial discourse.[65] European characterization of the 'Other' as African – rather than Nigerian, Ibo, Masai, etc. – led to characterization of the African 'self' as African, rather than as a tribal or religious identity.[66] Because of this largely negatively defined identity, a deep-seated anti-colonialism and a sense of cross-national racial identity condition African politics. In sum, he argues:

> African nationalist thought seems to regard traditional international law as having been naïve when it reduced all tensions to interstate relations. In African estimations, *three* levels of identity are relevant in diplomatic behaviour – a racial identity, a continental identity and the identities of sovereign states.[67]

Other postcolonial writers have endorsed this idea that racial and cultural identity are particularly salient issues in postcolonial societies.[68] The notions of identity and cultural self-determination become central to postcolonial theory – but have for the most part been played down in International Relations.[69] It can be argued that postcolonial states have unique histories of imperial occupation, which have important impacts on how these states relate to the international environment.

CONCLUSION

This chapter has developed two important ideas. First, it has shown that the discipline of International Relations, from the end of the Second World War to the early 1970s, continued to perceive Africa and the Third World in imperialist ways. While all these important texts attempted to take imperialism seriously, their efforts were circumscribed by a reliance on the same generalizations, images and preconceptions about the Third World that were shown to be present in the nineteenth century. Although the terms 'civilized' and 'barbarian' do not make frequent appearances in these texts, the stereotypes that underpinned this discourse are certainly prominent. The mainstream scholars quoted above viewed the Third World as constituted of malleable, backward nations, or as a passive site on which to play out the Cold War. However, there were dissenting voices in the discipline that explored a more sympathetic view.

Second, it has suggested that postcolonial states possess some unique characteristics, which may require an analytic apparatus separate from that which is used to analyse the Western states system. Scholars more sympathetic to the nuances of the postcolonial condition indicate the importance of culture and identity to postcolonial states. Postulating different, non-Western patterns of state development, these theorists are able to examine the behaviour and structure of postcolonial states with a view to their unique characteristics.

7 New Barbarians, Old Barbarians: Post-Cold War IR Theory. 'Everything Old is New Again'

The end of the Cold War wrought important changes in the popular and academic international imaginary. In the popular press, several trends emerged to diagnose the brave New World Order. Francis Fukuyama proclaimed the victory of liberalism and market capitalism, which he figured in Hegelian terms as the 'end of history'.[1] The global interpenetration of Western capital, with its accompanying media, communications and technological revolutions, inspired predictions of politico-cultural homogenization. This prompted greetings and warnings alike of a 'global culture'. Yet, the 'New World Order' proclaimed by George Bush Sr., which seemed to herald an era of benevolent unipolarism, faced a series of notable failures. Somalia, Rwanda and the former Yugoslavia alerted elite and popular perceptions alike to 'ethnic' conflicts which, many – inaccurately – argued had been 'suppressed' by the global geopolitics of the Cold War.[2] These trends were reflected in academic analyses. Though critical perspectives began to proliferate in the discipline in the late 1980s, the end of the Cold War caught most IR scholars by surprise.[3] What followed was a proliferation of paradigms offered to fit the brave new world. John Merscheimer and Kenneth Waltz insisted on the continuing relevance of realism.[4] Some argued for economic unification and the rise of the 'region-state'.[5] Charles and Clifford Kupchan advocated a return to the Concert of Europe model.[6] James Goldgeier and Michael McFaul, and Max Singer and Aaron Wildavsky, developed two of the world's paradigms that reinforced a colonial trope – it held that the developed West was peaceful and the developing non-West was a zone of conflict.[7] The most widely accepted model has been the 'two-worlds' thesis. The trend towards dualism has manifested itself again in post-Cold War international theory. Whether expressed as 'core/periphery', 'zones of peace and zones of conflict', 'the West v. the rest', this model has come to be accepted by many traditional scholars. Some have noted that the 'us/them' dichotomy, which now pervades IR theory, rests on imperial distinctions between the civilized West and its acolytes and the uncivilized, barbaric, postcolonial periphery.[8] In representing world politics as divided into realms of security and realms of insecurity, scholars must be conscious of the tenor of their diagnoses. The repetition of imperial stereotypes and the reintroduction of the 'civilized/barbarian' dichotomy have worrying implications for the post-Cold War IR imaginary.

In tracing the reappearance of the civilized/barbarian rhetoric in IR theory, I will look at Samuel Huntington's seminal article, 'The Clash of Civilizations?' and Paul Kennedy's 'Preparing for the Twenty-First Century'. I will also look at the popularization of these ideas in the works of Robert Kaplan and Benjamin Barber. In addition to indicating empirical concerns, I will concentrate on the rhetoric of civilized/barbarian in these works. The reintroduction of the civilized/barbarian dichotomy is important because of its historical legacy and the implications it has for theorizing about world politics in the post-Cold War world. The absent centre of these two-world theories of post-Cold War world order is the barbarian, and these theorists 'barbarize' the non-Western world in their descriptions. The reappearance of nineteenth-century stereotypes to describe the violent periphery of world politics implies a discursive Manicheanism in which the West is safe, secure and peaceful, and the non-West is marginal.

HUNTINGTON: BARBARIANS AT THE GATES

One of the major interventions in the post-Cold War search for a new paradigm is Huntington's 'Clash of Civilizations?' article in *Foreign Affairs*.[9] Testament to its impact is the cottage industry that has arisen around this argument. Huntington suggests, in this article and elsewhere, that culture will become the dominant axis of conflict in the twenty-first century, and civilizations the primary cultural groupings.[10] In addition to empirical concerns regarding his specific case studies and generalizations, there is a great deal of concern with the political impact of this article.[11] Jacinta O'Hagan's excellent chapter on Huntington elaborates a connection between his previous and current work. In particular, Huntington was the architect of the 'strategic hamlet' strategy during the Vietnam War.[12] After dealing with some of the empirical concerns of Huntington's critics, I will look at these troubling political implications of his argument. Shapiro in particular argues that the argument is 'historically and ethically impoverished'.[13] While we may be hesitant to accept the whole of Huntington's argument, his work does open space for important inquiry into the role of culture and identity in post-Cold War world politics.

Huntington argues that a civilization is an allegiance 'at the greatest level, less than that of humanity in general' to which an individual feels loyalty. Civilizations are distinguished by culture and can be understood as the field of beliefs which comprise one's identity with regards to 'the relations between God and man, the individual and the group, the citizen and the state, parents and children, husband and wife, as well as differing views of the relative importance of rights and responsibilities, liberty and authority, equality and hierarchy'.[14] Because these cultural beliefs are central to an individual's identity – which Huntington views as static and unitary – they cannot be compromised. As a result, he argues, the cultural, economic and political intervention of 'Western civilization' into non-Western civilizations has produced a xenophobic backlash in non-Western cultures. This is the crux of Huntington's predictions: non-Western civilizations are 'modernizing without Westernizing', which represents a relative decline in Western power and eventually a threat to Western identity, culture and power.[15]

If Iain Johnston had not first used the term 'cultural realism' to describe national differences in strategic culture, we might use it to describe Huntington's characterization of the world. Instead, we are left with 'civilizational realism'. Following Keohane's description of neorealism,[16] we might describe the precepts of Huntington's civilizational realism as follows:

1. civilizations are the key cultural groupings in world politics, led by core states supported by the kin-country syndrome;
2. states seek power, cultures seek conversion, and civilizations seek universalization;
3. all civilizations, and states within civilizations, make political

decisions according to their own cultural standards, but only the Western culture is rational.

Huntington's 'civilizational realism' is based on the assumption that the only possible outcome of the interaction of cultures is conflict.[17] Accordingly, civilizational difference produces cultural conflict in all areas of political and economic interaction. Trade between groups is dependent on their degree of cultural unity: 'economic integration depends on cultural commonality'.[18] International organizations are likewise dependent on this sense of cultural commonality: 'By and large, single civilization organizations do more things and are more successful than multi-civilizational organizations. This is true of both political and security organizations . . . '[19] Because a civilization's culture contains values that determine the relationship between individual and group, society and government, market and state, and so on, Huntington predicts that organizations that do not share similar values will be mired in philosophical discussions from mutually exclusive philosophical positions.

At the root of Huntington's argument, the conflict-prone nature of cultural interaction has two causes. The first is the classical realist assumption about the natural state of human society as conflictual.[20] Second, cultural interaction is conflictual because culture, and the identification with a specific culture or civilization, cannot be compromised.[21] Culture not only sharpens conflict,[22] it is described as the new realm of zero-sum competition. Huntington states plainly, 'cultural questions like these involve a yes or no, zero-sum choice'.[23] His description of cultural clash seems to disregard a large part of the historical record of exchange between civilizations – an exchange that can be productive as well as conflictual.[24] His recent contributions to *Foreign Affairs* seem to corroborate this perspective. In addition to any historical concerns, O'Hagan also points to the 'civilizational realism' of his article.[25] She concludes: 'there is some doubt as to whether Huntington is genuinely interested in inter-civilizational relations in their full complexity, or simply interested in "looking for enemies", trying to locate and justify the next threat'.[26]

Some of Huntington's critics have focused on his delineation of the seven civilizations which makes up the realm of global conflict.[27] Following Toynbee, Huntington divides the world's cultures into eight distinct civilizations: Western, Confucian, Japanese, Islamic,

Hindu, Slavic-Orthodox, Latin American and 'perhaps' African.[28] Toynbee had discounted Latin American civilization as an offshoot of Western civilization, and not included African civilization because it lacked a coherent literary tradition or single, unifying religion. Sub-Saharan Africa, in particular, was labelled 'savage' in the *Study of History*.[29] One criticism of Toynbee, which Huntington inherits, focuses on the portrayal of civilizations as discrete, bordered entities.[30] Toynbee and Huntington assume that the borders between civilizations are clear and mutually recognized.[31] Lewis and Wigen also indicate that civilizational identity is often blurred in these border zones and, even if borders were distinguishable, the history of civilizational interaction is a factor for which Huntington cannot account.[32]

Huntington's critics have pointed out that civilizations are neither unitary nor cohesive. The case against the West as a unified civilization is also pressing.[33] A number of scholars have posed the question, 'Whither the West?' – doubting if the North Atlantic alliance can survive the end of the Cold War.[34] Huntington side-steps this debate by arguing that the core states – America, China, India, Russia, and the like – act as the political focus of a particular civilization.[35] In this move, he resurrects the realist concern with great powers.

The case against the unity of an Islamic civilization is the strongest.[36] Scholars suggest that the Arabic, Turkic and Malay strains of Islamic civilization do not perceive themselves as being a community, and as such, are unlikely to come to each other's aid.[37] Fouad Ajami argues that 'the world of Islam divides and subdivides'[38] and that states determine world politics more than ephemeral cultural groupings.

Huntington's description of the 1991 Gulf War, and Saddam Hussein's attendant kin-country rally, has been taken to task on several fronts.[39] The most obvious example is that Hussein had no qualms about annexing another Arab country to Iraq. Huntington points to Muslim terrorists in Bosnia and Arab support of the Arabian Gulf War to claim that political contests will be decided on the basis of cultural affiliation. However, Ajami argues that Huntington has misunderstood the realist political manoeuvring of states as cultural affiliation.[40]

The 'kin-country syndrome' is refined in Huntington's *Clash of Civilizations* in which he develops a theory of interstate relations within individual civilizations. He classifies states in five categories within civilizations: 'member states, core states, lone countries, cleft countries, and torn countries'.[41] Core states, such as the US, China, India, Russia and Japan, act as the great power of their civilization, providing political direction and cultural leadership. Civilizations without core states are leaderless and thus dangerous.[42] Member states can be understood as middle powers, culturally and politically aligned with the core states. Lone countries is Huntington's term for so-called 'rogue states', figured in terms of cultural, rather than political, isolation.[43] A 'cleft country' is a sovereign state whose populace is divided between two civilizations. He cites as examples India, Sri Lanka, Malaysia and Singapore, China, the Philippines and Indonesia.[44] 'Torn countries' suffer a kind of cultural schizophrenia; the populace adheres to one civilization which the state's elite wishes to change to another civilization. Ataturk's transformation of Turkey and Peter the Great's attempted Westernization of Russia are paradigmatic of this pattern. Problematically, Huntington's theory makes no attempt to include postcolonial countries which have experienced imperial rule and whose culture is filtered through the imperial lens.

Through this portrayal of great and middle powers, natural alliances and rogue states, the state is reinstated as the *primus inter pares* actor of world politics. Though the earlier article had argued that civilizations would be the major actors, Huntington restores the state (and specifically, the United States) to the core of world politics.[45] Furthermore, inter-civilizational relations adopt a resemblance to European multipolar systems. Huntington argues specifically: 'the result is a highly complex pattern of international relations, comparably in many ways to those which existed in the eighteenth and nineteenth centuries in Europe . . . '[46] This refined typology reincorporates structuralist logic to civilizational realism.

While Huntington had dismissed the 'two worlds thesis' as too reductionist, the effect of his later predictions and his emphasis on conflict reinscribe this pattern. Emphasizing the dualistic tendency of political representations, Huntington affirms that 'People are always tempted to divide people into us and them, the in-group and the other, our civilization and those barbarians.'[47] Huntington acknowledges Said's criticism of the dualistic, essentialist tendency and argues that neither the West nor the non-West can be said to be unitary.[48] He seems, however, to undo this complication as soon as he makes it.

The polarization of 'East' and 'West' culturally is in part another consequence of the universal and unfortunate practice of calling European civilization Western civilization. Instead of 'East and West,' it is more appropriate to speak of 'the West and the rest' which at least implies the existence of many non-Wests. The world is too complex to be usefully envisioned for most purposes as simply divided economically between North and South or culturally between East and West.[49]

In one rhetorical move, Huntington acknowledges criticisms of the dualistic tendency in International Relations and reinscribes that dualism as the simplest and best way to describe the world. He states that there are multiple non-Wests, multiple Others, but he also asserts that the West is unitary. The West is united, if only against the non-Wests. In his words: 'in the clash of civilizations, Europe and America will hang together or hang separately . . . '[50] Given that earlier in his book he had stated that 'we know who we are only when we know who we are not and often only when we know whom we are against', he cannot be unaware of the impact of his division of the 'West and the rest' on the identity politics of international relations and International Relations.[51] Specifically offering a 'meta-geography' of world politics, Huntington aims to unify Western civilization around the leadership of the US and to unify the West against the threat of all others.

In reifying the West and the rest paradigm, Huntington reinscribes the 'two worlds' dichotomy. Even if the Other is multiple, it is still defined in terms of a binary structure. Huntington applies the civilized/barbarian discourse to this structure of distinction. He mobilizes the barbarian stereotypes in his description of the 'Other' civilizations – irrational, fundamentalist and violent – which have been circulated since the nineteenth century. He also portrays the West as the only truly 'civilized' ('developed') civilization.

Huntington's prime example of the threat to the Western civilizational order is Islam, for which he has received a great deal of criticism.[52] He argues that the historical record and quantitative analysis from a variety of 'disinterested sources' validate his conclusion.[53] Huntington characterizes an 'Islamic Resurgence' taking place in Islamic societies, in which Islam is regaining a prominent place in the culture of chiefly Arabic states.[54] This Resurgence has particular salience because of its anti-Western bias.[55] Huntington does not link anti-Westernism to anti-colonialism and thus misses a central foundation of postcolonial political culture. He describes Islam as weak in itself and predicts:

> The [Islamic] Resurgence will have shown that 'Islam is the solution' to the problems of morality, identity, meaning, and faith, but not to the problems of social injustice, political repression, economic backwardness, and military weakness. These failures could generate widespread disillusionment with political Islam, a reaction against it, and a search for alternative 'solutions' to these problems. Conceivably even more intensely anti-Western nationalisms could emerge, blaming the West for the failures of Islam.[56]

Whether or not Huntington is correct, he does not explore specifically what characteristics make Islam *not* the solution. To avoid Said's criticism that his argument is 'ideologically closed', Huntington must justify his pessimistic characterization of Islamic society.[57] Rather than enter into this particular religious or historical debate, following O'Hagan's analysis, I will focus on his comparison of Islam and Marxism. Huntington gives 'objective' criteria for the comparison:

> in its political manifestations, the Islamic Resurgence bears some resemblance to Marxism, with scriptural texts, a vision of the perfect society, commitment to fundamental change, rejection of the powers that be and the nation states, and doctrinal diversity ranging from moderate reformist to violent revolutionary.[58]

Huntington specifically endorses the comparison of Western/ Muslim tension to the Cold War.[59] In doing so, he seeks – and finds – an enemy that is powerful, threatening, anti-Western and, above all, familiar.

Islam is represented as threatening the West from a number of directions and on a variety of fronts. One of the vectors of anti-Western threat is demographic; another is terrorism. A final vector of threat is the 'hollow centre' of Islamic civilization. Huntington's diagnosis of the weakness of Islamic civilization is not the same as Ajami's criticism levelled at Huntington's categorization of Islam as a single civilization. Huntington asserts that Islamic states share a common civilizational culture. The weakness of Islamic civilization as a whole does not derive from internal differences, as Ajami asserts, but rather from the lack of leadership which would be provided by a core state. Huntington argues: 'the absence of an Islamic core state is a major contributor to the pervasive internal and external conflicts which characterize Islam. Consciousness without cohesion is a source of weakness to Islam and a source of threat to other civilizations.'[60]

One of the major trends that Huntington predicts, following his diagnosis of the bloody innards and borders of Islam, is an Islamic–Confucian, anti-Western alliance.[61] He argues that although these two civilizations would be as prone to conflict as any other two civilizations, the declining relative power of the West, and their mutual opposition to the West, create a sympathetic relationship.

> [A] common enemy creates a common interest. Islamic and Sinic societies which see the West as their antagonist thus have reason to cooperate with each other against the West . . . By the early 1990s a 'Confucian-Islamic connection' was in place between China and North Korea, on the one hand, and in varying degrees Pakistan, Iran, Iraq, Syria, Libya, and Algeria, on the other, to confront the West [on issues of human rights, economics, military capabilities].[62]

Some scholars have questioned the salience of this cooperation and the importance of an Islamic–Confucian connection.[63] However, in uniting these civilizations against the West, Huntington elides the multiple 'Others' into a single enemy. Thus, while criticizing dualism, his nuanced 'multiple' Others are figured as one, single enemy. The 'rest' unite in opposition to the 'West'.

Huntington's argument is wide-ranging and in some senses a moving target. Further, he has insulated himself from empirical criticisms with his caveat that:

> this book is not intended to be a work of social science . . . the test of its meaningfulness and usefulness is not whether it accounts for everything that is happening in global politics. Obviously it does not. The test is whether is provides a more meaningful and useful lens through which to view international developments than any alternative paradigm.[64]

Thus, he defuses any criticism about specific instances that challenge his theory and confines any challenge to a theory of similar scope and range.[65]

DEMOGRAPHY: PREPARING FOR THE NINETEENTH AND/OR THE TWENTY-FIRST CENTURY

The notion of 'demography as destiny' emerged several times in the twentieth century and again in popular and academic culture in the late 1990s. Demography has a long association with the rhetoric of imperialism, race and class, and civilized/barbarian distinctions. The science of demography is the study of populations – a science that Foucault links to the development of the modern state.[66] The stereotype of barbarians who are more fertile and populous than 'civilized' individuals is one of the underlying assumptions of demographic arguments. This is not to say that these demographic figures are inaccurate, only that demographic arguments are mobilized in periods when the West feels threatened – even though the demographic data have remained largely the same since the turn of the twentieth century.[67] Yet ever since the nineteenth century, an essential part of the barbarian stereotype had been overpopulation.

We must look also at the prescriptions, whether scientific, racist or paternalistic, to which demography leads us. The use of demography in International Relations has been traced in several works. Füredi's analysis of the changing perceptions of race in Western society pinpoints a fascination with demography in the interwar period.[68] Descriptions of the 'rising tide of colour' were popular currency. In the 1960s, this demographic interest emerged again, especially in the US, with the invention of an accessible birth control pill coupled with the movement towards decolonization – the so-called population explosion.[69] Whenever societies feel under threat from migration, immigration and multiculturalism, demography is used to justify these fears.[70] Just as mechanisms of surveillance were mobilized to control colonial populations, demography has represented a new mechanism of surveillance of the non-West and the West. By tracking the populations of both Western and non-Western populations, Western demographers can 'know' the comparative size and make-up of the two groups. When these data are analysed within the context of zero-sum gains, as Malthus, Huntington and Kennedy advocate, demography becomes a crucial predictor of stability and threat.

Both Huntington and Kennedy use demography to indicate the external threats to the Western developed world (particularly the United States) in the post-Cold War era. Traditional realists have long considered demographic strength as a factor of military power. Huntington argues that the present demographic predominance of the West (which is questionable in itself) is in jeopardy because of numbers, and also because of education: 'Quantitatively Westerners thus constitute a steadily decreasing minority of the world's population. Qualitatively, the balance between the West and other populations is also changing. Non-Western peoples are becoming healthier, more urban, more literate, and better educated.'[71] Not only are the numbers of non-Westerners increasing, but their 'quality' is also improving. This represents the inverse of the civilizing mission, a fear of the educated non-Westerner who will colonize the West. Coker uses the Freudian term 'return of the repressed' to describe this anxiety in the post-Cold War world.[72] However, this anxiety can be seen at all stages of the imperial project.[73] In addition to numerical or qualitative disadvantage, Huntington also points to the age differentials between Western and non-Western civilizations. The West and its allies, Japan and Russia, have populations which on average are steadily ageing. Non-Western civilizations, with a larger proportion of children, will benefit from 'future workers and soldiers'.[74] The imperial representation of non-Western individuals as numerous, fertile and violent becomes relegitimized through the lens of demography.

Following his prediction that the Islamic civilization will be the West's prime challenger, Huntington uses demographic evidence to bolster his characterization of the Islamic threat. Population growth in Muslim countries, and particularly the expansion of the 15–24-year-old age cohort, provides recruits for fundamentalism, terrorism, insurgency and migration. 'Economic growth strengthens Asian governments; demographic growth threatens Muslim governments and non-Muslim societies.'[75] He continues to chart the impact of this demographic trend, arguing that 'young people are the protagonists of protest, instability, reform, and revolution'.[76] While emigration to settler colonies (America, Canada, Australia) helped diffuse the youth cohort of the early nineteenth century, there is no such outlet for today's Muslim populations. In his conclusion he augurs a reversal of this trend. Because the West 'no longer has economic or demographic dynamism . . . [and as]

Asian and Muslim societies begin more and more to assert the universal relevance of their cultures, Westerns will come to appreciate more the connection between universalism and imperialism.'[77] Demography becomes one more symptom of Western decline – in both comparative and absolute terms. And, in the expression of these demographic threats, the anxiety of racial and cultural imperialism comes to be centred at the imperial core rather than in the postcolonial periphery. The 'return of the repressed' Huntington foresees is violent, life-threatening and imminent. Huntington's use of demography is not idiosyncratic.

In his recent work, Paul Kennedy draws a parallel between the turn of the eighteenth century and our own millennial *angst*. He is prompted by the writings of Thomas Malthus, whose famous 'Essay on Population' argued that food production technology increased at an arithmetic rate while population increased at a geometric rate.[78] From this dual concern with demography and technology, Kennedy diagnoses the post-Cold War situation and attempts to draw parallels between the dawn of the nineteenth and twenty-first centuries. The crux of Kennedy's argument is not the population crisis in general, but, like Malthus, the growth of the underclass.[79] Kennedy's key argument is that 'between now and 2025, around 95 per cent of global population growth will take place in developing countries'.[80] Kennedy is also careful to indicate that the danger is not spatially removed from the West or North. While it may 'appear that the main problem is *there*', Kennedy is quick to point out the dangers for the West in the form of environmental degradation, health risks and economic collapse.[81] In this geopolitics of fear, the 'return of the repressed' occurs through depletion and degradation of the global commons. It is all the more dangerous or threatening for its amorphous nature. Finally, Kennedy makes Huntington's point that children will become soldiers. The technology of warfare has advanced beyond attrition and sheer numbers no longer translate into military might. However, as Kennedy and Huntington agree, many well-known historical revolutions were prompted or supported by upsurges in the proportion of youth in society. The presence of large, young cohorts in developing countries is linked directly to violence.[82] Kennedy, however, does not link this violence to Islamic culture as Huntington does. And, given the historical precedents, it is perhaps not surprising that scholars firmly established in the status quo should express the anxiety of the *ancien régime*.

The developing countries have higher birth rates and smaller aged populations than the developed countries.[83] What is interesting about this analysis is that Kennedy lays the blame at the feet of 'Western health practices, especially immunization and antibiotics'.[84] The assumption that the success of Western medicine is not an absolute good is reminiscent of the rhetoric of social Darwinism, wherein nature and natural selection keep populations at sustainable levels. In sum, Kennedy argues that

> the greatest test for human society as it confronts the twenty-first century is how to find effective global solutions in order to free the poorer three-quarters of humankind from the growing Malthusian trap of malnutrition, starvation, resource depletion, unrest, enforced migration, and armed conflict – developments that will also endanger the richer nations, if not directly.[85]

His rhetoric echoes the 'civilizing mission' rhetoric in which Christian, European nations would 'free' the colonized natives from their barbarity.

The resurgence of demographic discourse indicates a parallel with Malthus's own time. However, rather than cite the similarity in empirical conditions, I would point to the similarity in political conditions. The industrial revolution brought a large underclass to urban centres. The rise of globalism has brought the global underclass to the West. The fear of the underclass – whether industrial or global – has prompted insecurity in the privileged sectors of the West, which is translated as a fear of increased fertility among the underclass and declining birth rates amongst the upper class. Malthus is relevant – not only because of his predictions, but also because of the fears they reveal.

This criticism does not impugn the validity of demography or the utility of using demography in international relations. However, the demographic trends have not changed substantially since the turn of the century. One of the core aspects of the barbarian stereotype, which links this demographic analysis specifically to imperial rhetoric in the nineteenth century, is the representation of the barbarian as over-sexual – and consequently, producing more children. It is no surprise, then, that when Malthus is translated into late twentieth-century discourse, the underclass which concerned him is represented as the global underclass. It is only during periods in which the West feels insecure that demographic data become a central component of arguments concerned with international relations. Kennedy describes this insecurity as a set of 'deep-rooted cultural and racial anxieties . . . the fear of population decline'.[86] Quite aside from the statistical validity of these predictions, we should note that demographic concerns are raised only when the West faces a challenge in world politics.[87]

THE REAL CLASH: AMERICA'S CLASH OF CULTURES

There is a dual audience for the 'clash of civilizations' argument. Plainly, Huntington's argument is directed at official US foreign policy circles: 'In acting as if this were a unipolar world, the United States is also becoming increasingly alone . . . with one or few partners, opposing most of the rest of the world's states and peoples.'[88] However, there is another, popular, audience. His argument is also an exhortation to the strengthening of US identity. Stephen Chan describes it as 'essentially a [nationalist] polemic . . . a work of partisanship, not of scholarship'.[89] Said concurs.[90] However, rather than dismiss the argument as a nationalist polemic, it is more useful to evaluate Huntington's exhortation and the threats he characterizes. He details several threats to US national identity, which come from a variety of directions: multiculturalism, demography and postmodernism.

Huntington argues that the US's cultural condition reflects its declining power in the realm of world politics. Though not mentioned until the final chapter of his book, multiculturalism becomes Huntington's prime target in the US's domestic establishment. 'Multiculturalism' has been termed 'identity politics' in other contexts and represents the inclination to focus on ethnic, racial and cultural identities over national identities. The criticism of the rise of multiculturalism and identity politics in US popular and academic culture is long-standing and recently inaugurated by Allan Bloom's *Closing of the American Mind*.[91] Huntington also argues against its influence, which he characterizes as follows:

> In the late twentieth century both [political and cultural] components of American identity have come under concentrated and sustained onslaught from a small but influential number of intellectuals and publicists. In the name of multiculturalism they have attacked the identification of the United States with Western civilization, denied the existence of a common American

culture, and promoted racial, ethnic, or other subnational cultural identities and groupings.[92]

Multiculturalism is both symptom and cause of the decline of a coherent and unitary US national identity. Identity politics are central to Huntington's conception of foreign policy because he argues that national identity structures national interest. As he argues in another *Foreign Affairs* article: 'Without a sure sense of national identity, Americans have become unable to define their national interests . . . '[93] Identity thus determines the direction of the kin-country syndrome in his civilizational realism. Culture is necessarily prior to cultural affinity; and cultural affinity is prior to international cooperation. He represents Hispanics as outside the domestic order, though physically located within US territory, because of what he sees as their lack of cultural assimilation.[94] Indeed, Huntington links the future of the West in general to the cultural strength of its core state: the United States. 'The futures of the West depend on Americans reaffirming their commitment to Western civilization. Domestically, this means rejecting the divisive siren calls of multiculturalism.'[95] Internal identity divisions – such as occurred during the Vietnam War – are interpreted as weakness in the international realm and thus undermine international prestige. Coker suggests a remedy in a paper that followed Huntington's at a 1994 conference: 'In a word, the West needs a new threat to define itself against, if only because it has difficulty understanding what it stands for.'[96] Following this prescription, Huntington portrays Muslim civilization as the external threat to Western civilization while multiculturalism is represented as the internal threat. He describes both of these 'Others' with a view to shoring up American identity by presenting it with immediate and dangerous threats.

James Kurth's article 'The *Real* Clash' responds to Huntington's 'Clash of Civilizations?' by arguing that the *real* clash is 'between Western civilization and a different grand alliance, one composed of the multicultural, and the feminist movements. It is, in short, a clash between Western and post-Western civilizations.'[97] Following Kennedy's description of non-military threats in military terms[98] and Huntington's description of identity politics as the realm of zero-sum, if soft, power,[99] Kurth describes American culture as an imperial battlefield:

African American, Latino Americans and Asian Americans . . .
form a sort of series of beachheads or even colonies of these
[African, Latin American, Confucian, and Islamic] civilizations
on the North American continent, and are now contesting the
hegemony there of Western civilization.[100]

This rhetoric of the empire striking back parallels Coker, Kennedy
and Huntington.[101] The anxiety about the 'return of the repressed'
is a common theme in much popular analysis of post-Cold War
politics.[102]

The second domestic threat to American and Western identity
according to Huntington and Kurth is more empirical. It 'comes
from immigrants from other civilizations who reject assimilation
and continue to adhere to and propagate the values, customs, and
cultures of their home societies'.[103] Huntington argues that these
culturally threatening domestic groups are also those that pose a
demographic threat to Western homogeneity: Muslims in Europe
and Hispanics in America. Because culture and identity politics
are represented as zero-sum contests based on relative demographic
power, not only is conflict endemic between states and civilizations
but also within states. Because, in Kurth and Huntington's view,
America is the core state of the predominant civilization, the
threats posed by multiculturalism supported by demographic
growth are pressing and dangerous.

Kurth and Huntington represent multiculturalism, feminism
and postmodernism as threats to the hegemonic, masculine,
white, European identity on which, they argue, the US is based.
That identity is, in turn, equated with the values of liberalism and
capitalism. Their argument suggests that the assertion of a female
and/or multicultural identity involves the rejection of liberal and
capitalist values.[104] Kurth suggests an immediate remedy. He points
to the turn of the twentieth century, when the US faced a large
influx of immigrants. In response to the reality of a large number
of multicultural citizens, the American elite 'undertook a massive
and systematic program of Americanization, imposing on the new
immigrants and on their children the English language, Anglo-
American history, and American civics'.[105] Kurth admits that this
process was so 'relentless and even ruthless [that] many individuals
were oppressed and victimized by it, and many rich and meaningful
cultural islands were swept away'.[106] However, the price was
legitimized retroactively by American success in the Second World

War. American identity – in the sense of sameness and unity – produced American strength. Huntington extends this view to argue that American identity produces American interests which determine American policy. Diversity amongst identity groups leads to fragmented policy.

Huntington argues that the US stands for the American Creed of political culture and Western civilization generally. However, Huntington also believes in the power of the enemy to consolidate national identity. This view of identification – that the constitution of the self requires the rejection of the Other – shapes Huntington's analysis of cultural politics and his condemnation of multiculturalism. I want to make two points: first, that Huntington argues that Americans, other than Huntington himself, are looking for an Other to shore up their cultural identity and national interests; and second, that Huntington makes an 'Other' out of multiculturalism to shore up domestic identity.

Huntington understands identity to represent homogeneity and the primacy of national identity over racial or ethnic allegiances, gender or sexual preferences. He argues that because multiculturalism has failed to maintain American identity, 'identity and unity will depend on a continuing consensus on political ideology'.[107] In other words, shared political ideology will take the place of shared cultural values. The end of the Cold War is responsible, in part, for the lack of identification – because of the loss of the Soviet Union as an enemy.[108] The attention paid to ethnic conflicts in the post-Cold War era does not provide Americans with an immediate danger. Huntington points to the Oklahoma City bombing as an indication of America's post-Cold War malaise. The initial reaction to the bombing was anti-Muslim – it was first reported that 'dark-skinned, bearded men' were seen driving away from the scene.[109] Americans, Huntington argues, had expected an external, Muslim enemy. The actual culprits, Timothy McVeigh, and a right-wing militia group, left America bewildered. The common condemnation of McVeigh only united Americans against 'one of their own'.

Huntington's anti-Islamic and anti-multicultural agenda stems from his understanding of identity formation. 'We know who we are only when we know who we are not and often only when we know who we are against.'[110] 'People', Huntington argues, 'define their identity by what they are not'.[111] Indeed, the need of an 'Other' is justified by psychology in general and American history specifically.[112] The implication he draws from this understanding of identity is interesting. Because American culture is under threat from outside and inside its borders, it is declining. Cultural decline leads to the diffusion of a homogeneous identity, which renders national interests opaque and muddles foreign policy goals. American cultural decline produces and is produced by a decline in the coherence of American identity. Diffusion of American identity is a symptom of a decline in power, but also contributes to that decline. Huntington's response is thus to describe two 'Others' – one internal, the other external – to bolster and reconstitute American unity, identity and culture for his popular audience. Thus, while decrying multiculturalism and identity politics, Huntington's articles can be seen as a nationalistic intervention in contemporary identity politics. His 'clash of civilizations' connects international relations to domestic identity, culture, and power – but not unproblematically.

POPULAR ACCOUNTS OF THE 'TWO WORLDS' MODEL

Huntington's 'clash of civilizations' argument has enjoyed a great deal of critical engagement within International Relations. Because it reflects the two most prominent trends in the post-Cold War world – international conflicts and cultural or identity politics – many sympathetic readings have extended his argument into the realm of popular culture. Barber and Kaplan represent the popular incarnation of Huntington and Kennedy. Their use of similar rhetoric – with similar intentions – has particular salience for the popularization of the civilization/barbarian discourse in the late 1990s.

BARBER AND HUNTINGTON

Barber was among the first political scientists in the post-Cold War era to argue that the trends towards globalization and fragmentation were not only related, but mutually constituted. He uses the terms 'McWorld' and 'Jihad' to represent the social spheres of globalization and fragmentation. These spheres are neither mutually exclusive nor physical spaces. Rather, McWorld and Jihad are both states of social life in which either unification or fragmentation takes precedence. Similar to this spatial disjuncture, Barber diagnoses a general shift from national time – understood as simultaneity in Anderson's sense[113] – to an obsession with the global, multinational and ahistoric field of popular culture and capital. Barber argues that globalized Western culture has moved beyond national culture and historical development. In an argument that Huntington later adopts, he contends that the process of globalization and homogenization is inherently alienating.[114] The backlash to the imposition of homogeneous images and products within the global market induces individuals to identify with smaller and smaller groups.[115]

Barber's political agenda is democratic and he evaluates these tendencies towards unification and fragmentation for its potential for democracy. He identifies 'the *information-technology* imperative' to describe how the globalization of popular media and the communications revolution have fostered the unification of global culture and the globalization of capital. Barber also analyses Islamic culture and its prospects for democracy. Although it differs from 'Clash of Civilizations' in several important respects – not the least of which is its identity politics – 'Jihad v. McWorld' can be seen as the popular analogue to Huntington's 'clash of civilizations' argument. By tracing the ways in which the argument slips and shifts when moved into the popular realm, we can trace the dynamics of identity politics in international relations and the popular international imaginary.

Barber traces four 'imperatives', which he believes drive globalization: the market imperative; the resource imperative; the information-technology imperative; and the ecological imperative. An international division of labour and the near-universal extension of capital in all spaces of the globe – even virtual spaces – have discredited the notion of autarky. While a scientific consensus has not yet formed on ecological sustainability, it is generally recognized in popular and elite culture that the environment and environmental resources are global factors that cannot be ignored.[116] The information-technology imperative has also been theorized in International Relations. However, as Barber notes, in political science this analysis has focused primarily on the 'hardware' of globalization: the technology that facilitates world-wide communication. Cultural studies, postcolonial studies and human geography have been more oriented towards the 'software' of globalization.[117] Popular media images, television programmes and films not only sell products to the globe, they also disseminate the cultural mores of the West. The spread of American ideals has been a focus of many non-Western and Western nationalist scholars. While he may overstate the case, Barber's (re)introduction of popular culture to international relations is important. 'McWorld', Barber's shorthand for the sphere of globalization, 'permits private corporations whose only interest is their revenue stream to define by default the public goods of the individuals and communities they serve'.[118] Because the investigation of popular culture in IR theory is a relatively new phenomenon, I will look more closely at this particular argument.

Barber's evidence of the influence of popular culture on politics in a post-Cold War era is compelling. Proponents of nationalism have long argued that cultural autarky is central to political autonomy.[119] Barber's core assumption is that 'more and more people around the world watch films that are less and less varied. Nowhere is American monoculture more evident and more feared than in its movies and videos.'[120] The global dominance – not to say hegemony – of American cinema and television products has important political ramifications. Barber claims that American cultural ideals are hegemonic, because even in indigenous, non-Western countries, filmmaking is 'rooted in the glamour of the seductive lifestyle trinity: sex, violence, and money . . . mainly devoted to low-budget imitations or blockbuster replicas of Hollywood fare'.[121] One might argue for the uniqueness of Indian or Hong Kong cinema, but the draw of American films internationally makes his larger point that American images, stereotypes and narratives are internationally predominant.[122] For example, even within the Western community, 'America now controls well over 80 per cent of the European market, while Europe has less than 2 per cent'.[123] Barber reproduces these results across the globe in an appendix.[124] He argues that if this is true for cinema, it is doubly true for television, which reaches even more households across the globe. 'The Americanization of global television is proceeding even faster than the globalization of American films.'[125] As evidenced by the most popular shows in the world, *Baywatch* and *Hercules/Zena Warrior Princess*, it is not high culture that circulates globally but the lowest common denominator of Western culture. The dominance of American media represents, for Barber, evidence of an 'imagineered' international imaginary, which is increasingly homogeneous and Western. Public, civic-oriented behaviour is being eclipsed by private, consumer-oriented media, which Barber deplores as damaging to democracy. It is also damaging to nationalism and national identities. When participating in this American-dominated McWorld, Barber describes the position as 'nowhere' and 'everywhere'. 'Universal images assault the eyes and global dissonances assault the ears in a heart-pounding tumult that tells you everything except which country you are in. Where are you? You are in McWorld.'[126]

The social sphere of McWorld is best described as a 'theme park', not in the literal but the figurative sense of any social space that is consumer-oriented, fantastic and strangely homogeneous.[127] Thus, just as Mitchell argues for an 'exhibitionary order' in colonial Egypt and Britain, Barber argues for a 'Disneyfied Order' across the globe. In describing this, Barber points to shopping malls, theme restaurants and media–business partnerships that promulgate products as ideas across cultures.[128] Euro-Disney and Japan-Disney are the most obvious examples. Shopping malls in particular are a spatial inversion of the 'exhibitionary order': rather than the world being represented within the exhibition, the mall is represented *as* the world.[129]

Barber's recollection of the theme park echoes the previous analysis of nineteenth- and early twentieth-century world exhibitions.[130] The world exhibitions displayed national, imperial and industrial successes to metropolitan crowds. World exhibitions were not hegemonic, unproblematic sites of ideological display, however. The 'exhibitionary order' was faced with class, national and racial tensions. These tensions were resolved through the participation of the audience in the spectacle of the exhibition.[131] But, as Barber argues, such participation is lacking in today's theme parks. In McWorld, 'all you can do is buy a ticket to watch: watch without consequences, watch without engagement, watch without responsibility'.[132] In the contemporary world, the theme park of postmodernity is decentralized, enjoyed not as a community spectacle but as individual consumers. At most, culture is experienced not as a national identity, but as 'a small world' or as the provider of different booths at the food court. McWorld's theme parks display private, commercial successes and the universality of consumers – in short, an anti-national message. This leads Huntington and Barber to theorize the small worlds that purposefully isolate themselves from this postmodernity.[133]

Barber argues that viewing American stories may not convert other cultures. However, he asserts, the globalization of American media 'inculcates secularism, passivity, consumerism, vicariousness, impulse buying and an accelerated pace of life . . . Stories told to a tribe around the campfire, whatever their content, knit people together and reflect a common heritage.'[134] Huntington has argued that, in fact, the promulgation of American pop culture cannot be seen as imperialism because consumerism and market capitalism are not at the heart of the American Creed.[135]

Given Huntington's attempt to describe Islam as America's 'Other', I would like to highlight Barber's popular characterization of Islam. Fostered by religious 'anti-modernism', Barber describes the Islamic scepticism of Western values and material or cultural products. Again, using military terminology, Barber argues that fundamentalism 'has been a literal war on the values, culture, and institutions that make up liberal society'.[136] Like Huntington, Barber elides the West with modernism and argues: 'Islam regards Western secular culture and its attending values as corrupting to and morally incompatible to with its own.'[137] However, he makes several valuable and important points about Islamic fundamentalism. First, Islamic fundamentalism has its roots, at least in the modern age, in colonialism – or rather anti-colonialism. He recalls the rhetoric of Hassan Al-Banna, the founder of the Muslim Brotherhood, who promulgated anti-Western fundamentalism in the 1920s.[138] Second, he spends very little time on Islam as such, but moves quickly to fundamentalism within America. By citing American and Western parallels to the fundamentalist movement – specifically, the contemporary Christian Right and the historical Puritan movement – Barber opens the theoretical space to sympathize with the 'Other'. By describing American 'martyrs' – such as Timothy McVeigh – as part of an American Jihad, Barber represents the 'Other' as internal as well as external.[139] Jihad is not just 'out there'. In being 'in here', Jihad is part of a non-national, non-spatial pattern of alienation, and becomes understandable as a reaction to the process of globalization for 'us' as well as 'them'. In contrast, Huntington portrays Islamic fundamentalists in stereotypically 'barbaric' terms, which precludes the possibility of empathy. The 'Other' is undesirable, wholly unlike 'us', and so is definitively beyond redemption. Barber, on the other hand, represents Islamic fundamentalism as part of an understandable, historically and contextually situated social and religious tradition, which has analogues in Western and American culture.[140] Barber's argument approaches a more nuanced understanding of identity and undoes the 'othering' rhetoric of Huntington. In part, Barber's depiction of American *and* Islamic Jihads can be seen as a remedy for Huntington's essentialist description.

KAPLAN AND KENNEDY

Just as Barber can be seen as a popularizer of Huntington, Robert Kaplan states specifically that his book can be understood as 'a brief romp through a swath of the globe, in which I try to give personal meaning to the kinds of issues raised in Paul Kennedy's *Preparing for the Twenty-first Century*'.[141] Kaplan is a travel writer who envisages a new, authentic and realistic travelogue which 'confront[s] the real world, slums and all, rather than escape into an airbrushed version of a more rustic past . . . which folds international studies into a travelogue'.[142] This folding of international studies has some interesting potential. Kaplan rewrites in the American international imaginary many of the Orientalist tropes popular in the eighteenth and nineteenth centuries, notably; climate as character, darkness v. light, development v. under-development, history as progress and Westernization. He paints the periphery as violent, unstable and anarchic in specific contrast to American national space which – apart from the inner cities – is peaceful, stable and ordered.[143]

Kaplan's 'Journey to the Frontiers of Anarchy' can be criticized on similar empirical and theoretical grounds to Huntington and Kennedy. One might object that Kaplan does not intend to write International Relations (and, in fact, disavows political science in general). It could be argued that because he reads historians exclusively, he is a prisoner of their stereotypes. However, I would argue that, apart from these criticisms, Kaplan's work can be analysed as an artifact of popular culture. In his reinscription of nineteenth-century stereotypes of the barbarian, these stereotypes are reintroduced into the American popular imaginary and gain political import to the extent that they are used in public discourse. However, like Barber, Kaplan provides a more nuanced understanding of identification and the rise of 'politicized Islam'. Given the extent to which Kaplan is widely read, I would argue that he is crucial to understanding Africa's representation in the American international imaginary.[144] Indeed, he counts Bill Clinton among his readers.[145] To avoid repetition, I will concentrate on Kaplan's descriptions of West Africa and Egypt.

Like the imperialist writings of the late nineteenth century, Kaplan argues that the threat from Africa is 'more elemental: *nature unchecked* . . . To understand the events of the next fifty years, then, one must understand environmental scarcity, cultural and racial clash, geographic destiny, and the transformation of war.'[146] Kaplan connects the demographic growth identified by Kennedy and mobilized by Huntington to the resource and ecological perspectives cited by Barber.[147] He also recruits Malthus to warn Western audiences of West African population growth.[148] Like Malthus, Kaplan cites statistics that locate the population explosion in the underclass, in the underdeveloped world.[149] Kaplan also adds an important dimension to popular demographic discourse. He argues:

> Demographic pressures never reveal themselves as such . . . The crush of humanity invites scarcity, whether in food, water, housing, or jobs. Scarcity fuels discontent, wearing the mask in this [Egyptian] case of politicized Islam.[150]

As with Kennedy, demographic increases are linked with the 'carrying capacity' of the region's natural resources. Kaplan describes the African earth as 'seething with fecundity and too much of it . . . '[151] He describes the physical results of this fecundity – children – as being as 'numerous as ants'.[152] The stereotypes of the tropical earth as being too fertile and children as being insects are more familiar to the nineteenth century than the twentieth.

Kaplan also resurrects the imperialist discourse that treats geography as destiny. This is not to argue that environmental scarcity and regional geopolitics have an unimportant role in international relations.[153] Indeed, he cites Thomas Homer-Dixon and popularizes his thesis that environmental factors – and the constellation of issues related to resource scarcity and population growth – will become the 'core foreign policy challenge' in the post-Cold War world.[154] However, Kaplan implies that climate determines character. In general, he writes, 'Africa is nature writ large.'[155] 'Now the threat is more elemental: *nature unchecked*.'[156] These descriptions reinscribe the dichotomy between European man who is the master of the environment and African man who is a slave to his environment. As he states in an argument that echoes Rousseau and Montesquieu, 'it is almost certainly not accidental that Africa is both the poorest and hottest region of the world'.[157] He describes his train journey in Egypt as a 'time machine', using the Hegelian metaphor in which distance from Europe indicates movement back in history.[158] Local individuals are described as having the same colour as the soil – as well as its fecundity. The elision of population and nature is reminiscent of nineteenth-century divisions between civilized and barbarian – in terms of both sexual and population restraint and society's relation to nature. Because this division has rarely been utilized to emancipate – except in the paternalistic variation of the civilizing mission – we must be wary of reinscribing these stereotypes in popular or academic culture.

Despite his refusal to acknowledge a specific connection between his own travel writing and Huntington's 'clash of civilizations' rhetoric, Kaplan does mention Huntington specifically. Kaplan recounts the core argument of 'clash of civilizations' and highlights Fouad Ajami's criticism. However, if Kaplan disagrees with Huntington's description of Islam, he does use his notion of culture and civilizational conflict in his analysis of troubled areas.[159] Specifically, Kaplan describes Islamic culture as providing a moral foundation for Turkish and Egyptian society – despite environmental, social and political conditions similar to those in West Africa. Against Huntington's description of Turkey as a 'torn country',[160] Kaplan describes Islamic organizations holding together the social fabric of newly urbanized peasants and providing a social and moral superstructure that minimizes their alienation.[161] His analysis is incisive and worth quoting at length:

> Whereas rural poverty is age-old and almost a 'normal' part of the social fabric, urban poverty is socially destabilizing . . . Islamic extremism is the psychological defense mechanism of many urbanized peasants threatened with the loss of traditions in pseudo-modern cities where their values [and communal identities] are under attack . . . Islam's very militancy makes it attractive to the downtrodden. It is the one religion that is prepared to *fight*. A political era driven by environmental stress, increased cultural sensitivity, unregulated urbanization, and refugee migrations is an era divinely created for the spread and intensification of Islam, already the world's fastest growing religion.[162]

Rather than a country in which elite and popular civilizations clash, as Huntington has portrayed Turkey, Kaplan argues that Islam – and religion in general – has provided an answer to the displacement of urban migration and the alienation of changing social structures. However, while refuting Huntington's specific diagnosis of Turkey, Kaplan's description of the move towards cultural renaissance is the same as Barber's and Huntington's. In the alienation of the postcolonial, globalized culture, there is a general trend to smaller, more coherent identity groupings. Kaplan's description of Islam is more sympathetic, but there remains a consensus on the centrality of identity politics in contemporary world politics. In representing Islam as a rational alternative to alienation, Kaplan makes the rise in Islamic fundamentalism appear understandable and rational.[163] Like Barber, he cites the Muslim Brotherhood and Hassan el-Banna as a 'useful barometer' of political conditions in Egypt.[164] While the Muslim Brotherhood has had a violent history – a fact that Barber neglects – the organization has changed in character since 1970. In tactics similar to many counter-governmental organizations in developing countries, the Muslim Brotherhood has turned from violence to welfare to convert potential followers. The Muslim Brotherhood 'is a benevolent neighborhood force, operating clinics, welfare organizations, schools, and hospitals that arose to fill a void created . . . in general by modernism'.[165] Kaplan thus describes an Islamic, religious organization that is acting rationally and even compassionately. This is the benign face of modernization without Westernization, which Huntington occludes. By resisting the stereotype of Islamic fundamentalist as violent, irrational and barbaric, Kaplan presents a sympathetic view of the Islamic other. By not 'othering' the 'Other', Kaplan allows a more nuanced analysis and opens the possibility for dialogue in the place of civilizational conflict.

Kaplan's 'folding' of travelogue and international studies also provides for more personal encounters with the 'Other'. Because stereotypes can never be perfectly applied to individuals, Kaplan's selective one-to-one encounters have a paradoxical effect. On the one hand, he reinscribes nineteenth-century stereotypes on those individuals whom he does not meet. However, when Kaplan does meet individuals face-to-face, he is prompted to engage with them and come to understand them. These conversations restrict the 'othering' of the 'Other'. The stereotype that appears clear from a distance becomes unreliable in personal interaction. Kaplan's depictions of the 'frontiers of anarchy' have shaped the contemporary international imaginary of the non-West. While we must be wary of his reinscription of nineteenth-century stereotypes, the form of his travelogue *cum* international studies has great potential for theorizing contact with 'Others'.

CONCLUSION: THE REAL CLASH OF IDENTITY POLITICS

The contrast between popular and academic representations of identity politics is telling. On the one hand, Huntington's effort to describe external and internal 'Others' to shore up domestic identity and thus domestic power relies on demographic and imperialist rhetoric from the nineteenth century. Dossa argues that this trend in US policy circles 'is an attempt to *mentally construct, and in practice reconstruct, the Third World as the place of evil it was imagined to be in the heyday of imperialism in the nineteenth century*'.[166] Barber and Kaplan, on the other hand, manage to portray the 'Other' in far more sympathetic and subtle ways. I do not want to argue that either argument is more faithful to the reality of Islamic fundamentalism or demographic shift. What I want to emphasize is the political intent of each message. While Huntington's description of the clash of civilizations allows only for conflict between cultures, Kaplan and Barber open up spaces for dialogue and cooperation. Huntington argues that cultural similarity will structure the success of all international organizations, trade agreements and the international balance of power. In focusing on the local and individual, Kaplan and Barber cite the specific strengths and weakness of cultural solutions to common problems – criticizing 'us' and 'them' in a similar fashion. Huntington portrays the Islamic–Confucian alliance and multiculturalism as America's chief enemies, and urges a process of Americanization domestically and wariness internationally. Declaring multiculturalists and feminists enemies of America is not the same as describing the Christian Right as a fundamentalist movement. The former places multiculturalists outside of the community, whereas the latter identities common processes of alienation and provokes comparisons with other fundamentalist movements outside the Western community. Kaplan and Barber offer a framework for inter-cultural encounters which is based on dialogue rather than conflict, citing lessons to be learned and taught by Western civilization and America in particular.

I would make one final criticism of the 'two worlds' model of post-Cold War international relations. The 'two worlds' model is a direct heir to the realist tradition of parsimony. Many IR scholars, and critical theorists in particular, have taken realism to task for the deification of parsimony. This debate relates to debates in IR with regards to theory-building. However, this particular dualistic simplification fails to reflect the many diverse political conditions present in the 'non-West'. Rhetorically, the 'two worlds' model acts as a form of identity politics: while creating a unified 'enemy', the dualist model also attempts to render 'our' world unproblematic. In addition to the diverse and serious problems faced by many 'Third World' nations – whether or not we see these problems as the inheritance of imperialism – International Relations needs to consider seriously the problems facing 'the West'. While this is plainly a positive move, we much be wary of theories that portray the Third World as derivative, homogeneous or outside its historical context. I would argue that while IR should direct more of its attention to the periphery, we should be wary of recreating imperialist stereotypes when we do so.

8 Conclusion: The Return of Culture, Identity, Civilization and Barbarians to International Relations

In recent IR theory, there has been a great deal of concern for self-reflection, at both a personal and disciplinary level. Tracing the impact of the 'civilized/barbarian' discourse across time illuminates, on the one hand, how the discipline has changed its epistemological focus, and, on the other, how it remains concerned with the same central questions: war, power and security. For the majority of the twentieth century, IR was concerned chiefly with the international system as an objective social realm. War was operationalized. Power was quantified in terms of economic, military and diplomatic strength. Security was theorized as a zero-sum game. The advent of post-positivism has shifted the focus of the discipline towards the textual and discursive aspects of power and security. While early IR theorists sought to define 'civilization', this project illustrates that the 'civilized/barbarian' discourse has shifted and changed to meet the contemporary political imagination. The rhetoric of the preservation of 'civilization' against the threat of the 'barbarian' remains a staple in political discourse. By understanding its origin in the 'civilizing mission', we might better understand uses to which this rhetoric is applied today.

The concept of 'civilization' – as a marker of both progress and belonging – was central to nineteenth- and early twentieth-century IR theory. The community of 'civilized' nations was constituted, reified and policed through the legalistic standard of 'civilization', as well as a matrix of imperialist, racial, class and gendered discourses. 'Civilization' and 'barbarism' defined the members of international society and, in part, regulated the status they were accorded. Early idealist thinkers took the defence of universal 'civilization' against warfare itself to be one of the prime tasks of IR theory. Realist thinkers adopted the more pluralistic sense of 'civilizations' as social groupings. English School scholars have also taken 'barbarians' in particular to be an essential part of IR theory – but this dimension of their work has not been adopted by mainstream IR. However, apart from world-systems theory, which has come to examine 'civilizations' as potential units of analysis, the notions of 'civilization' and 'barbarians' largely faded from the discipline's view until the end of the Cold War. A number of thinkers – both popular and academic – reasserted the 'civilized/barbarian' dichotomy in the post-Cold War world. Whether figured as 'core/periphery', 'liberal zones of peace/realist zones of conflict' or 'West/the rest', the description of contemporary world politics in these terms has the effect of the 'civilized/barbarian' division. Scholars such as Samuel Huntington and Paul Kennedy, and popular writers such as Benjamin Barber and Robert Kaplan, use imperialist stereotypes and concepts to describe the contemporary international society. As I have shown, the representation of groups as 'barbaric' has specific, negative, material and political effects. Imperialism was a central concern of early IR theorists. However, the realist move towards parsimonious theories of international relations removed imperialism from its specific historical context. European imperialism was no longer figured as a specific case of expansion and exploitation. Instead, imperialism was defined as any policy by a state wishing to change the current power configuration. This theoretical move had the effect of retroactively legitimizing European imperialism as a natural result of an anarchic system. It also has the result of removing from view the impact of European imperialism on the contemporary postcolonial international society.

The connection between identity, culture and power has been shown in any number of academic circles. This study of 'culture' takes two primary forms in contemporary international relations. First, culture is studied as the norms, values and ideas that institutions or nations share in common. Traditionally subsumed under foreign policy analysis or country-specific studies, recent scholars have examined the ideational context of national and international institutions. The study of strategic culture, for example, is a fast-growing sub-field of study. Scholarship in this area has concentrated for the most part on elite or policy-forming cultures. Second, culture is studied as a field of representations in which identities and social meanings are constructed, contested and reified. Familiar to postcolonial theory, cultural studies, human and cultural geography, and women's studies, this definition of culture is implicit in a great deal of work done by critical theorists. Students of critical security studies and critical geopolitics represent the leading edge of this sub-field. Critical scholarship has focused a great deal of fresh attention on popular culture, which this project reflects.

The concept of 'race' was central to nineteenth- and early twentieth-century imperialist ideology. Initially figured as a hierarchy that legitimized European rule, the anxiety of racial mixing or racial demographics came to 'colour' the imperial effort. Racial politics were important to early IR scholars. The Holocaust discredited racial politics, although traces can still be found during the era of decolonization. American anxiety about its own racial tension was projected onto its competition with the Soviets for control of the non-aligned countries. Explicit racial politics has been peripheral to IR theory since the 1970s, with very few exceptions. While recent scholarly attention has been drawn to race in the context of postcolonial theory, International Relations has been slow to study this important, if problematic, concept. The combination of the 'civilized/barbarian' discourse and stereotypes of racial 'Others' gives cause for concern. I also hope to have indicated the importance of this concept to IR theory and the popular international imaginary. The use of 'race' in IR theory certainly deserves a more sustained interrogation. One aspect of racial discourse, which is particularly salient to post-Cold War popular culture, is demographic rhetoric. While demographic data have not changed significantly since the turn of the nineteenth century, demographic rhetoric often appears when groups feel threatened. Because demographic threats are sometimes linked to racial stereotypes, we must be wary of the reintroduction of this rhetoric in IR theory.

'Identity' is a leading theme in contemporary politics and scholarship. Many scholars from a variety of disciplines and perspectives are engaging with the concept of 'identity'. While traditional studies had concentrated on a simple, dualistic relationship between the 'self' and the 'Other', contemporary critical theorists have problematized this relationship in any number of ways. The 'self/Other' dichotomy has faced theoretical and empirical critiques. The most recent scholarship views 'identity' as an ongoing process of definition which is always contested, always incomplete and always multiple. While critics of this view argue that such an ephemeral definition makes analysis difficult, critical scholars have argued that it is the very difficulty of this complex concept that makes it useful. Attempting to complicate 'identity' by placing it in a historical, socio-political, cultural perspective seeks to redress the imbalance of generalizations of empirical social science. Against the essentializing tendencies of Said, several scholars have indicated how one can avoid reifying the 'self/Other' dichotomy. Darby illustrates how fiction can disrupt the 'self/Other' dualism. Kaplan and Barber demonstrate how personal encounters disrupt stereotypes. Todorov depicts the 'self/Other' relationship from a number of perspectives. Der Derian and Campbell show how the 'self/Other' relationship shifts and changes over time. This project has sought to undermine the 'iron law of dualism' by examining how one particular dualism – 'civilized/barbarian' – has changed meaning, location and politics over time.

Following postcolonial theory, this project aims to show the importance of imperialism, race and identity to contemporary politics. As Darby suggests, there can be a productive interface between IR theory and postcolonial theory. While postcolonial theory concentrates primarily on literary texts and the power of representation, IR emphasizes the material forces of domination. One such intersection that seems especially valuable is in representations of war. A number of scholars have worked in this direction. Shapiro has indicated the importance of popular culture to contemporary American cartography. Campbell has also traced the history of the shifting American 'enemies'. Other scholars, such as Der Derian, Bethke Elshtain, Dalby, Booth and Klein, have looked at the meaning ascribed to the war/politics confrontation.

By tracing the ways that the 'barbarian' stereotype was mobilized in a number of wars, the stakes involved in the politics of representation become clear. Imperial ideology used the 'civilizing mission' rhetoric to justify warfare against 'barbarians'. In many cases, technology or strategy that was considered immoral when used against 'civilized' Europeans was considered necessary against the 'barbarian'. During the First World War, all sides of the conflict circulated the same message: 'we' are fighting for the protection of 'civilization' against the 'barbarians'. However, as the war dragged on, Europe began to suspect that it was barbaric itself. The interwar period saw a frantic reassertion of the civilizing mission, embodied in the Covenant of the League of Nations and the Mandate System. The machinations of Hitler, and the Second World War in general, disrupted the distinction between 'civilized' and 'barbarian'. In part, the mentality of Nazi rule, especially in the East, was derived from the mechanisms of imperialism. The West represented itself as again fighting for the preservation of civilization. The barbarity of Nazi rule was familiar to colonial subjects, something Césaire and Fanon point out with great clarity and force. Anti-colonialism and decolonization marked the retreat of the 'civilized/barbarian' dichotomy in representations of warfare for some time.

However, we find some of the same images, tropes and descriptions marshalled in contemporary representations of 'ethnic', 'tribal', or 'intractable' conflicts. In post-Cold War scholarship, the 'discovery' of ethnic wars or wars of a 'third kind' resembles nineteenth-century descriptions of imperial warfare. However, as Kaplan portrays West Africa, in contemporary popular culture, both sides are barbaric. Ethnic conflicts are portrayed as irrational and incomprehensible from a Western point of view. Ethnic conflicts are represented as natural features of the postcolonial periphery, often as a result of colonial borders. Although some scholars working from the vantage of international ethics urge a reconsideration of intervention as a viable international institution, the majority of mainstream theorists argue, like Huntington, that these wars are fundamentally 'irresolvable' and consequently counsel non-intervention. Whether one favours intervention or non-intervention, the genealogy of imperialist ideology and the paternalistic rhetoric of the civilizing mission are especially germane to this public debate.

IMPLICATIONS

Barbarians and Civilization contributes to several contemporary conversations in IR theory. From one vantage, *Barbarians and Civilization* engages critically with Huntington's 'clash of civilization' rhetoric. It has shown that, when situated in its discursive and historical context, the 'civilized/barbarian' dichotomy is familiar to both popular and academic culture. Despite the degree to which Huntington attempts to present his terms and argument as unproblematic, the genealogy of his discourse has shown the extent to which 'civilization' and 'barbarians' have been used in political, ideological and unstable ways for imperialist ends since the nineteenth century. Using critical analysis, it has also shown that Huntington's arguments act as a polemic against 'identity politics' and multiculturalism in the West and the United States. Huntington describes internal enemies who are as much to blame as the 'Islamic–Confucian' connection for American decline. IR scholars must take care to engage both aspects of Huntington's argument.

Barbarians and Civilization also shows that popular culture is a valuable source of international relations. This project has focused on one theme in popular culture – the 'barbarians' – from its usage in the nineteenth through the twentieth centuries. It has shown the importance of popular culture as a reflection of international politics. However, it has also shown the importance of popular culture and national identity in the realm of international relations. Analysis of the popular international imaginary can provide a deeper, more nuanced understanding of international relations by focusing not only on the elites who 'do' international politics, but also on the populace who endorse or reject these policies. One contemporary example of the importance of the popular international imaginary is the 'two worlds' model. Circulated by academics and popular press alike, the model is fast becoming accepted in post-Cold War international relations. We must be wary that descriptions of a peaceful, Western core and a violent, non-Western periphery are not understood to mean a division between the spheres of civilization and spheres of barbarism. As is indicated by the contemporary description of 'ethnic' or 'tribal' conflict, we are in danger of dividing the world theoretically into the realm of the understandable 'West' and the pre-modern, incomprehensible 'non-West'. While there may be characteristics of postcolonial states about which we wish to generalize, we must be wary of relying on imperialist stereotypes or colonial rhetoric which has the effect of reifying power relations.

From another vantage, *Barbarians and Civilization* has sought to continue the research started by Doty, Manzo and Darby on the interaction between postcolonial and IR theories. Postcolonial and critical theories of identity and culture have been shown to be particularly illuminating. Further, the postcolonial tendency to focus on texts supplements IR theory, which traditionally concerns itself with material rather than ideational dominance. By not emphasizing the ideational or representational aspects of power, IR cannot understand many relations of dominance or sites of resistance.

This genealogy of the 'civilized/barbarian' discourse illustrates the power of discourse and ideas in international politics. IR theory itself can act as a powerful form of identity politics. Often moored to a 'nation', it defines the world in which all national 'selves' act. If it is not moored to a 'nation', IR theory has the potential to represent all nations as 'Others', which may preclude the potential for cross-national, inter-civilizational dialogue. As suggested by critical theorists, we must examine how the 'self/Other' dyad is constructed, resisted and reified – and how we can complicate those representations and disrupt that power.

Epilogue: New Barbarians, New Civilizations, and No New Clashes[1]

The recent attack on the World Trade Center has been called the 'end of the post-Cold War era' and has inaugurated another war-related era: the 'war against terror'. The flux of the post-Cold War era has been fixed with a new economy of danger. What is striking about this rhetoric is the invocation of the tropes of 'civilized' and 'barbarian'. The adoption of this discourse represents an acceptance of the logic of Huntington's clash of civilizations. At its heart, I would argue, is the formation of a new articulation of America's role in the world and of American identity. While this discourse draws on familiar tropes in American history and policy, the new global mission represents a new articulation of the American mission. As I have argued, the real result of the clash of civilizations discourse is a division of the world into 'civilized' and 'barbarian' spheres. The attendant politics of this are evidenced in the United States' military action in Afghanistan. The 'barbarian' sphere – now associated with terrorism – is open to the violence of the 'civilized'. The invocation of the civilized/barbarian is explicit in statements made by the US administration. Policy-makers are quick to point out that these events do not indicate Huntington's 'clash of civilizations'; nevertheless, in doing so, these public figures reinforce the model.

In statements made in the first week of the post-11 September era, President Bush repeatedly referred to the terrorists as 'barbarians' and the growing US-led coalition as the 'civilized world'. This division between civilization and barbarians is important and has a long history, which I have elaborated above. In rhetorically distancing these terrorists as 'barbarians', the administration hopes that all manner of extra-legal international violence will be tolerated by the society of nations and that other Muslim countries may be appeased and co-opted to the American alliance. The US is shoring up this image of itself as the 'crusader' of civilization, at war not with the general barbarian of Islam, but the specific barbarian of the terrorist. This rhetorical image is difficult to build in face of the powerful rhetoric of the Taliban and Osama Bin Laden on the one hand, and Samuel Huntington on the other.

WAR ON TERROR: NOT THE CLASH OF CIVILIZATIONS

The analysis of US foreign policy is muddied by the inconsistency of statements made by different administration officials. President Bush in particular has made statements that were almost immediately retracted, such as the infamous remark about a new 'crusade'.[2] It is thus a challenge to distinguish a persistent discourse from those false starts, slips of the tongue and mis-speakings. Though this chapter could also discuss the closing of public space for criticism of US foreign policy read as the external face of American patriotism,[3] for purposes of clarity and parsimony I will focus on official statements.

One of the most consistent messages of the Bush administration has been that the 'war on terror' is *not* a clash of civilizations. The persistence of this assertion testifies to the power and pervasiveness of this model of the post-world order – in both Western and non-Western policy circles. Huntington's argument has been taken by Islamic policy-makers and scholars as indicative of current US policy orientation.[4] Because this conflict resembles Huntington's predictions, the American-led coalition wants to avoid the actualization of the 'kin-country syndrome', wherein co-civilizational states rally to the call of 'jihad'. In the rhetorical moves of the Bush administration, we see a common acceptance of the clash of civilizations model.

The promulgation of Huntington's model is furthered by his recent article 'The Age of Muslim Wars'. As always, Huntington is bold in his statements: 'Contemporary global politics is the age of Muslims wars . . . Muslims wars have replaced the cold war as the principal form of international conflict.'[5] While not necessarily a clash of civilizations in itself, he argues that 'reactions to September 11 and the American response were strictly along civilizational lines'.[6] While Huntington has tempered his view of Islamist groups, such as the Muslim Brotherhood in Egypt, he remains adamant that Islam is not the solution to the 'problems' of globalization and development. However, this argument remains unsubstantiated. In short, Huntington sees the attacks of 11 September and the subsequent reactions of state proving his two most controversial predictions: the expression of Muslim violence and the alliance of the West against the rest. Huntington's attempt to link this conflict with eternal cycles of civilizational struggle faces several competing narratives.

There are a number of interesting attempts to link the events of 11 September with the American responses to different histories and contexts. Osama Bin Laden attempts to connect the attack on America to its foreign policy in the Middle East and Persian Gulf. American foreign policy towards Palestine has been inconsistent since 11 September as competing interest groups and public perceptions wage an image war in the American popular imagination. On the one hand, Palestinian support is seen as a necessary American concession to gain the tacit support of Egypt, Saudi Arabia and other Persian Gulf States. On the other hand, Israeli spokespeople have been working overtime to restate their position that the Palestinian Authority is linked to terrorism. The Bush administration vacillated several times between 11 September and December 2001, while the Israeli government takes harsher and more violent actions. It has not escaped the attention of the Arab world that the attacks made on Arafat's helicopters were made by American-supplied Apache helicopters, similar to those used in Afghanistan.[7]

The connection between American support in Israel and American attacks in Afghanistan is easy to see in the Muslim world. This is an argument distinctly rejected by the Americans. Secretary of State Colin Powell distinguishes between the terrorist attack and US foreign policy: 'I think every civilized nation in the world recognizes that this was an assault not just against the United States, but against civilization.'[8] Huntington too attempts to distance US foreign policy from Muslim rage.[9] One of Bush's infamous mis-statements concerned the war against terrorism as a new crusade, an image that resonates deeply with Arab populations, although in the way that is antithetical to Bush's wishes. This attempted reassertion of a Christian community was quickly recanted, and the safe 'civilized' community came to dominate American public discourse. Huntington links the terrorist attacks to a history of violence by Muslims, which he connects to the end of the Cold War.[10] Such nostalgia for the simplicity and 'rationality' of the Cold War is uniquely American.[11]

However, we must ask whether this decision is made for cultural reasons or calculation of national interest. Strategically, it is not in the US's national interest to alienate the entire Muslim community of one billion and countless important states (Saudi Arabia, Egypt, India, Malaysia, etc.). Consequently, we see US and British officials quick to distance Al-Quaeda from 'true' Islam, and Afghanistan's Taliban from their religious roots. President Bush quickly distanced the terrorists from Islam:

> These acts of violence against innocents violate the fundamental tenets of the Islamic faith . . . The face of terror is not the true faith of Islam. That's not what Islam is about. Islam is peace. These terrorists don't represent peace. They represent evil and war. When we think of Islam we think of a faith that brings comfort to a billion people around the world.[12]

In the support of the US attacks by Islamic countries, we see the influence of raw discursive power on foreign policy. It is only through public discourse that Americans could bomb an Islamic country in the Arab world without massive retaliation; it is simply inexplicable any other way. While 'realist', military and economic power certainly plays a large role, it is through diplomacy and careful management of the public image that America is able to intervene in this way. Islamic leaders have been complicit in the construction of the Taliban and Al-Quaeda as terrorists and thus barbarian in order to distance bin Laden's call for jihad from their own populations. Consequently, while the war against terrorism may not be a specific clash of civilizations, public figures on both sides of the conflict have accepted the logic of the clash.

In the face of an attack on the United States by a self-identified Islamic fundamentalist group, the president and members of the cabinet have consistently stated that the attacks on Al-Quaeda, the Taliban and Afghanistan do not represent a clash of civilizations. As argued above, Huntington's now infamous description of the post-Cold War era describes a world in which countries clash due to conflicts over values, which leads to civilizational groups acting as security alliances.[13] Precisely relevant to the terror attacks on America is Huntington warning of the danger of Islamic civilization. He identifies two reasons for concern: a population surge which has little outlet, and the failure of Islam to provide solutions to the problems of underdevelopment.[14] As I have noted, there is a greater population surge in sub-Saharan Africa than in the Islamic countries. Further, several authors, both 'Islamic' and Western, have argued that Islam can provide the solution to the problems of underdevelopment.[15]

Huntington does not simply promote the clash of civilizations.

He links three sets of 'clashes': the clash of civilizations, which is figured as the West vs. the rest; the real clash, which is between the West and the post-West (feminism, multiculturalism and postmodernism); and the real global clash, between civilization and barbarism. It is this third clash which crowns his book.[16] And, it is this final rhetoric which we see invoked in the current American administration. Stemming from Ancient Greece, the image of the barbarian comes from Greek descriptions of the Persians who could not speak Greek and consequently could not participate in the Greek *polis*.[17] The barbarian has ever thus been represented as beyond the bounds of the political community. While the savage may be 'noble' and consequently fetishized, he is never assimilated in the community. The use of this trope closes all non-violent responses and any possibility of negotiation. We see the reiteration of this trope in the lack of both formal and informal communication between the Americans and the Taliban. Neither is speaking the language of the other. The administration attempts to use the language of just war and national interest. Osama bin Laden has reiterated his use of the language of 'jihad' and defence of the holy lands. However, what results from this rhetoric is a new cultural containment, whereby the West makes war against individuals or groups, but not values or religions.

The constant danger to society thus becomes 'the return of the repressed', a term that has recently found its way back into International Relations with the end of the Cold War.[18] This is evident in the American-sponsored *mujahadeen* turning into the American-targeted Taliban. The US government has recently established an 'interim' government, although it is too early to tell the effects of this latest imposition.

In sum, the 11 September attacks on the United States and the subsequent reactions illustrate precisely the real politics at stake in IR theory. The US attack on Afghanistan would have been politically unfeasible without a rhetorical justification that could distance US foreign policy from itself and Muslims from Muslim causes. The rhetorical well of the trope of barbarism is so deep that the call to a civilizational war against barbarians proves able to trump other narratives. This illustrates the importance of the discourse of civilization/barbarians in the post-Cold War world. It is imperative that we continue to reassert the complexity of these images, their long histories imprecated in the process of European colonialism and the uses to which they have been put in the past.

Notes

CHAPTER 1

1. *Al-Ahram Weekly*, 4–10 December 1997.
2. *Al-Ahram Weekly*, 27 November–3 December 1997.
3. *Al-Ahram Weekly*, 27 November–3 December 1997.
4. *Al-Ahram Weekly*, 4-10 December 1997.
5. *Al-Ahram Weekly*, 20–26 November 1997.
6. *Ibid.*
7. Bobby S. Sayyid, *A Fundamental Fear: Eurocentrism and the Emergence of Islam* (London: Zed Books, 1997), p. 47.
8. Samuel P. Huntington, *Clash of Civilizations and the Remaking of the World Order* (New York: Simon and Schuster, 1996), p. 321.
9. Post-structural theory is a wide school, which embraces a number of different perspectives and varied methodologies. For the purposes of this chapter, I take post-structural theory to represent a philosophical position which emphasizes: 'the instability of meanings and of intellectual categories, and [seeks] to undermine any theoretical system that claimed to have universal validity . . . [post-structural theorists] set out to dissolve the fixed binary oppositions of structuralist thought . . .' Chris Baldick, *The Concise Oxford Dictionary of Literary Terms* (Toronto: Oxford University Press, 1990), pp. 175–6.
10. Edward Said, *Orientalism* (New York: Vintage, 1978), p. 54.
11. Jacinta O'Hagan, *Conceptualizing the West in International Relations: From Spengler to Said* (NY: Palgrave, 2002).
12. David Campbell and Michael J. Shapiro, 'Introduction: From Ethical Theory to Ethical Relation', *Moral Spaces: Rethinking Ethics and World Politics* (Minneapolis: University of Minnesota Press, 1999), p. xi.
13. Philip Darby and A.J. Paolini, 'Bridging International Relations and Postcolonialism', *Alternatives*, Vol. 19, No. 1 (1994) p. 378.
14. Philip Darby, *The Fiction of Imperialism: Reading Between International Relations and Postcolonialism* (London: Cassell, 1998), p. 3.
15. Darby and Paolini, 'Bridging International Relations and Postcolonialism', pp. 371–97.
16. Albert Paolini, *Navigating Modernity: Postcolonialism, Identity, and International Relations*, ed. Anthony Elliot and Anthony Moran (Boulder, CO: Lynne Rienner, 1999).
17. *Ibid.*, p. 375.
18. Roxanne Lynn Doty, *Imperial Encounters: The Political Representation in North-South Relations* (Minneapolis: University of Minnesota Press, 1996), p. 168.
19. See Fred Halliday, *Islam and the Myth of Confrontation: Religion and Politics in the Middle East* (London: I.B. Taurus, 1996); Fouad Ajami, 'The

Summoning', *Foreign Affairs*, Vol. 72, No. 4 (September/October 1993), pp. 2–9; Fawas Gerges, *America and Political Islam: Clash of Cultures or Clash of Interests?* (New York: Cambridge University Press, 1999).

CHAPTER 2

1. Samuel P. Huntington, *The Clash of Civilizations and the Remaking of the World Order* (New York: Simon and Schuster, 1996) p. 321.
2. Naeem Inayatullah and David L. Blaney, 'Knowing Encounters: Beyond Parochialism in International Relations Theory', *The Return of Culture and Identity in IR Theory*, ed. Yosef Lapid and Friedrich Kratochwil (Boulder, CO: Lynne Rienner, 1996), p. 81.
3. Huntington, *Clash of Civilizations*, p. 21.
4. Samuel P. Huntington, 'The Erosion of American National Interests', *Foreign Affairs*, Vol. 76, No. 5 (September 1997), pp. 30–1.
5. William E. Connolly, *Identity/Difference: Democratic Negotiations of Political Paradox* (Ithaca, NY: Cornell University Press, 1991), p. x.
6. Etienne Balibar, 'Racism and Nationalism', *Race, Nation, Class: Ambiguous Identities*, trans. Chris Turner (London: Verso, 1990), p. 49.
7. Anne McClintock, *Imperial Leather: Race, Gender and Sexuality in the Colonial Contest* (New York: Routledge, 1995), pp. 61–5.
8. Shapiro and Hall provide the most accessible explanations of this dynamic, in Stuart Hall, 'Introduction: Who Needs "Identity"?', *Questions of Cultural Identity*, ed. Stuart Hall (London: Sage, 1996), pp. 2–5; Michael J. Shapiro, *Violent Cartographies: Mapping Cultures of War* (Minneapolis: University of Minnesota Press, 1997), pp. 94–6.
9. Hall, 'Introduction: Who Needs "Identity"?', p. 4.
10. Roxanne Lynn Doty, *Imperial Encounters: The Political Representation in North–South Relations* (Minneapolis: University of Minnesota Press, 1996).
11. Edward Said, *Orientalism* (New York: Random House, 1978), p. 54.
12. R.B.J. Walker, *Inside/Outside: International Relations as Political Theory* (Cambridge: Cambridge University Press, 1993), p. 66.
13. John Agnew and Stuart Corbridge, *Mastering Space: Hegemony, Territory and International Political Economy* (London: Routledge, 1995); Martin Lewis and Kären Wigen, *The Myth of Continents: A Critique of Metageography* (Berkeley: University of California Press, 1997); Said, *Orientalism*, p. 54; Shapiro, *Violent Cartographies*.
14. Hall, 'Introduction: "Who Needs Identity"?', p. 4.
15. McClintock has criticized postcolonial scholars for over-generalizing the relationship between the self and the Other: McClintock, *Imperial Leather*, pp. 61–5.
16. Shapiro, *Violent Cartographies*, pp. 41–4.
17. David Campbell, *Writing Security: United States Foreign Policy and the Politics of Identity*, 2nd edition (Minneapolis: University of Minnesota Press, 1998), p. 9.
18. Hall, 'Introduction: "Who Needs Identity"?', p. 13.

19. Judith Butler, *Gender Trouble: Feminism and the Subversion of Identity* (New York: Routledge, 1990), p. 25.

20. Roxanne Lynn Doty, 'Sovereignty and the Nation: Constructing the Boundaries of National Identity', *State Sovereignty as a Social Construct*, ed. Thomas J. Biersteker and Cynthia Weber (Cambridge: Cambridge University Press, 1996), pp. 166–8.

21. Daniele Conversi, 'Reassessing Current Theories of Nationalism: Nationalism as Boundary Maintenance and Creation', *Nationalism and Ethnic Politics*, Vol.1, No. 1 (Spring 1995), pp. 77–9; Doty, 'Sovereignty and the Nation'.

22. Iver B. Neumann, *Uses of the Other: 'The East' in European Identity Formation* (Minneapolis: University of Minnesota Press, 1999), p. 5.

23. Allan Bloom, *The Closing of the American Mind* (Toronto: Simon and Schuster, 1987).

24. Neumann, *Uses of the Other*, p. 8; Vamik D. Volkan, *The Need to Have Enemies and Allies: From Clinical Practice to International Relations* (Northwale, NJ: Jason Aronson Press, 1988); Vamik D. Volkan, *Psychodynamics of International Relationships: Vol. I: Concepts and Theories*, ed. Vamik D. Volkan, Demetrios A. Julius, Joseph V. Montville (Toronto: Lexington Books, 1990).

25. Neumann, *Uses of the Other*, p. 10; Michael Dillon, *Politics of Security: Towards a Political Philosophy of Continental Thought* (London: Routledge, 1996).

26. Neumann, *Uses of the Other*, p. 15.

27. Iver B. Neumann and Jennifer M. Welsh, 'The Other in European Self-definition: An Addendum to the Literature on International Society', *Review of International Studies*, Vol. 17, No. 1 (1991), p. 329.

28. Walker, *Inside/Outside*, p. 49.

29. Robert J.C. Young, *Colonial Desire: Hybridity in Theory, Culture and Race* (London: Routledge, 1995), p. 30.

30. R.B.J. Walker, 'The Concept of Culture in the Theory of International Relations', *Culture and International Relations* ed. Jongsuk Chay (New York: Praeger, 1990), pp. 4–5.

31. Arthur Herman, *The Idea of Decline in Western History* (Toronto: Free Press, 1997), p. 259.

32. *Ibid.*, p. 6.

33. Modris Eksteins, *Rites of Spring: The Great War and the Birth of the Modern Age* (Toronto: Lester and Orpen Dennys, 1989), pp. 77–9.

34. Oswald Spengler, *The Decline of the West*, ed. Helmut Werner, trans. Sophie Wilkins (New York: Alfred A. Knopf, 1962), p. 24; Young, *Colonial Desire*, p. 37.

35. Friedrich Nietzsche, *The Will to Power*, ed. Walter Kaufmann, trans. Walter Kauffman and R.J. Hollingdale (New York: Vintage, 1967), p. 75.

36. Walker, 'The Concept of Culture in the Theory of International Relations', p. 6.

37. Sujata Chakrabarti Pasic, 'Culturing International Relations Theory: A Call for Extension', *The Return of Culture and Identity to IR Theory*, ed. Yosef Lapid and Friedrich Kratochwil (Boulder, CO: Lynne Rienner Publishers, 1996), p. 97.

38. Michel Foucault, *Power/Knowledge: Selected Interviews and Other Writings, 1972–1977*, ed. Colin Gordon, trans. Colin Gordon, Leo Marshall, John Mepham and Kate Soper (Brighton: Harvester Press, 1980).
39. John Fiske, *Reading the Popular* (Boston: Unwin Hyman, 1989), pp. 2–4.
40. Philip Darby, *The Fiction of Imperialism* (London: Cassell, 1998), p. 13.
41. Edward W. Said, *Culture and Imperialism* (New York: Random House, 1993), p. 310.
42. Michael J. Shapiro, 'Introduction to Part I', *Challenging Boundaries: Global Flows, Territorial Identities*, ed. Michael J. Shapiro and Hayward R. Alker (Minneapolis: University of Minnesota Press, 1996), p. 3.
43. Michael J. Shapiro, *The Politics of Representation: Writing Practices in Biography, Photography, and Policy Analysis* (Madison: University of Wisconsin Press, 1988), p. 7.
44. John Stuart Mill, 'Civilization', *Essays on Politics and Culture*, ed. Gertrude Himmelfarb (Garden City, NY: Anchor Book, 1962), p. 49.
45. Young, *Colonial Desire*, p. 31.
46. *Ibid.*, pp. 30–1.
47. Alice L. Conklin, *A Mission to Civilize: The Republican Idea of Empire in France and West Africa, 1895–1930* (Stanford: Stanford University Press, 1997), p. 14.
48. Spengler, *The Decline of the West*, p. 28.
49. I would like to thank Eddie Keene for first pointing this out to me.
50. See McClintock on Irish and Welsh racism and the parallels to the discourse of the lower classes in Britain. McClintock, *Imperial Leather*, pp. 52–60.
51. Silvia Federici, 'The God that Never Failed: The Origins and Crises of Western Civilization', *Enduring Western Civilization: The Construction of the Concept of Western Civilization and its 'Others'*, ed. Silvia Federici (London: Praeger, 1995), p. 65.
52. Ronald L. Meek, *Social Science and the Ignoble Savage* (New York: Cambridge University Press, 1976), pp. 14–23.
53. *Ibid.*, p. 33.
54. P.J. Marshall and Glyndwr Williams, *The Great Map of Mankind: British Perceptions of the World in the Age of Enlightenment* (Toronto: J.M. Dent, 1982), p. ii.
55. Said, *Orientalism*, p. 177.
56. Gerrit W. Gong. *The Standard of 'Civilization' in International Society* (Oxford: Clarendon Press, 1984), p. 23.
57. Said, *Culture and Imperialism*, p. 8.
58. *Ibid.*, p. 107; Michael Harbsmeier, 'Early Travels to Europe: Some Remarks on the Magic of Writing', *Europe and Its Others*, ed. Francis Barker, Peter Hulme, Margaret Iverson, Diana Loxley Proceedings of the Essex Conference on the Sociology of Literature, Vol. I (July 1984) (Colchester: University of Essex, 1985), p. 72.
59. Gong, *The Standard of 'Civilization'*, p. 10.
60. Neumann and Welsh, 'The Other in European Self-definition', p. 348.
61. Eric Hobsbawm, *The Age of Capital, 1848–1875* (New York: Random House, 1975), p. 80.

62. Gong, *The Standard of Civilization*, pp. 29–30.
63. See Homi K. Bhabha, 'Of Mimicry and Man: The Ambivalence of Colonial Discourse', *The Location of Culture* (New York: Routledge, 1996), pp. 85–92.
64. Ali Mazrui, 'The Moving Cultural Frontier of World Order: From Monotheism to North–South Relations', *Culture, Ideology, and World Order*, ed. R.B.J. Walker (Boulder, CO: Westview Press, 1984), p. 35.
65. Nietzsche, *Will to Power*, p. 464.
66. Harbsmeier, 'Early Travels to Europe', p. 7; Eric Cheyfitz, *The Poetics of Imperialism: Translation and Colonization from 'The Tempest' to 'Tarzan'*, expanded edition (Philadelphia: University of Pennsylvania Press, 1991), p. 89.
67. Helen H. Bacon, *Barbarians in Greek Tragedy* (New Haven: Yale University Press, 1961), p. 10, n. 8.
68. Julia Kristeva, *Strangers to Ourselves*, trans. Leon S. Roudiez (New York: Columbia University Press, 1991), p. 51.
69. Aristotle, 'Politics', *Basic Works of Aristotle*, ed. Richard McKeon (New York: Random House, 1941), Book I, ch. 2., p. 1128.
70. Homi Bhabha, 'The Other Question', *Location of Culture* (New York: Routledge, 1994).
71. Neumann, *Uses of the Other*, p. 47. The connection to Huntington – who attempts to connect a logic of culture with a logic of *raison d'état* – is particularly interesting.
72. David Fausett, *Images of the Antipodes in the Eighteenth Century: A Study in Stereotyping* (Amsterdam: Rodopi B.V., 1994), pp. 11–13.
73. Neumann, *Uses of the Other*, p. 39. Harbsmeier, *Early Travels to Europe*.
74. Neumann, *Uses of the Other*, ch. 5; Larry Wolff, *Inventing Eastern Europe: The Map of Civilization on the Mind of the Enlightenment* (Stanford: Stanford University Press, 1994), chs. 7–8.
75. Gustav Jahoda, *Images of Savages: Ancient roots of modern prejudice in Western Culture* (New York: Routledge, 1999), p. 16.
76. Harbsmeier, *Early Travels to Europe*, p. 78.
77. Bernard W. Sheehan, *Savages and Civility: Indians and Englishmen in Colonial Virginia* (New York: Cambridge University Press, 1980), p. 2.
78. Hayden White, 'The Noble Savage Theme as Fetish', *Tropics of Discourse* (Baltimore: Johns Hopkins University Press, 1978).
79. Fausett, *Images of the Antipodes*, p. 193; Tzvetan Todorov, *The Conquest of America: The Question of the Other*, trans. Richard Howard (Norman, OK: University of Oklahoma Press, 1999), pp. 16–17.
80. Todorov, *The Conquest of America*, p. 5.
81. Michel de Montaigne, *Essays*, trans. J.M. Cohen (London: Penguin Books, 1958 [English, 1603]), pp. 105–19.
82. *Ibid.*, p. 114.
83. *Ibid.*, p. 108.
84. Gong, *The Standard of Civilization*, p. 8.
85. Montaigne, *Essays*, p. 109.
86. *Ibid.*, p. 113.
87. Lisa Lowe, *Critical Terrains: French and British Orientalisms* (Ithaca, NY: Cornell University Press, 1991), p. 56.

88. Montesquieu, *Persian Letters*, trans. C.J. Betts (London: Penguin Books, 1993), p. 160 (Letter 81).
89. *Ibid.*, p. 66 (Letter 19).
90. Jean-Jacques Rousseau, *Émile: or On Education*, trans. Allan Bloom (New York: Basic Books, 1979), p. 118.
91. Should there be any doubt about the sexualized/gendered notion of 'civilization', one need only compare Émile's education with Sophie's.
92. Jean-Jacques Rousseau, 'Essay on the Origin of Languages', *On the Origin of Language*, trans. John M. Moran and Alexander Gode (Chicago: University of Chicago Press, 1966 [1749]), p. 46.
93. See also V.G. Kiernan, 'Noble and Ignoble Savages', *Exoticism in the Enlightenment*, ed. G.S. Rousseau and Roy Porter (New York: Manchester University Press, 1990), pp. 86–116.
94. Gong, *The Standard of Civilization*, p. 36; Meek, *Social Science and the Ignoble Savage*; Barbara Arneil, *John Locke and America: The Defence of English Colonialism* (Oxford: Clarendon Press, 1996), pp. 27–31.
95. Edward G. Keene, 'International Theory and Practice in the Seventeenth Century: A New Interpretation of the Significance of the Peace of Westphalia'. Paper presented at International Studies Association Annual Conference, 1997.
96. Said, *Orientalism*, pp. 57–5.
97. Lowe, *Critical Terrains*.
98. Martin Wight, 'De systematibus civitatum', *Systems of States*, ed. Hedley Bull (Leicester: Leicester University Press, 1977), p. 34.
99. Martin Wight, *International Theory: The Three Traditions*, ed. Gabriele Wight (Leicester: Leicester University Press, 1991), pp. 57–63.
100. Wight, 'De systematibus civitatum', p. 69.
101. Wight, *International Theory*, p. 42.
102. Hedley Bull and Adam Watson, 'Introduction', *The Expansion of International Society*, ed. Hedley Bull and Adam Watson (Oxford: Clarendon Press, 1984), p. 6.
103. Neumann and Welsh, 'The Other in European Self-definition', p. 328.
104. Friedrich Nietzsche, *The Birth of Tragedy and The Genealogy of Morals*, trans. Francis Golffing (New York: Doubleday, 1956), pp. 174–5.
105. Kristeva describes how Persians became integral to Ancient Greek society while remaining outsiders. Kristeva, *Strangers to Ourselves*, pp. 54–9.
106. Lewis and Wigen. *The Myth of Continents: A Critique of Metageography*, pp. 53–62.
107. Matthew Arnold, *Culture and Anarchy* (New Haven: Yale University Press, 1960 [1869]).

CHAPTER 3

1. V.G. Kiernan, *The Lords of Human Kind: Black Man, Yellow Man, and White Man in an Age of Empire* (New York: Columbia University Press, 1986), p. 28.
2. I found similar statements in Clark, Goldgeier and McFaul, Holsti, Kissinger and Vasquez. Ian Clark, *The Hierarchy of States: Reform and Resistance in the International Order* (Cambridge: Cambridge University

Press, 1989), pp. 124–5; James M. Goldgeier and Michael McFaul, 'A Tale of Two Worlds: Core and Periphery in the post-Cold War Era', *International Organizations*, Vol. 46, No. 2 (Spring 1992) pp. 474–5; K.J. Holsti, 'Governance without Government: Polyarchy in Nineteenth-Century European International Politics', *Governance without Government*, ed. James Rosenau and Ernst-Otto Czempiel (Cambridge: Cambridge University Press, 1992), p. 49; Henry Kissinger, *Diplomacy* (London: Simon and Schuster, 1994), p. 79; John A. Vasquez, *The War Puzzle* (Cambridge: Cambridge University Press, 1993), p. 272.

3. Adam Watson, 'European International Society and its Expansion', *Expansion of International Society*, ed. Hedley Bull and Adam Watson (Oxford: Oxford University Press, 1984), p. 30.

4. Daniel R. Headrick, *The Tools of Empire: Technology and European Imperialism in the Nineteenth Century* (New York: Oxford University Press, 1981), p. 83.

5. Adam Watson, *The Evolution of International Society: A Comparative Historical Analysis* (New York: Routledge, 1992); Holsti, 'Governance without Government', pp. 48–50.

6. Hedley Bull and Adam Watson, 'Introduction', in *Expansion of International Society*, ed. Hedley Bull and Adam Watson (Oxford: Clarendon Press, 1984), p. 6.

7. Marc Ferro, *Colonization: A Global History*, trans. K.D. Prithipaul (New York: Routledge, 1997) (orig. French 1994).

8. John Agnew and Stuart Corbridge, *Mastering Space: Hegemony, Territory and International Political Economy* (New York: Routledge, 1995), p. 56.

9. Gerrit Gong, *The Standard of 'Civilization' in International Society* (Oxford: Clarendon Press, 198), p. 238.

10. Timothy Mitchell, *Colonising Egypt* (New York: Cambridge University Press, 1988), p. 82.

11. There is a rich literature on gender and sexuality in the colonial scene. In this project, I will primarily be using the works of Stoler, McClintock, Doty and Darby. These scholars represent the cutting-edge of research that intersects International Relations but does not represent the entire field of study.

12. Ferro, *Colonization*, p. 14.

13. Ashis Nandy, *The Intimate Enemy: Loss and Recovery of Self under Colonialism* (Delhi: Oxford University Press, 1983), p. 11.

14. John Locke, 'An Essay Concerning the True Original, Extent and End of Civil Government', *Treatise of Civil Government and A Letter Concerning Toleration*, ed. Charles L. Sherman (New York: Appleon-Century-Crofts, 1937; first published 1688), p. 20.

15. W.E.B. du Bois, 'To the Nations of the World', *W.E.B. du Bois: A Reader*, ed. David Levering Lewis (New York: Holt and Company, 1995), pp. 639–41; William Olson and A.J.R. Groom, *International Relations Then and Now: Origins and Trends in Interpretation* (New York: HarperCollins, 1991), pp. 39–42.

16. J.A. Hobson, *Imperialism: A Study* (Ann Arbor: University of Michigan Press, 1965); Olson and Groom, *International Relations Then and Now*, pp. 38–9.

17. V.G. Kiernan, *The Lords of Human Kind: Black Man, Yellow Man, and White Man in an Age of Empires* (New York: Columbia University Press, 1986), p. 23.
18. Georg Wilhelm Friedrich Hegel, *The Philosophy of History*, trans. J. Sibree (New York: Dover Publications, 1956), p. 103.
19. Shiraz Dossa, 'Philosophical History and the Third World: Hegel on Africa and Asia', *European Values in International Relations*, ed. Vilho Harle (New York: Pinter, 1990), p. 100.
20. Hegel, *The Philosophy of History*, p. 91.
21. *Ibid.*, p. 95.
22. Edward Said, *Culture and Imperialism* (New York: Random House, 1993), p. 51.
23. Roxanne Lynn Doty, *Imperial Encounters: The Political Representation in North–South Relations* (Minneapolis: University of Minnesota Press, 1996), p. 4.
24. *Ibid.*, p. 8.
25. Allan Bloom, *The Closing of the American Mind* (Toronto: Simon and Schuster, 1987), p. 80.
26. Neumann's recent work provides a brilliant exploration of the interaction between the Ottoman Empire and Europe. See Iver B. Neumann, *Uses of the Other: 'The East' in European Identity Formation* (Minneapolis: University of Minnesota Press, 1999), pp. 39–63.
27. Anthony Sattin, *Lifting the Veil: British Society in Egypt 1768–1956* (London: J.M. Dent, 1988), p. 3.
28. Said, *Culture and Imperialism*, p. 58.
29. Alice L. Conklin, *A Mission to Civilize: The Republican Idea of Empire in France and West Africa, 1895–1930* (Stanford: Stanford University Press, 1997), p. 17.
30. Said, *Culture and Imperialism*, p. 98.
31. Lisa Lowe, *Critical Terrains: French and British Orientalisms* (Ithaca, NY: Cornell University Press, 1991), p. 8.
32. *Ibid.*, pp. ix–xi.
33. Hegel, *The Philosophy of History*, p. 115.
34. Arthur Goldschmidt, Jr, *Modern Egypt: The Formation of a Nation-State* (Boulder, CO: Westview, 1988), p. 29.
35. Kiernan, *The Lords of Human Kind*, p. 118.
36. Robert D. Kaplan, 'The Coming Anarchy', *Atlantic Monthly*, Vol. 274, No. 2 (February 1994), p. 54.
37. Richard K. Ashley, 'The Geopolitics of Geopolitical Space: Toward a Critical Social Theory of International Politics', *Alternatives*, Vol. 12, No. 3 (1987), pp. 420–2.
38. T.O. Lloyd, *The British Empire 1558–1995*, 2nd edition (Oxford: Oxford University Press, 1996), pp. 114–15.
39. Gong, *The Standard of Civilization*, pp. 14–15. The rule of law was a requirement of the standard of 'civilization', and in its original French, civilization was used to describe the condition of civil law in contrast to lawlessness.
40. Kiernan, *The Lords of Human Kind*, p. 33.
41. Conklin, *A Mission to Civilize*, pp. 5–6.

42. Philip Darby, *The Fiction of Imperialism: Reading Between International Relations and Postcolonialism* (London, Cassell, 1998), p. 25.
43. Joseph Conrad, *The Heart of Darkness* (Toronto: Bantam Books, 1969; first published 1910).
44. During decolonization this ambiguity would be exploited to resist imperialism – citing that the violence necessary to the rule of the colonies was in itself barbaric. Aimé Césaire, *Discourse on Colonialism*, trans. Joan Pinkham (New York: Monthly Review Press, 1972), p. 59.
45. Kiernan, *The Lords of Human Kind*, pp. 216–17.
46. V.G. Kiernan, *Colonial Empires and Armies, 1815–1960* (Kingston: McGill-Queen's University Press, 1998), p. 178.
47. Homi K. Bhabha, 'Of Mimicry and Man: The Ambivalence of Colonial Discourse', *The Location of Culture* (New York: Routledge, 1994), p. 86.
48. Ann Laura Stoler, 'Rethinking Colonial Categories: European Communities and the Boundaries of Rule', *Colonialism and Culture*, ed. Nicholas B. Dirks (Ann Arbor: University of Michigan Press, 1992), p. 321.
49. Ann Laura Stoler, *Race and the Education of Desire: Foucault's History of Sexuality and the Colonial Order of Things* (Durham, NC: Duke University Press, 1995), p. 108.
50. Kiernan, *Colonial Empires and Armies, 1815–1960*, p. 111.
51. Ronald Hyam, *Britain's Imperial Century 1815–1914: A Study in Empire and Expansion* (London: Macmillan, 1993), p. 301.
52. Lloyd, *The British Empire 1558–1995*, p. 178.
53. Kenneth N. Waltz, 'Anarchic Orders and Balances of Power', *Neorealism and its Critics*, ed. Robert O. Keohane (New York: Columbia University Press, 1986), p. 98.
54. K.J. Holsti, *Peace and War: Armed Conflicts and International Order 1648–1989* (Cambridge: Cambridge University Press, 1991).
55. Gregory F. Trevorton, 'Finding an Analogy for Tomorrow', *Orbis*, Vol. 37, No. 1 (1993); Charles A. Kupchan and Clifford A. Kupchan, 'Concerts, Collective Security and the Future of Europe', *International Security*, Vol. 16, No. 1 (1991), p. 115.
56. Gong, *The Standard of Civilization*, p. 58.
57. Hedley Bull, 'European States and African Political Communities', *The Expansion of International Society*, ed. Hedley Bull and Adam Watson (Oxford: Clarendon Press, 1984).
58. Lloyd, *The British Empire 1558–1995*, p. 4.
59. Adam Watson, 'European International Society and its Expansion', *The Expansion of International Society*, ed. Hedley Bull and Adam Watson (Oxford: Clarendon Press, 1984), p. 30.
60. K.J. Holsti, *The State, War, and the State of War* (Cambridge: Cambridge University Press), 1996, p. 21.
61. Jürgen Osterhammel, *Colonialism: A Theoretical Overview*, trans. Shelley L. Frisch (Princeton, NJ: Markus Wiener, 1997 first published in German in 1995), p. 44.
62. Kiernan, *Colonial Empires and Armies, 1815–1960*, pp. 155–65.
63. Chris Hables Gray, *Postmodern War: The New Politics of Conflict* (New

York: Guilford Press, 1997), p. 131; Headrick, *The Tools of Empire*, pp. 102–3.

64. Kiernan, *Colonial Empires and Armies, 1815–1960*, p. 163.
65. Michael Mann, 'Authoritarian and Liberal Militarism: A Contribution from Comparative and Historical Sociology', in Steve Smith, Ken Booth and Marysia Zalewskim eds, *International Theory: Positivism and Beyond* (Cambridge: Cambridge University Press, 1996), pp. 234–5.
66. Gong, *The Standard of Civilization*, p. 247; Shapiro, *Violent Cartographies*, pp. 1–16.
67. Lloyd, *The British Empire 1558–1995*, p. 178.
68. Timothy Mitchell, *Colonising Egypt* (New York: Cambridge University Press, 1988), p. 82.
69. Ferro, *Colonization: A Global History*, p. 66.
70. Said, *Culture and Imperialism*, pp. 118–19.
71. Vivant Denon, *Travels in Upper and Lower Egypt*, Vols. I–III, trans. Alan Aikin (New York: Arno Press, 1973; first English Translation 1803), pp. iii–iv.
72. Thomas Walsh, *Journal of the Late Campaign in Egypt: Including Descriptions of that Country* (London: Hansard, 1803; republished by Gregg Int'l Publishers, Weastmead, 1972), p. vii.
73. Lowe, *Critical Terrains*, p. 78.
74. Conklin, *A Mission to Civilize*, p. 2.
75. Michel Foucault, *Discipline and Punish: The Birth of the Prison*, trans. Alan Sheridan (New York: Vintage, 1977), pp. 102–3.
76. A common occurrence in universities.
77. Foucault, *Discipline and Punish*, p. 201.
78. *Ibid.*, pp. 212–15.
79. Thomas C. Shelling, *The Strategy of Conflict* (Cambridge, MA: Harvard University Press, 1963), pp. 9–13.
80. Mitchell, *Colonising Egypt*, p. 35.
81. I would like to thank Daniel Nexon for pointing out the geographical source, which Mitchell fails to do. Gulru Necipoglu, *Architecture, Ceremonial, and Power: The Topakapi Palace in the Fifteenth and Sixteenth Centuries* (Cambridge, MA: MIT Press, 1991).
82. Stoler, *Race and the Education of Desire*; Said, *Orientalism*.
83. Timothy Mitchell, 'Orientalism and the Exhibitionary Order', *Colonialism and Culture*, ed. Nicholas B. Dirks (Ann Arbor: University of Michigan Press, 1992), pp. 289–90; Mitchell, *Colonising Egypt*.
84. Gong, *The Standard of Civilization*, p. 14.
85. Denon, *Travels in Upper and Lower Egypt*, Vol. I, ch. VIII, pp. 257–8.
86. Edward William Lane, *An Account of the Manners and Customs of the Modern Egyptians Written in Egypt During the Years 1833–1835* (London: East–West Publications, 1978), p. 15.
87. Walsh, *Journal of the Late Campaign in Egypt*, p. 236.
88. Gustave Flaubert, *Flaubert in Egypt: A Sensibility on Tour*, trans. and ed. Francis Steegmuller (Toronto: Bodley Head, 1972; first published 1850), p. 79.
89. Mitchell, *Colonising Egypt*, p. 68.

90. I am examining this theme through a genealogy of the passport in my current project.
91. Foucault, *Discipline and Punish*, p. 200.
92. Mitchell, *Colonising Egypt*, p. 34.
93. Stoler, *Race and the Education of Desire*, pp. 32, 102–6.
94. Richard F. Burton, *Personal Narrative of a Pilgrimage to Al-Madinah and Meccah*, ed. Isabel Burton (New York: Dover Publications Inc. 1964; first edition 1863; memorial edition 1893), Part I, ch. II, p. 18.
95. Flaubert, *Flaubert in Egypt*, p. 103.
96. Burton, *A Personal Narrative of a Pilgrimage*, p. 1. 'In the autumn of 1852 . . . I offered my services to the Royal Geographic Society of London, for the purpose of removing that opprobrium to modern adventure, the *huge white blot* which our maps still notes the Eastern and the Central regions of Arabia.'
97. Said, *Culture and Imperialism*, p. 211. I will look at the sexual metaphors of 'discover' and 'possession' in the next section, in addition to the connection between racial, gendered and class-based discourses.
98. Benedict Anderson, *Imagined Communities: Reflections on the Origin and Spread of Nationalism*, 2nd edition (London: Verso, 1991), p. 173.
99. Mitchell, *Colonising Egypt*, p. 46.
100. Ali Behdad, *Belated Travelers: Orientalism in the Age of Colonial Dissolution* (Durham, NC: Duke University Press, 1994), pp. 13–14.
101. *Ibid.*, pp. 68–9; Lowe, *Critical Terrains*, pp. 75–86.
102. Burton, *A Personal Narrative of a Pilgrimage*, p. 2.
103. Flaubert, *Flaubert in Egypt*, p. 42.
104. See 'Colonial Passing'. McClintock notes that the privilege of colonial passing is uniquely male. McClintock, *Imperial Leather*, pp. 69–71.
105. Anderson, *Imagined Communities*, p. 122.
106. Cited in McClintock, *Imperial Leather*, pp. 62–3.
107. Bhabha, 'Of Mimicry and Man'.
108. It should be noted that the World Exhibitions took place chiefly in France, England and America and not other European colonial powers. Yengoyan argues this is due to differences in worldview, best shown in the difference between French 'civilization' and German '*Kultur*'. 'A culture model is bounded, limited, not expansive, and hardly universalistic in scope . . . A civilization model is the basis of universalistic exhibitions . . . The civilizing process which is the basis of western civilization in theory is not contained, bounded or limited.' For a deeper exploration of this division between German and Anglo-French notions of civilization, see Patrick Thaddeus Jackson's doctoral thesis: 'Occidentalism: The Symbolic Technology of German Reconstruction'.
109. Eric Hobsbawm, 'The Invention of Tradition', *Nationalism*, ed. John Hutchinson and Anthony D. Smith (Oxford: Oxford University Press, 1994), pp. 76–8.
110. Aram A. Yengoyan, 'Culture, Ideology and World's Fairs', *Fair Representations: World's Fairs and the Modern World*, ed. Robert W. Rydell and Nancy Gwinn (Amsterdam: VU University Press, 1994), p. 82.
111. McClintock, *Imperial Leather*, p. 37.

112. Hobsbawm, *The Age of Capitalism*, p. 204.
113. Mitchell, 'Orientalism and the Exhibitionary Order', p. 290.
114. David Strang, 'Contested Sovereignty: The Social Construction of Colonial Imperialism', *Sovereignty as a Social Construct*, ed. Thomas J. Biersteker and Cynthia Weber (Cambridge: Cambridge University Press, 1996), p. 35.
115. Marilyn Wan, 'Naturalized Seeing/Colonial Vision: Interrogating the Display of Races in Late Nineteenth Century France', Master's Thesis, Fine Arts, University of British Columbia, 1992, p. 20.
116. Burton Benedict, 'Rituals of Representation: Ethnic Stereotypes and Colonized Peoples at World's Fairs', *Fair Representations: World's Fairs and the Modern World*, ed. Robert W. Rydell and Nancy Gwinn (Amsterdam: VU University Press, 1994), p. 28.
117. McClintock, *Imperial Leather*, p. 59.
118. Wan, 'Naturalized Seeing/Colonial Vision', pp. 29–50.
119. Allan Pred, *ReCognizing European Modernities: A Montage of the Present* (New York: Routledge, 1995), p. 37.
120. Mitchell, *Colonising Egypt*, p. 291.
121. Ronald Hyam, *Britain's Imperial Century, 1815–1914: A Study of Empire and Expansion* (London: Macmillan, 1993), pp. 280–92; McClintock, *Imperial Leather*, pp. 23–30.
122. Wan, 'Naturalized Seeing/Colonial Vision', p. 60.
123. Leila Kinney and Zeynep Çelik, 'Ethnography and Exhibitionism', *Assemblages*, Vol. 13 (1990), p. 38, cited in Said, *Culture and Imperialism*.
124. Hobsbawm, *Age of Capitalism*, p. 125.
125. Anderson, *Imagined Communities*, p. 184.
126. Michel Foucault, 'Governmentality', *The Foucault Effect: Studies in Governmentality*, ed. Graham Burchell, Colin Gordon and Peter Miller (Chicago: University of Chicago Press, 1991), pp. 101–2.
127. Thomas Robert Malthus, 'An Essay on the Principle of Population (1798)', *The Works of Thomas Robert Malthus*. Vol. I, ed. E.A. Wrigley and David Souden (London: William Pickering, 1986), p. 9.
128. *Ibid.*, p. 33.
129. Anderson, *Imagined Communities*, p. 164.
130. *Ibid.*, p. 39.
131. *Ibid.*, pp. 18–20.
132. Michael S. Teitelbaum and Jay M. Winter, *The Fear of Population Decline* (Toronto: Academic Press, 1985), pp. 36–40.
133. Lowe, *Critical Terrains*, p. 78.
134. Stoler explores how imperialism was represented as a bourgeois practice, but in fact required members from every class and the tension this endows. Stoler, *Race and the Education of Desire*, ch. IV.
135. Anderson, *Imagined Communities*, pp. 80, 113–14; Balibar, 'Racism and Nationalism'.
136. McClintock, *Imperial Leather*, pp. 54–5.
137. V.G. Kiernan, *European Empires from Conquest to Collapse: 1815–1960* (Leicester: Leicester University Press 1982), p. 156.
138. Darby, *The Fiction of Imperialism*, p. 66.
139. Susie Prestney, 'Inscribing the Hottentot Venus: Generating the Data

for Difference', *At the Edge of International Relations: Postcolonialism, Gender and Dependency*, ed. Phillip Darby (London: Continuum, 1997), pp. 86–105.
140. Anderson, *Imagined Communities*, p. 150.
141. Stoler, *Race and the Education of Desire*, p. 96.
142. R.J. Vincent, 'Race in International Relations', *Culture, Ideology and World Order*, ed. R.B.J. Walker (Boulder, CO: Westview Press, 1984), pp. 44–6.
143. McClintock, *Imperial Leather*, pp. 22–56.
144. R.J. Vincent, 'Racial Equality', *The Expansion of International Society*, ed. Hedley Bull and Adam Watson (Oxford: Clarendon Press, 1984), p. 240.
145. Ann Laura Stoler, 'Rethinking Colonial Categories: European Communities and the Boundaries of Rule', *Colonialism and Culture*, ed. Nicholas B. Dirks (Ann Arbor: University of Michigan Press, 1992), p. 27.
146. John Laffey, *Civilization and its Discontented* (Montreal: Black Rose Books, 1993), p. 70.
147. Kiernan, *European Empires*, p. 316.
148. Denon, *Travels in Upper and Lower Egypt*, p. 210.
149. Walsh, *Journal of the Late Campaign in Egypt*, pp. 257, 261.
150. Lowe, *Critical Terrains*, p. 8.
151. Kiernan, *Colonial Empires and Armies*, p. 16.
152. Kiernan, *The Lords of Human Kind*, p. 317.
153. Denon, *Travels in Upper and Lower Egypt*, pp. 219–20.
154. Said, *Culture and Imperialism*, p. 111.
155. Denon, *Travels in Upper and Lower Egypt*, pp. 232–3.
156. Edward William Lane, *An Account of the Manners and Customs of the Modern Egyptians during the Years 1833–1835* (London: East–West Publications, 1978), p. 297.
157. *Ibid.*, p. 298.
158. Said, *Orientalism*, p. 188. 'Woven through all of Flaubert's Oriental experiences, exciting or disappointing, is an almost uniform association between the Orient and sex.'
159. Behdad, *Belated Travelers*, p. 49.
160. Flaubert (15 January 1850) p. 81.
161. Flaubert (1853), in Lowe, *Critical Terrains*, p. 75.
162. Lowe, *Critical Terrains*, p. 76.
163. Stoler, *Race and the Education of Desire*, p. 42.
164. Said, *Orientalism*, p. 190.
165. Burton, *Personal Narrative of a Pilgrimage*, p. 60.
166. McClintock, *Imperial Leather*, p. 31.
167. Burton, *Personal Narrative of a Pilgrimage*, p. 58.
168. Hyam, *Britain's Imperial Century*, p. 103.
169. Michel Foucault, 'Body/Power', *Power/Knowledge: Selected Interviews and Other Writings* (Brighton: Harvester Press, 1980), pp. 55–62.
170. Burton, *Personal Narrative of a Pilgrimage*, p. 17.
171. Stoler, *Race and the Education of Desire*, p. 102.
172. Hyam, *Britain's Imperial Century*, p. 292.

173. Lloyd, *The British Empire 1558–1995*, p. 178.
174. Benedict Anderson, *Imagined Communities: Reflections on the Origin and Spread of Nationalism*, 2nd edition (London: Verso, 1991), p. 6.
175. Ashis Nandy, *The Intimate Enemy: Loss and Recovery of Self under Colonialism* (Delhi: Oxford University Press, 1983), p. 32. 'They were overwhelmed by the experience of being colonial rulers. As a result, the long-term cultural damage colonialism did to the British society was greater.' Aimé Césaire, *Discourse on Colonialism*, trans. Joan Pinkham (New York: Monthly Review Press, 1972), p. 13.
176. Said, *Orientalism*, p. 40.
177. Kiernan, *The Lords of Human Kind*, p. 131.

CHAPTER 4

1. Christopher Coker, *War and the 20th Century: A Study of War and Modern Consciousness* (London: Brassey's, 1994), p. 2.
2. W.I. Langer, *The Diplomacy of Imperialism* (New York: Alfred Knopf, 1951), p. 85.
3. Hugh Tinker, *Race, Conflict and the International Order: From Empire to United Nations* (London: Macmillan Press, 1977), p. 39.
4. Frank Füredi, *The Silent War: Imperialism and the Changing Perception of Race* (London: Pluto Press, 1998), pp. 18–19.
5. R.J. Vincent, 'Race in International Relations', *Culture, Ideology and World Order*, ed. R.B.J. Walker (Boulder, CO: Westview Press, 1984), pp. 45–7.
6. Allan Chase, *The Legacy of Malthus: The Social Costs of the New Scientific Racism* (Chicago: University of Illinois Press, 1980), pp. 90–2.
7. Ivan Hannaford, *Race: The History of an Idea in the West* (Baltimore: Johns Hopkins University Press, 1996), p. 265.
8. *Ibid.*, p. 348.
9. Tinker, *Race, Conflict and the International Order*, p. 43.
10. Füredi, *The Silent War*, p. 68.
11. Michael S. Teitelbaum and Jay M. Winter, *The Fear of Population Decline* (Toronto: Academic Press, 1985), pp. 129–33.
12. *Ibid.*, p. 224.
13. Robert G.L. Waite, *The Psychopathic God: Adolf Hitler* (New York: Da Capo Press, 1977), p. 279.
14. Walter Kaufmann, *Nietzsche: Philosopher, Psychologist, Antichrist*, 4th edition (Princeton, NJ: Princeton University Press, 1974), p. 8.
15. Friedrich Nietzsche, *The Gay Science with a Prelude in Rhymes and an Appendix of Songs*, trans. Walter Kaufmann (New York: Random House, 1974 [1882]), pp. 181 [125]. The brackets refer to original date of publication and section number respectively.
16. Kaufmann, *Nietzsche: Philosopher, Psychologist, Antichrist*, pp. 337–71; Friedrich Nietzsche, *Beyond Good and Evil: Prelude of a Philosophy of the Future*, trans. R.J. Hollingdale (London: Penguin Books, 1990 [1886]), pp. 74–81.
17. Jacques Derrida, 'Structure, Sign and Play in the Discourse of the Human

Sciences', *Writing and Difference*, trans. Alan Bass (Chicago: University of Chicago Press, 1978), pp. 278–93.

18. Friedrich Nietzsche, 'The Genealogy of Morals', *The Birth of Tragedy and The Genealogy of Morals*, trans. Francis Golffing (New York: Doubleday, 1956 [1887]), pp. 151 [3]. The brackets refer to original date of publication and section number respectively.

19. Coker, *War and the 20th Century*, pp. 43–4.

20. Friedrich Nietzsche, *The Will to Power: An Attempt at a Revaluation of All Values*, ed. Walter Kaufmann, trans. Walter Kaufmann and R.J. Hollingdale (New York: Vintage, 1967 [1901]), p. 267 [481]. The brackets refer to original date of publication and section number respectively.

21. *Ibid.*, p. 278 [515].

22. *Ibid.*, pp. 55 [90].

23. *Ibid.*, pp. 290–1 [535–7].

24. Kaufmann, *Nietzsche: Philosopher, Psychologist, Antichrist*, p. 288.

25. Friedrich Nietzsche, *Thus Spoke Zarathustra: A Book for All and None*, trans. Walter Kaufmann (London: Penguin Books, 1966 [1883]), p. 47.

26. Nietzsche, *The Will to Power*, p. 3.

27. *Ibid.*, p. 465 [870]. 'The root of all evil: that the slavish morality of meekness, chastity, selflessness, absolute obedience has triumphed – ruling natures were thus condemned.'

28. Nietzsche, 'The Genealogy of Morals', pp. 174–5 [11].

29. Nietzsche, *The Will to Power*, p. 464 [868].

30. Kaufmann, *Nietzsche: Philosopher, Psychologist, Antichrist*, p. 196.

31. *Ibid.*, p. 362.

32. Nietzsche, 'The Genealogy of Morals', pp. 170–1.

33. See Shapiro and Bhabha on Lacan and Fanon. Michael J. Shapiro, *Violent Cartographies: Mapping Cultures of War* (Minneapolis: University of Minnesota Press, 1997), p. 95; Homi K. Bhabha, 'The Other Question: Stereotype, Discrimination and the Discourse of Colonialism', *The Location of Culture* (New York: Routledge, 1994), p. 77.

34. Nietzsche, *The Will to Power*, pp. 478–9 [900].

35. Nietzsche, 'The Genealogy of Morals', pp. 167–8 [7].

36. Nietzsche, quoted in Kaufmann, *Nietzsche: Philosopher, Psychologist, Antichrist*, p. 45.

37. Kaufmann in Nietzsche, *The Will to Power*, pp. xvi–xix.

38. Walter A. Kaufmann, *Nietzsche: Philosopher, Psychologist, Antichrist* (New York: Meridian Books, 1956), pp. 300–1.

39. Daniel Jonah Goldhagen, *Hitler's Willing Executioners: Ordinary Germans and the Holocaust* (New York: Alfred Knopf, 1996), pp. 53–64.

40. Arthur Herman, *The Idea of Decline in Western History* (Toronto: The Free Press, 1997), pp. 244–5.

41. Modris Eksteins, *Rites of Spring: The Great War and the Birth of the Modern Age* (Toronto: Lester and Orpen Dennys, 1989), pp. 79–80.

42. Oswald Spengler, *The Decline of the West*, ed. Helmut Werner, trans. Sophie Wilkins (New York: Alfred Knopf, 1962 [Vol. I, 1918, Vol. II 1922]), p. 73.

43. Nietzsche, *The Will to Power*, p. 75 [121].
44. Sigmund Freud, 'The Future of an Illusion', *Sigmund Freud: Civilization, Society and Religion*, ed. Albert Dickson, trans. James Strachey (New York: Penguin Books, 1985 [1927 Ger., 1928 Eng.]), p. 184.
45. Spengler, *The Decline of the West*, p. 24.
46. *Ibid.*, p. 28.
47. G. Kurt Johannsen and H.H. Kraft, *Germany's Colonial Problem* (London: Thornton Butterworth, 1937), pp. 24, 27–32. Although the authors argue that a 'colonial guilt lie' accompanies the 'war guilt lie' in the Versailles settlement, they do not justify Germany's claim to colonies on the basis of the civilizing mission. Instead, they cite the economic, demographic, and territorial needs of Germany within Europe.
48. Christopher Coker, *Twilight of the West* (Boulder, CO: Westview Press, 1998), p. 18.
49. See Jack Weatherford, *Savages and Civilization: Who Will Survive?* (New York: Crown Publishers, 1994).
50. Sigmund Freud, 'An Autobiographical Study', *Sigmund Freud: Historical and Expository Works on Psychoanalysis*, ed. Albert Dickson, trans. James Strachey (London: Penguin Books, 1986 [1925 Ger., 1927 Eng.]), p. 244. See also 'On the History of the Psychoanalytic Movement', *Sigmund Freud: Historical and Expository Works on Psychoanalysis*, ed. Albert Dickson, trans. James Strachey (London: Penguin Books, 1986 [1925 Ger., 1927 Eng.]), p. 73.
51. Nietzsche, 'The Genealogy of Morals', pp. 189–230 (Second Essay).
52. Sigmund Freud, 'Thoughts for the Times on War and Death', *Sigmund Freud: Civilization, Society and Religion*, ed. Albert Dickson, trans. James Strachey (New York: Penguin Books, 1985 [1915 Ger., 1918 Eng.]), p. 61.
53. Sigmund Freud, 'Civilization and Its Discontents', *Sigmund Freud: Civilization, Society and Religion*, ed. Albert Dickson, trans. James Strachey (New York: Penguin Books, 1985 [1930 Ger., 1930 Eng.]), pp. 325–9.
54. Lacanian psychoanalysis works from this basis to speculate on the universal 'Self'/'Other' structure of all identity. See Jacques Lacan, 'The Field of the Other and Back to the Transference', *The Four Fundamental Concepts of Psychoanalysis*, ed. Jacques-Alain Miller, trans. Alan Sheridan (New York: Norton, 1977 [1973]).
55. Freud, 'Civilization and Its Discontents', p. 69.
56. Freud, 'Thoughts for the Times on War and Death', p. 65.
57. Freud, 'Civilization and Its Discontents', p. 314.
58. Freud, 'Thoughts for the Times on War and Death', p. 66.
59. Jean Bethke Elshtain, 'Freud's Discourse of War/Politics', *International/ Intertextual Relations: Postmodern Readings of World Politics*, ed. James Der Derian and Michael J. Shapiro (Toronto: Maxwell Macmillan, 1989), p. 55.
60. Sigmund Freud, 'Why War?', *Sigmund Freud: Civilization, Society and Religion*, ed. Albert Dickson, trans. James Strachey (New York: Penguin Books, 1985 [1933 Eng., Published under the auspices of the League of Nations, correspondence with Albert Einstein; publication forbidden in Germany]), pp. 355–8.

61. Nietzsche, *The Will to Power*, p. 487 [922]. 'What means one has to employ with rude peoples, and that "barbarous" means are not arbitrary and capricious, becomes palpable in practice as soon as one is placed, with all one's European pampering, in the necessity of keeping control over barbarians, in the Congo or elsewhere.'

62. Freud, 'Why War?' p. 362.

63. See Daniel Pick, *Faces of Degeneration: Aspect of a European Disorder 1848–1918* (Cambridge: Cambridge University Press, 1993).

64. Christopher Coker, 'The New World (Dis)Order', *The International System after the Collapse of the East-West Order*, ed. Armand Cleese, Richard Cooper, and Yoshikazu Sakamoto (London: Martinus Nijhoff, 1994), p. 37.

65. *Ibid.*, p. 90.

66. Eksteins, *Rites of Spring*, p. 56.

67. Sigmund Freud, 'Group Psychology and the Analysis of the Ego', *Sigmund Freud: Civilization, Society and Religion*, ed. Albert Dickson, trans. James Strachey (New York: Penguin Books, 1985 [1915 Ger., 1918 Eng.]), pp. 103–4.

68. Elshtain, 'Freud's Discourse of War/Politics', p. 54.

69. Friedrich Nietzsche, 'Twilight of the Idols', *Twilight of the Idols and The Anti-Christ*, trans. R.J. Hollingdale (New York: Penguin Books, 1990 [1889]), p. 33 [8].

70. Nietzsche, 'The Genealogy of Morals', p. 149.

71. Coker, 'The New World (Dis)Order', pp. 4–5.

72. Defining and debating modernism is a cottage industry in itself. In this project, I follow Eksteins' definition, see Eksteins, *Rites of Spring*.

73. Daniel Pick, *War Machine: The Rationalisation of Slaughter in the Modern Age* (New Haven: Yale University Press, 1993), p. 153.

74. Coker, *The Twilight of the West*, p. 35.

75. Brian Bond, *War and Society in Europe 1870–1970* (Montreal: McGill-Queen's University Press, 1998), p. 100.

76. Eksteins, *Rites of Spring*, pp. 63–4.

77. Robert G.L. Waite, *The Psychopathic God: Adolf Hitler* (New York: Da Capo Press, 1977), p. 200.

78. Coker, 'The New World (Dis)Order', p. 66.

79. Benedict Anderson, *Imagined Communities: Reflections on the Origins and Spread of Nationalism*, 2nd edition (London: Verso, 1991), pp. 33–6.

80. Pick, *War Machine*, p. 147.

81. Cate Haste, *Keep the Home Fires Burning: Propaganda in the First World War* (London: Penguin Books, 1977), p. 78.

82. Pick, *War Machine*, p. 140.

83. Philip M. Taylor, *Munitions of the Mind: A History of Propaganda from the Ancient World to the Present Era*. 2nd edition (New York: St. Martin's Press, 1995), p. 2.

84. William E. Connolly, *Identity/Difference: Democratic Negotiations of Political Paradox* (Ithaca, NY: Cornell University Press, 1991), p. 93.

85. It is true that there was a strong pacifist movement during the First World War, but even these pacifists used and reinforced the propagandist

language and popular symbols: 'primitive', 'savage', 'barbarous', 'civilized', 'cultured'. See Pick, *War Machine*, p. 151.

86. Eksteins, *Rites of Spring*, p. 196.
87. I.F. Clarke, 'Introduction: The Paper Warriors and their Fights of Fantasy', *The Tale of the Next Great War, 1871–1914: Fictions of Future Warfare and the Battles Still-to-come*, ed. I.F. Clarke (Syracuse, NY: Syracuse University Press, 1995), p. 8.
88. Bond, *War and Society in Europe 1870–1970*, p. 77.
89. Hannah Arendt, *The Origins of Totalitarianism* (New York: Harcourt Brace Javonavich, 1973 [1948]), pp. 216–19.
90. Bond, *War and Society in Europe*, p. 77.
91. Haste, *Keep the Home Fires Burning*, p. 127.
92. Harold D. Lasswell, *Propaganda Technique in the World War* (New York: Alfred Knopf, 1927), p. 68.
93. Pick, *War Machine*, p. 140.
94. Homi Bhabha, 'The Other Question: Stereotype, Discrimination and the Discourse of Colonialism', *The Location of Culture* (New York: Routledge, 1994), p. 66.
95. V.G. Kiernan, *European Empires from Conquest to Collapse, 1815–1960* (Montreal: McGill-Queen's University Press, 1998), pp. 180–1.
96. Haste, *Keep the Home Fires Burning*, pp. 89–90.
97. Pick, *War Machine*, p. 157.
98. Bond, *War and Society in Europe*, p. 100.
99. Coker, *War and the 20th Century*, p. 6.
100. Bond, *War and Society in Europe*, p. 178 n 33.
101. Michael Walzer, *Just and Unjust Wars: A Moral Argument with Historical Illustrations* (New York: Basic Books, 1977), p. 147.
102. Chris Hables Gray, *Postmodern War: The New Politics of Conflict* (New York: Guilford Press, 1997), pp. 130–1.
103. John Keegan, *A History of Warfare* (London: Pimlico, 1993), p. 362.
104. Coker, *War and the 20th Century*, p. 230.
105. *Ibid.*, p. 6.
106. Haste, *Keep the Home Fires Burning*, pp. 95–6.
107. Bond, *War and Society in Europe*, pp. 114–15.
108. Lasswell, *Propaganda Technique in the World War*, p. 85.
109. *Ibid.*, p. 86.
110. Gwynne Dyer, *War – Past, Present, and Future* (New York: Crown, 1985), p. 83.
111. Eksteins, *Rites of Spring*, p. 147.
112. Paul Fussell, *The Great War and Modern Memory* (New York: Oxford University Press, 1975), p. 174.
113. V.G. Kiernan, 'Colonial Africa and its Armies', *Imperialism and Its Contradictions*, ed. Harvey J. Kaye (New York: Routledge, 1995), p. 86.
114. Lasswell, *Propaganda Technique in the World War*, p. 85.
115. Kiernan, 'Colonial Africa and its Armies', p. 84. Since Kiernan cites Wavell, who argues that coloured troops from Napoleon's *Armée Chopte* were used on the Italian peninsula – for which I could find no corroboration. I am left to argue that although it may not be the first time that coloured troops were used in battle in modern

Europe, it was certainly the first time that their use was culturally significant.

116. Melvin E. Page, 'Black Men in a White Men's War', *Africa and the First World War*, ed. Melvin E. Page (London: Macmillan Press, 1987), pp. 8–9.

117. *Ibid.*, p. 19.

118. J.A. Hobson, *Imperialism: A Study* (New York: Gordon Press, 1975 [1902]), pp. 256–7.

119. Kiernan, 'Colonial Africa and its Armies', p. 85.

120. *Ibid.*, p. 86.

121. Page, 'Black Men in a White Men's War', p. 18.

122. Eksteins, *Rites of Spring*, p. 235.

123. Albert Grundlingh, *Fighting Their Own War: South African Blacks and the First World War* (Johannesburg: Ravan Press, 1987), p. 97.

124. Joe Harris Lunn, 'Kande Kamara Speaks: An Oral History of the West African Experience in France 1914–18', *Africa and the First World War*, ed. Melvin E. Page (London: Macmillan Press, 1987), p. 36.

125. Kiernan, *Colonial Empires and Armies, 1815–1960*, p. 186.

126. Covenant of the League of Nations. Art. 22.

127. Gong, *The Standard of Civilization*, p. 238; Hedley Bull and Adam Watson, 'Conclusion', *The Expansion of International Society*, ed. Hedley Bull and Adam Watson (Oxford: Clarendon Press, 1984), p. 426.

128. Joseph A. Schumpeter, *Imperialism and Social Classes,* ed. Paul M. Sweezy, trans. Heinz Nordern (New York: Augustus M. Kelly, 1951), p. 6.

129. T.O. Lloyd, *The British Empire 1558–1995*, 2nd edition (London: Oxford University Press, 1996), p. 256.

130. Hedley Bull, 'The Revolt Against the West', *The Expansion of International Society*, ed. Hedley Bull and Adam Watson (Oxford: Clarendon Press, 1984), p. 221.

131. Anderson, *Imagined Communities*, pp. 113–30.

132. Alfred Zimmern, *The Study of International Relations: An Inaugural Lecture delivered before the University of Oxford on 20 February 1931* (Oxford: Clarendon, 1931), pp. 26–7.

133. E.H. Carr, *The Twenty Years' Crisis: An Introduction to the Study of International Relations*, 2nd edition (New York: St. Martin's Press, 1966), p. 97.

134. William Olson and A.J.R. Groom, *International Relations Then and Now: Origins and Trends in Interpretation* (New York: HarperCollins, 1991), p. 79; Brian C. Schmidt, 'Lessons from the Past: Reassessing the Interwar Disciplinary History of International Relations', *International Studies Quarterly*, Vol. 42, No. 3 (September 1998), p. 452.

135. Carr, *Twenty Years' Crisis*, p. 36.

136. This can be seen not only in the wartime experiences of Morgenthau, but in the pre-war writings of Carr, Toynbee and Zimmern.

137. Carr, *Twenty Years' Crisis*, p. 154.

138. Martin Wight, *International Theory: The Three Traditions*, ed. Gabriele Wight (Leicester: Leicester University Press, 1991), p. 61.

CHAPTER 5

1. Arnold J. Toynbee, *Survey of International Affairs 1933* (Oxford: Oxford University Press, 1934), p. 111.
2. Christopher Coker, *War and the 20th Century: A Study of War and Modern Consciousness* (London: Brassey's, 1994), p. 77.
3. This applies chiefly to the realists of the contemporary generation (1930–48), and was seen as a corrective to idealistic statesmen, such as the American Frank Kellogg and the French Aristide Briand, who drew up the Briand-Kellog Pact (1928), which outlawed war.
4. Hans J. Morgenthau, *Politics among Nations: The Struggle for Power and Peace* (New York: Alfred Knopf, 1948), p. 13. The first sentence of ch. 1 is: 'International politics, like all politics, is a struggle for power.'
5. Hedley Bull, 'The Challenge of the Third Reich: Introduction', *The Challenge of the Third Reich: The Adam von Trott Memorial Lectures*, ed. Hedley Bull (Oxford: Clarendon Press, 1986), p. 10.
6. William Olson and A.J.R. Groom, *International Relations Then and Now: Origins and Trends in Interpretation* (New York: HarperCollins, 1991), p. 81.
7. Frederick L. Schuman, *International Politics: An Introduction to the Western State System* (New York: McGraw-Hill, 1933), p. viii.
8. Georg Schwarzenberger, *Power Politics: An Introduction to the Study of International Relations and Post War Planning* (London: Camelot Press, 1941), p. 114.
9. Hannah Arendt, *The Origins of Totalitarianism* (New York: Harcourt, Brace, Jovanovich, 1973), p. 470.
10. Adolf Hitler, *Mein Kampf*, trans. Helmut Riperger (New York: Reynal and Hitchcock, 1939), p. 296.
11. See R.J. Vincent, 'Racial Equality', *The Expansion of International Society*, ed. Hedley Bull and Adam Watson (Oxford: Clarendon Press, 1984) pp. 253–4; R.J. Vincent, 'Race in International Relations', *Culture, Ideology and World Order*, ed. R.B.J. Walker (Boulder, CO: Westview Press, 1984), p. 45. These two articles are the notable exceptions.
12. Hitler, *Mein Kampf*, pp. 138–9.
13. Arendt, *The Origins of Totalitarianism*, p. 392.
14. *Ibid.*, p. 344.
15. Adolf Hitler, 'Most Secret. Directive No. 1 for the Conduct of War: 31 August', *The War, 1939–45: A Documentary History*, ed. Desmond Flower and James Reeves (New York: Da Capo Press, 1997), p. 2; Count von Ribbentrop, 'German Ambassador in Moscow, 21 June 1941', *The War, 1939–45: A Documentary History*, ed. Desmond Flower and James Reeves (New York: Da Capo Press, 1997), p. 206.
16. Adolf Hitler, 'Adolf Hitler to the German High Command, 3 November 1939', *The War, 1939–45: A Documentary History*, ed. Desmond Flower and James Reeves (New York: Da Capo Press, 1997), p. 48.
17. Hitler, *Mein Kampf*, p. 135.
18. *Ibid.*, pp. 609–10 (italics in original).
19. Toynbee, *Survey of International Affairs 1933*, p. 111.

20. R.R. Kuczynski, *'Living-Space' and Population Problems* (Oxford Pamphlets on World Affairs, No. 8) (Oxford: Oxford University Press, 1939), p. 31.
21. Adolf Hitler, *Hitler's Tabletalk 1941–44*, trans. Norman Cameron and R.H. Stevens (Oxford: Oxford University Press, 1953), p. 661 (26 August 1942).
22. Hitler, *Mein Kampf*, pp. 627 (bold in original).
23. Hitler, *Tabletalk*, p. 663 (26 August 1942).
24. Olson and Groom, *International Relations Then and Now*, p. 98.
25. Martin Wight, *International Theory: The Three Traditions*, ed. Gabriele Wight and Brian Porter (London: Leicester University Press, 1991), pp. 172, 225, 239.
26. E.H. Carr, *Conditions of Peace* (New York: Macmillan, 1942), p. 10.
27. E.H. Carr, *International Relations between the Two World Wars, 1919– 1939* (London: Macmillan, 1947), p. 42.
28. Chris Brown, *International Relations Theory: New Normative Approaches* (London: Harvester Wheatsheaf, 1992), pp. 43, 73–5.
29. R.C.K. Ensor, *Herr Hitler's Self-Disclosure in Mein Kampf* (Oxford Pamphlets on World Affairs, No. 3) (Oxford: Clarendon Press, 1939), p. 29.
30. Hitler, *Tabletalk*, p. 697.
31. Olson and Groom, *International Relations Then and Now*, p. 106.
32. Alfred Zimmern, *The Study of International Relations, An Inaugural Lecture Delivered before the University of Oxford on 20 February 1931* (Oxford: Clarendon Press, 1931), p. 19.
33. Toynbee, *Survey of International Affairs 1933*, p. 202.
34. *Ibid.*, p. 111.
35. R.B.J. Walker, *Inside/Outside: International Relations as Political Theory* (Cambridge: Cambridge University Press, 1993), ch. 2.
36. This ignores Machiavelli's strong moral component. See Walker, *Inside/Outside*.
37. Carr, *International Relations Between the Two World Wars*, p. 235.
38. Aimé Césaire, *Discourse on Colonialism*, trans. Joan Pinkham (New York: Monthly Review Press, 1972), p. 14.
39. Toynbee, *Survey of International Affairs 1933*, p. 121.
40. Arthur Herman, *The Idea of Decline in Western History* (Toronto: Free Press, 1997), p. 282.
41. Olson and Groom, *International Relations Then and Now*, p. 105.
42. Alfred Zimmern, *The Prospects of Civilization* (Oxford Pamphlets on World Affairs, No. 1), (Oxford: Clarendon Press, 1939), p. 29.
43. Arnold J. Toynbee, *A Study of History: Volume IX* (London: Oxford University Press, 1954), p. 500.
44. Wight, *International Theory: The Three Traditions*, p. 265.
45. Arendt, *Origins of Totalitarianism*, p. 124.
46. Max Weber, 'The Uniqueness of Western Civilization', *Max Weber on Capitalism, Bureaucracy and Religion*, ed. and trans. Stanislav Andreski (London: Allen and Unwin, 1983), p. 24.
47. Max Weber, 'The Economic Foundations of 'Imperialism', *From Max Weber: Essays in Sociology*, ed. and trans. H.H. Gerth and C. Wright Mills (New York: Oxford University Press, 1958), pp. 163–5.

48. Michael D. Burleigh, *Ethics and Extermination: Reflections on Nazi Genocide* (New York: Cambridge University Press, 1997).

49. Peter du Preez, *Genocide: The Psychology of Mass Murder* (New York: Boyars/Bowerdean, 1994), pp. 16–19.

50. Allan Chase, *The Legacy of Malthus: The Social Costs of the New Scientific Racism* (Chicago: University of Illinois Press, 1980), pp. 14–23.

51. V.G. Kiernan, *Colonial Empires and Armies 1850–1960* (Kingston: McGill-Queen University Press, 1998), p. 93.

52. Christopher Coker, *The Twilight of the West* (Boulder, CO: Westview Press, 1998), p. 35.

53. Martin Gilbert, *The Second World War* (Toronto: Stoddart, 1989), p. 554.

54. Carr, *International Relations Between the Two World Wars* p. 97.

55. See Oxford Pamphlets on World Affairs, published 1939–45.

56. Hedley Bull, 'The Challenges of the Third Reich: Introduction', *The Challenge of the Third Reich: The Adam von Trott Memorial Lectures*, ed. Hedley Bull (Oxford: Clarendon Press, 1986), p. 10.

57. Churchill describes his motives for strategic bombing in the Second World War, despite heavy civilian casualties. 'This is a military and not a civilian war. You and others may desire to kill women and children. We desire to destroy German military objectives. My motto is "Business before Pleasure".' Stephen A. Garret, 'Political Leadership and "Dirty Hands": Winston Churchill and the City Bombing of Germany', *Ethics of Statecraft: The Moral Dimensions of International Affairs*, ed. Cathal J. Nolan (London: Praeger, 1995), p. 80.

58. Michael Burleigh and Wolfgang Wippermann, *The Racial State: Germany 1933–45* (Cambridge: Cambridge University Press, 1991), p. 39.

59. *Ibid.*, p. 10.

60. Paul Weindling, 'Understanding Nazi Racism: Precursors and Perpetrators', *Confronting the Nazi Past: New Debates on Modern German History*, ed. Michael Burleigh (London: Collin & Brown, 1996), p. 67.

61. The phrase 'internal colonization' is used idiosyncratically by Hitler in *Mein Kampf* to refer to a system of land usage (pp. 133–6). Coker's usage in *War and the 20th Century* is more common – referring to a racially-based, hierarchical system of governance within a country, using imperial modes of governance usually reserved for non-European colonies.

62. Coker, *War and the 20th Century*, p. 233.

63. Robert G.L. Waite, *The Psychopathic God: Adolf Hitler* (New York: Da Capo Press, 1977), p. 275.

64. Zygmunt Bauman, *Modernity and the Holocaust* (Ithaca, NY: Cornell University Press, 1989), p. 52.

65. Adolf Hitler quoted in *Nazi Culture: Intellectual, Cultural and Social Life in the Third Reich*, ed. George L. Mosse, trans. Salvator Attanasio (New York: Grosset and Dunlap, 1966), p. 8.

66. Burleigh and Wippermann, *The Racial State*, p. 44.

67. Michael Burleigh, *Germany Turns Eastward: A Study of Ostforschung in the Third Reich* (New York: Cambridge University Press, 1988), pp. 9, 22–5.

68. Arendt, *Origins of Totalitarianism*, p. 207.
69. Burleigh and Wippermann, *The Racial State*, p. 52.
70. *Ibid.*, p. 95.
71. Hitler, *Mein Kampf*, p. 56
72. Bauman, *Modernity and the Holocaust*, p. 8.
73. Burleigh and Wippermann, *The Racial State*, pp. 46, 48, 51.
74. *Ibid.*, p. 52.
75. Daniel Jonah Goldhagen, *Hitler's Willing Executioners: Ordinary Germans and the Holocaust* (New York: Alfred Knopf, 1996), p. 469.
76. George L. Mosse, 'Introduction', *Nazi Culture: Intellectual, Cultural and Social Life in the Third Reich*, ed. George L. Mosse, trans. Salvator Attansio (New York: Grosset and Dunlap, 1966), pp. 59–60.
77. Goldhagen, *Hitler's Willing Executioners*.
78. Mosse, 'Introduction', *Nazi Culture*, p. 133.
79. Hitler, *Mein Kampf*, pp. 118–19, 177–81; Bond, *War and Society in Europe 1870–1970*, p. 188.
80. William E. Connolly, *Identity/Difference: Democratic Negotiations of Political Paradox* (Ithaca, NY: Cornell University Press, 1991), pp. 65–6.
81. Burleigh and Wippermann, *The Racial State*, p. 36.
82. There is an interesting parallel to the British treatment of colonial subjects with regard to British citizenship, and particularly the right of residence in England. *Ibid.*, p. 45.
83. Goldhagen, *Hitler's Willing Executioners*, pp. 135, 168–70.
84. *Ibid.*, p. 471.
85. Rolf-Dieter Müller and Gerd R. Ueberschär, *Hitler's War in the East, 1941–45: A Critical Assessment*, trans. Bruce D. Little (Providence: Berghahn Books, 1997), p. 210; Hitler, *Tabletalk*, trans. Norman Cameron and R.H. Stevens (Oxford: Oxford University Press, 1953), p. 24 (8/9 August 1941).
86. Bond, *War and Society in Europe 1870–1970*, p. 181.
87. Omer Bartov, *The Eastern Front, 1941–45, German Troops and the Barbarisation of Warfare* (London: Macmillan, 1985), p. 155.
88. Omer Bartov, 'Savage War', *Confronting the Nazi Past: New Debates on Modern German History*, ed. Michael Burleigh (London: Collins & Brown, 1996), p. 128.
89. R.R. Kuczynski, '*Livings-Space' and Population Problems* (Oxford Pamphlets on World Affairs No. 8) (Oxford: Clarendon Press, 1939), p. 31.
90. Arthur Salter, *The Dual Policy* (Oxford Pamphlets on World Affairs No. 11) (Oxford: Clarendon Press, 1939), pp. 25–7.
91. Hitler, *Mein Kampf*, p. 620.
92. 'Hitler, at Charleville [on 5 June 1940 – before the commencement of *Operation Barbarossa*], spoke to his generals of his admiration of Britain's rule in India.' Martin Gilbert, *The Second World War* (Toronto: Stoddart, 1989), p. 83.
93. Eberhard Jäckel, *Hitler's Weltanschauung: A Blueprint for Power*, trans. Herbert Arnold (Middleton: Wesleyan University Press, 1972), pp. 27–46.
94. Hitler, *Tabletalk*, p. 24. However, as pointed out by Broszat, this

policy did not receive a great deal of encouragement from the prospective rural immigrants. Martin Broszat, 'The Third Reich and the German People', *The Challenge of the Third Reich: The Adam von Trott Memorial Lectures*, ed. Hedley Bull (Oxford: Clarendon Press, 1986), p. 87.

95. Hitler, *Tabletalk*, p. 15.
96. *Ibid.*, p.33.
97. *Ibid.*, p. 87.
98. *Ibid.*, p. 493.
99. *Ibid.*, p. 615.
100. *Ibid.*, p. 588.
101. Waite, *The Psychopathic God*, p. 79.
102. Hitler, *Tabletalk*, p. 258.
103. Jürgen Förster, 'The Relation between *Operation Barbarossa* as Ideological War of Extermination and the Final Solution', *The Final Solution: Origins and Implementation*, ed. David Cesarani (New York: Routledge, 1994), p. 89.
104. Omer Bartov, *Hitler's Army: Soldiers, Nazis, and War in the Third Reich* (New York: Oxford University Press, 1992), p. 16.
105. Bartov, *The Eastern Front*, p. 106.
106. Todorov makes the same observation of early explorers to the New World. Tzvetan Todorov, *The Conquest of America: The Question of the Other*, trans. Richard Howard (Norman, OK: University of Oklahoma Press, 1999), pp. 34–44.
107. Bartov, *Hitler's Army*, p. 118.
108. Gilbert, *The Second World War*, p. 160.
109. Bond, *War and Society in Europe 1870–1970*, p. 182.
110. Himmler, 'October 1943', *The War, 1939–45: A Documentary History*, ed. Desmond Flower and James Reeves (New York: Da Capo Press, 1997), p. 830.
111. Burleigh and Wippermann, *The Racial State*, pp. 67–8.
112. Goldhagen, *Hitler's Willing Executioners*, p. 152.
113. Bartov, *Hitler's Army*, p. 126.
114. General Von Mellehthin, 'The Battle of Kursk, 4 July 1942', *The War, 1939–45: A Documentary History*, ed. Desmond Flower and James Reeves (New York: Da Capo Press, 1997), p. 829.
115. Hitler, 'Last Order of the Day, 16 April 1945', *The War 1939–45: A Documentary History*, ed. Desmond Flower and James Reeves (New York: Da Capo Press, 1997), p. 1003.
116. 'Ribbentrop to Count Schulenburg, German Ambassador in Moscow, 21 June 1941', *The War 1939–45: A Documentary History*, ed. Desmond Flower and James Reeves (New York: Da Capo Press, 1997), p. 206.
117. Hitler, 'Planning for National Suicide, March 1945', *The War 1939–45: A Documentary History*, ed. Desmond Flower and James Reeves (New York: Da Capo Press, 1997), p. 856.
118. Gilbert, *The Second World War*, p. 528.
119. Coker, *War and the 20th Century*, p. 18.
120. Schwarzenberger, *Power Politics*, p. 41.
121. Ali A. Mazrui, 'The Moving Cultural Frontier of World Order: From

Monotheism to North-South Relations', *Culture, Ideology and World Order*, ed. R.B.J. Walker (Boulder, CO: Westview Press, 1984), p. 35.
122. Aimé Césaire, *Discourse on Colonialism*, trans. Joan Pinkham (New York: Monthly Review Press, 1972 [1955]), p. 14.
123. Frantz Fanon, *The Wretched of the Earth*, trans. Constance Farrington (New York: Grove Press, 1963), p. 101.
124. *Ibid.*, p. 250.
125. Césaire, *Discourse on Colonialism*, p. 21.
126. Frantz Fanon, *Black Skin, White Masks*, trans. Charles Lam Markmann (New York: Grove Press, 1967 [1952]), p. 11.
127. Césaire, *Discourse on Colonialism*, p. 20.
128. Fanon, *The Wretched of the Earth*, pp. 267–9.

CHAPTER 6

1. K.J. Holsti, *The Dividing Discipline: Hegemony and Diversity in International Theory* (Boston: Unwin Hyman, 1985), p. 64.
2. Joseph Stalin, 'Stalin on Foreign Policy', *Crisis and Continuity in World Politics: Readings in International Relations*, ed. George Lanyi and Wilson McWilliams (New York: Random House, 1966), p. 207.
3. Frederick L. Schuman, *International Politics: An Introduction to the Western State System* (New York: McGraw-Hill, 1933), p. 375.
4. *Ibid.*, p. 375.
5. *Ibid.*, p. 376.
6. *Ibid.*, p. 375.
7. See Marc Ferro, *Colonization: A Global History*, trans. K.D. Prithipaul (New York: Routledge, 1997).
8. Schuman, *International Politics*, p. 399.
9. *Ibid.*, p. 426.
10. *Ibid.*, p. 422.
11. *Ibid.*, p. 427.
12. *Ibid.*, p. 429.
13. Hans J. Morgenthau, *Politics among Nations: The Struggle for Power and Peace*, 2nd edition (New York: Alfred E. Knopf, 1954 [1948]), p. 36.
14. *Ibid.*, p. 36.
15. William Olson and A.J.R. Groom, *International Relations Then and Now: Origins and Trends in Interpretation* (New York: HarperCollins, 1991), p. 146.
16. Philip Darby and A.J. Paolini, 'Bridging International Relations and Postcolonialism', *Alternatives*, Vol. 19 (1994), pp. 379–80.
17. Morgenthau, *Politics among Nations*, p. 85.
18. *Ibid.*, p. 57.
19. *Ibid.*, p. 335.
20. Olson and Groom, *International Relations Then and Now*, p.104.
21. *Ibid.*, p. 57.
22. Roxanne Lynn Doty, *Imperial Encounters: The Political Representation in North–South Relations* (Minneapolis: University of Minnesota Press, 1996), p. 162.

23. Amitav Acharya, 'The Periphery as the Core', *Critical Security Studies*, ed. Keith Krause and Michael C. Williams (Minneapolis: University of Minnesota Press, 1997), p. 300.
24. *Ibid.*, pp. 305–7.
25. Darby and Paolini, 'Bridging International Relations and Postcolonialism', p. 381.
26. Schuman, *International Politics*, p. 101.
27. *Ibid.*, p. 101.
28. *Ibid.*, p. 101.
29. *Ibid.*, p. 641.
30. *Ibid.*, p. 103.
31. *Ibid.*, p. 315.
32. Ali Mazrui, *Towards a Pax Africana: A Study of Ideology and Ambition* (London: Weidenfeld and Nicolson, 1967), p. 166.
33. Schuman, *International Politics*, pp. 315–34.
34. *Ibid.*, p. 317.
35. Georg Schwarzenberger, *Power Politics: A Study of World Society*, 3rd edition (London: Stevens and Sons, 1964), p. 65.
36. *Ibid.*, p. 39.
37. *Ibid.*, p. 40 (italics in original).
38. *Ibid.*, p. 64.
39. *Ibid.*, p. 64.
40. *Ibid.*, p. 66.
41. *Ibid.*, p. 514.
42. *Ibid.*, p. 494 (emphasis added).
43. Schuman, *International Politics*, p 101.
44. Roxanne Lynn Doty, 'The Bounds of "Race" in International Relations', *Millennium: Journal of International Relations*, Vol. 22, No. 3 (Summer 1993), pp. 443–61.
45. Schwarzenberger, *Power Politics*, pp. 496–8.
46. *Ibid.*, p. 514.
47. K.J. Holsti, *International Politics* (Toronto: Prentice Hall, 1967), p. 22.
48. *Ibid.*, p 23.
49. K. J. Holsti, *Peace and War: Armed Conflicts and International Order 1648–1989* (Cambridge: Cambridge University Press, 1991), p. 272.
50. *Ibid.*, p. 72.
51. *Ibid.*, p. 75.
52. A.F.K. Organski, *World Politics*, 2nd edition (Toronto: Random House, 1968), p. vii.
53. *Ibid.*, p. 9.
54. *Ibid.*, p. 224.
55. Martin W. Lewis and Kären E. Wigen, *Myth of Continents: A Critique of Metageography* (Berkeley: University of California Press, 1997), p. 42.
56. Organski, *World Politics*, p. 231.
57. Jean-Jacques Rousseau, 'Essay on the Origin of Languages', *On the Origin of Language*, trans. John H. Moran (Chicago: University of Chicago Press, 1966), pp. 31–49.
58. David Arnold, 'Inventing Tropicality', *The Problem of Nature* (Oxford: Blackwell, 1996), p. 142.

59. Organski, *World Politics*, p. 245.
60. *Ibid.*, p. 254.
61. *Ibid.*, p. 479.
62. *Ibid.*, pp. 229–30, 236–7.
63. Samuel P. Huntington, *Political Order in Changing Societies* (New Haven: Yale University Press, 1968), p. 46.
64. Mazrui, *Towards a Pax Africana*, p. 3.
65. *Ibid.*, p. 52.
66. *Ibid.*, p. 48.
67. *Ibid.*, p. 125.
68 Ezekiel Mphahlele, 'The Fabric of African Cultures', *Foreign Affairs*, Vol. 42, No. 2 (July 1964), p. 627.
69. Darby and Paolini, 'Bridging International Relations and Postcolonialism', p. 375.

CHAPTER 7

1. Francis Fukuyama, *The End of History and the Last Man* (New York: Avon Books, 1992); Francis Fukuyama, 'The Trouble with Names', *Foreign Policy*, Vol. 119 (Summer 2000), p. 61.
2. K.J. Holsti, *The State, War, and the State of War* (Cambridge: Cambridge University Press, 1996), p. 123.
3. John Lewis Gaddis, 'International Relations and the End of the Cold War', *International Security*, Vol. 17, No. 1 (1992), pp. 5–58; Jim George, 'Of Incarceration and Closure: Neorealism and the New World Order', *Millennium: Journal of International Studies*, Vol. 22, No. 2 (Winter 1993); Friedrich Kratochwil, 'The Embarrassment of Changes: Neorealism as the Science of *Realpolitik* without Politics', *Review of International Studies*, Vol. 19, No. 1 (Spring 1993).
4. John J. Merscheimer, 'Back to the Future: Instability in Europe after the Cold War', *International Security*, Vol. 15, No. 1 (Summer 1990), pp. 5–56; John J. Merscheimer, 'Why We Will Soon Miss the Cold War', *Atlantic Monthly*, Vol. 266, No. 2 (August 1990), pp. 35–50; Kenneth N. Waltz, 'The New World Order', *Millennium: Journal of International Studies*, Vol. 22, No. 1 (Summer 1993), pp. 187–95; Kenneth Waltz, 'The Emerging Structure of International Politics', *International Security*, Vol. 18, No. 2 (Fall 1993).
5. Kenichi Ohmae, 'Rise of the Region State', *Foreign Affairs*, Vol. 72, No. 1 (Spring 1993).
6. Charles A. Kupchan and Clifford A. Kupchan, 'Concerts, Collective Security, and the Future of Europe', *International Security*, Vol. 16, No. 1 (Summer 1991), pp. 114–61; R.N. Rosecrance, 'A New Concert of Powers', *Foreign Affairs*, Vol. 71, No. 2 (Spring 1992); Gregory F. Trevorton, 'Finding an Analogy for Tomorrow', *Orbis*, Vol. 37, No. 1 (Winter 1993).
7. James M. Goldgeier and Michael McFaul, 'A Tale of Two Worlds: Core and Periphery in the post-Cold War Era', *International Organization*, Vol. 46, No. 2 (Spring 1992), pp. 461–91; Max Singer and Aaron

Wildavsky, *The Real World Order: Zones of Peace and Zones of Turmoil* (Chatham, NJ: Chatham House, 1993).

8. Roxanne Lynn Doty, *Imperial Encounters: The Political Representation in North–South Relations* (Minneapolis: University of Minnesota Press, 1996), p. 152.

9. An earlier draft is reprinted in *The International System after the Collapse of the East/West Order*, ed. A. Cleese, R. Cooper and Y. Sakamoto (London: Martinus Nijhoff, 1994). Huntington expands and refines his argument in later articles and in the book of similar title. Samuel P. Huntington, 'The Clash of Civilizations?', *Foreign Affairs*, Vol. 72, No. 3 (Summer 1993); Samuel P. Huntington, 'If Not Civilizations, What?', *Foreign Affairs*, Vol. 72, No. 5 (November/December 1993).

10. Huntington, 'The Clash of Civilizations?', p. 22.

11. Jacinta O'Hagan, 'Civilisational Conflict? Looking for Cultural Enemies', *Third World Quarterly*, Vol. 16, No. 1 (1995), p. 19.

12. Jacinta O'Hagan, 'Conceptions of the West in International Relations Thought: From Oswald Spengler to Edward Said', Unpublished PhD dissertation, Australia National University, 1998, p. 231.

13. Michael Shapiro, *Violent Cartographies: Mapping Cultures of War* (Minneapolis: University of Minnesota Press, 1997), p. 33.

14. Huntington, 'Clash of Civilizations?' p. 25.

15. *Ibid.*, p. 49.

16. Robert O. Keohane, 'Realism, Neorealism and the Study of World Politics', *Neorealism and its Critics*, ed. Robert O. Keohane (New York: Columbia University Press, 1986), p. 7.

17. Yosef Lapid, 'Culture's Ship: Returns and Departures in International Relations Theory', *The Return of Culture and Identity in IR Theory*, ed. Yosef Lapid and Friedrich Kratochwil (Boulder, CO: Lynne Rienner, 1996), p. 8.

18. Samuel P. Huntington, *The Clash of Civilizations and the Remaking of the World Order* (New York: Simon and Schuster, 1996), p. 135.

19. *Ibid.*, p. 131.

20. *Ibid.*, p. 130.

21. O'Hagan, 'Civilisational Conflict?', p. 28.

22. Huntington, *The Clash of Civilizations and the Remaking of the World Order*, p. 208.

23. *Ibid.*, pp. 130.

24. This potential is explored by postcolonial theorists. Merryl Wyn Davies, Ashis Nandy and Ziauddin Sardar, *Barbaric Others: A Manifesto on Western Racism* (Boulder, CO: Pluto Press, 1993), p. 92.

25. O'Hagan, 'Civilisational Conflict?', p. 19.

26. *Ibid.*, p. 35.

27. Fouad Ajami, 'The Summoning: "But They Said, We Will Not Hearken"', *Foreign Affairs*, Vol. 72, No. 4 (September/October 1993), p. 2; Jeanne J. Kirkpatrick, 'The Modernizing Imperative: Tradition and Change', *Foreign Affairs*, Vol. 72, No. 4 (September/October 1993), p. 22; O'Hagan, 'Civilisational Conflict?', p. 22; Martin W. Lewis and Kären E. Wigen, *The Myth of Continents: A Critique of Metageography* (Berkeley: University of California Press, 1997), p. 135.

28. Huntington, 'Clash of Civilizations?', p. 25.
29. Arnold J. Toynbee, *Study of History*, Vol. I, ed. D.C. Somervell (New York: Dell, 1946), p. 79.
30. Ajami, 'The Summoning', p. 2; O'Hagan, 'Civilisational Conflict?', pp. 21–4.
31. Arnold Toynbee, 'The Psychology of Encounters', *Civilization on Trial and The World and the West* (New York: Meridian Books, 1958), p. 279.
32. Lewis and Wigen, *The Myth of Continents*, p. 127.
33. Ajami, 'The Summoning', p. 3; O'Hagan, 'Civilisational Conflict?', pp. 30–4.
34. Coker, *Twilight of the West*, Introduction; Kishore Mahbubani, 'The Dangers of Decadence', *Foreign Affairs*, Vol. 72, No. 4 (September/October 1993), p. 14.
35. Huntington, *The Clash of Civilizations and the Remaking of the World Order*, p. 157.
36. Ajami, 'The Summoning', p. 8.
37. Mahbubani, 'The Dangers of Decadence', pp. 12–13.
38. Ajami, 'The Summoning', p. 9.
39. O'Hagan, 'Civilisational Conflict?', p. 23; Ajami, 'The Summoning', p. 8; Kirkpatrick, 'The Modernizing Imperative', p. 23; Albert L. Weeks, 'Do Civilizations Hold?', *Foreign Affairs*, Vol. 72, No. 4 (September/October 1993), p. 25; David Campbell, *Politics without Principle: Sovereignty, Ethics, and the Narratives of the Gulf War* (Boulder, CO: Lynne Rienner, 1993).
40. Ajami, 'The Summoning', pp. 7–9.
41. Huntington, *The Clash of Civilizations and the Remaking of the World Order*, p. 135.
42. *Ibid.*, p. 157.
43. *Ibid.*, p. 136.
44. *Ibid.*, p. 138.
45. Samuel P. Huntington, 'The Lonely Superpower', *Foreign Affairs*, Vol. 78, No. 2 (March/April 1999), p. 36.
46. Huntington, *The Clash of Civilizations and the Remaking of the World Order*, p. 219.
47. *Ibid.*, p. 32.
48. *Ibid.*, p. 33.
49. *Ibid.*, p. 33.
50. *Ibid.*, p. 321.
51. *Ibid.*, p. 21.
52. Huntington, 'Clash of Civilizations?', p. 35.
53. Huntington, *The Clash of Civilizations and the Remaking of the World Order*, p. 258.
54. Huntington capitalizes 'Islamic Resurgence' to highlight what he sees as the historical parallels to the 'Protestant Reformation'. See Huntington, *The Clash of Civilizations and the Remaking of the World Order*, p. 109.
55. *Ibid.*, p. 213.
56. *Ibid.*, p. 121.

57. Edward W. Said, 'Response', *Social Text*, Vol. 40, No. 1 (1994), p. 23.
58. Huntington, *The Clash of Civilizations and the Remaking of the World Order*, p. 111.
59. *Ibid.*, p. 212.
60. *Ibid.*, p. 177.
61. Huntington, 'Clash of Civilizations?', p. 46.
62. Huntington, *The Clash of Civilizations and the Remaking of the World Order*, p. 185.
63. Mahbubani, 'The Dangers of Decadence', p. 13.
64. Huntington, *The Clash of Civilizations and the Remaking of the World Order*, pp. 13–14.
65. Huntington, 'If Not Civilizations, What?', p. 194.
66. Michel Foucault, 'Governmentality', *The Foucault Effect: Studies in Governmentality*, ed. Graham Burchell, Colin Gordon and Peter Miller (Chicago: University of Chicago Press, 1991), p. 100.
67. Massimo Livi-Bacci, *A Concise History of World Population*, 2nd edition, trans. Carl Ipsen, (New York: Blackwell, 1997), pp. 160–1.
68. Frank Füredi, *The Silent War: Imperialism and the Changing Perception of Race* (London: Pluto Press, 1998), pp. 68–75.
69. Allan Chase, *The Legacy of Malthus: The Social Costs of the New Scientific Racism* (Chicago: University of Illinois Press, 1980), pp. 382–405.
70. See for an excellent summary: Michael S. Teitelbaum and Jay M. Winter, *The Fear of Population Decline* (Toronto: Academic Press, 1985).
71. Huntington, *The Clash of Civilizations and the Remaking of the World Order*, pp. 84–5.
72. Christopher Coker, *War and the 20th Century: A Study of War and Modern Consciousness* (London: Brassey's, 1994), p. 29.
73. Teitelbaum and Winter, *The Fear of Population Decline*, pp. 39–40.
74. Huntington, *The Clash of Civilizations and the Remaking of the World Order*, p. 86.
75. *Ibid.*, p. 103.
76. *Ibid.*, p. 117.
77. *Ibid.*, p. 310.
78. Paul Kennedy, *Preparing for the Twenty-First Century* (Toronto: HarperCollins, 1993), pp. 4–6.
79. Thomas Robert Malthus, *An Essay on the Principle of Population (1798)*, ed. E.A. Wrigley and David Souden (London: William Pickering, 1986), p. 33.
80. Kennedy, *Preparing for the Twenty-First Century*, p. 24.
81. *Ibid.*, p. 32.
82. *Ibid.*, p. 35.
83. *Ibid.*, p. 36.
84. *Ibid.*, p. 25.
85. *Ibid.*, p. 13.
86. *Ibid.*, p. 39.
87. Teitelbaum and Winter, *The Fear of Population Decline*, pp. 134–6.
88. Huntington, 'The Lonely Superpower', pp. 40–1.
89. Stephen Chan, 'Too Neat and Under-Thought a World Order: Huntington and Civilisations', *Millennium: Journal of International Studies*, Vol. 27, No. 1 (1997), p. 138.

90. Said, 'Response', pp. 22–3.
91. Allan Bloom, *The Closing of the American Mind* (Toronto: Simon and Schuster, 1987), p. 379.
92. Huntington, *The Clash of Civilizations and the Remaking of the World Order*, p. 305.
93. Samuel P. Huntington, 'The Erosion of American National Interests', *Foreign Affairs*, Vol. 76, No. 5 (September 1997), p. 29.
94. Brook Larmer 'Face of the Future', *Newsweek*, 12 July 1999 (http://newsweek.com/nw-srv/issue/02_99b/printed/int/us/latino_1.htm) Accessed 18 October 1999.
95. Huntington, *The Clash of Civilizations and the Remaking of the World Order*, p. 307.
96. Coker, *War and the 20th Century*, p. 35.
97. James Kurth, 'The *Real* Clash', *National Interest*, (Fall 1994), p. 3.
98. Kennedy, *Preparing for the Twenty-First Century*, p. 14.
99. Huntington, *The Clash of Civilizations and the Remaking of the World Order*, p. 91.
100. Kurth, 'The *Real* Clash', p. 12.
101. Huntington, *The Clash of Civilizations and the Remaking of the World Order*, p. 310.
102. Kathryn Manzo, *Creating Boundaries: The Politics of Race and Nation* (Boulder, CO: Lynne Rienner, 1996), p. 39.
103. Huntington, *The Clash of Civilizations and the Remaking of the World Order*, p. 304.
104. Kurth, 'The *Real* Clash', p. 14.
105. *Ibid.*, p. 13.
106. *Ibid.*
107. Huntington, 'The Erosion of American National Interests', p. 34.
108. *Ibid.*, p. 31.
109. Benjamin R. Barber, *Jihad vs. McWorld: How Globalism and Tribalism Are Reshaping the World* (New York: Ballantine Books, 1995), p. 215.
110. Huntington, *The Clash of Civilizations and the Remaking of the World Order*, p. 21.
111. *Ibid.*, p. 67.
112. Huntington, 'The Erosion of American National Interests', pp. 30–1.
113. Benedict Anderson, *Imagined Communities: Reflections on the Origin and Spread of Nationalism* (London: Verso, 1991), p. 93.
114. Barber, *Jihad vs. McWorld*, ch. 10.
115. Benjamin R. Barber, 'Jihad vs. McWorld', *Atlantic Monthly*, Vol. 269, No. 3 (March 1992), p. 60.
116. See 'Environmental Scares: Plenty of Gloom', *The Economist*, 20 December 1997, pp. 19–21; 'A Cooling Off Period', *The Economist*, 29 November 1997, pp. 83–5.
117. Recent moves in this regard include: Robert W. Gregg, *International Relations on Film* (Boulder, CO: Lynne Rienner, 1998); Shapiro, *Violent Cartographies*, ch. 4.
118. Barber, *Jihad vs. McWorld*, p. 98.
119. Quebec's demand for political sovereignty is based in part on its need to defend its francophone culture. Barber, *Jihad vs. McWorld*, p. 178.

120. *Ibid.*, p. 89.
121. *Ibid.*, p. 90.
122. For up-to-date box office gross earnings, with percentage foreign and domestic, see Gitesh Pandya, www.boxofficeguru.com/intl.html, Accessed 20 March 1999.
123. Barber, *Jihad vs. McWorld*, p. 92.
124. *Ibid.*, pp. 307–9.
125. *Ibid.*, p. 101.
126. *Ibid.*, p. 99.
127. *Ibid.*, p. 128.
128. *Ibid.*, p. 136.
129. *Ibid.*, p. 130; John Fiske, 'Shopping for Pleasure', in John Fiske, *Reading the Popular* (Boston: Unwin Hyman, 1989), pp. 13–42.
130. Barber, *Jihad vs. McWorld*, p. 129.
131. Allan Pred, *Recognizing European Modernities: A Montage of the Present* (New York: Routledge, 1995), p. 38.
132. Barber, *Jihad vs. McWorld*, p. 136.
133. *Ibid.*, p. 60.
134. *Ibid.*, p. 97.
135. Huntington, *The Clash of Civilizations and the Remaking of the World Order*, p. 58.
136. Barber, *Jihad vs. McWorld*, p. 206.
137. *Ibid.*, p. 209.
138. *Ibid.*, p. 210.
139. *Ibid.*, p. 215.
140. *Ibid.*, p. 212.
141. Robert D. Kaplan, *The Ends of the Earth: From Togo to Turkmenistan, From Iran to Cambodia – a Journey to the Frontiers of Anarchy* (New York: Vintage, 1996), p. xiii.
142. *Ibid.*, p. xiv.
143. Robert D. Kaplan, 'The Coming Anarchy', *Atlantic Monthly*, Vol. 274, No. 2 (February 1994), pp. 44–76.
144. See press conference by President Clinton and President Mandela, Garden of Tuynhius, Cape Town, Office of the Press Secretary, 27 March 1998.
145. Yahuda Sadowski, *Theorists of Global Chaos* (Washington: Brookings Institute, 1997), p. 13. In one famous incident, Bill Clinton invoked Kaplan to justify his veto of a plan to intervene militarily in Bosnia.
146. Kaplan, *The Ends of the Earth*, p. 54.
147. *Ibid.*, p. 117.
148. *Ibid.*, p. 48.
149. Kaplan, 'The Coming Anarchy', p. 59.
150. Kaplan, *The Ends of the Earth*, pp. 117–18.
151. *Ibid.*, p. 3.
152. Kaplan, 'The Coming Anarchy', p. 55.
153. Barry Buzan, *People, States and Fear: An Agenda for International Security Studies in the Post-Cold War Era*, 2nd edition (Boulder, CO: Lynne Rienner, 1991), pp. 187–202; Thomas F. Homer-Dixon, 'On the Threshold: Environmental Changes as Causes of Acute Conflict', *International Security* (Fall 1991).

154. Kaplan, 'The Coming Anarchy', p. 58. Former Vice President Al Gore read Kaplan's article and shortly afterwards Kaplan was invited to speak with Gore about these issues.
155. Kaplan, *The Ends of the Earth*, p. 5.
156. Kaplan, 'The Coming Anarchy', p. 54.
157. Kaplan, *The Ends of the Earth*, p. 7.
158. *Ibid.*, p. 102.
159. Kaplan, 'The Coming Anarchy', pp. 60–3; Kaplan, *The Ends of the Earth*, p. 8.
160. Huntington, *The Clash of Civilizations and the Remaking of the World Order*, p.148 (on Islam in Turkey).
161. Kaplan, *The Ends of the Earth*, p. 99.
162. Kaplan, 'The Coming Anarchy', p. 66; Kaplan, *The Ends of the Earth*, p. 107. Same paragraph in both sources.
163. Kaplan, *The Ends of the Earth*, p. 110.
164. *Ibid.*, p. 108.
165. *Ibid.*, p. 109.
166. Shiraz Dossa, 'Philosophical History and the Third World: Hegel on Africa and Asia', *European Values in International Relations*, ed. Vilho Harle (New York: Pinter, 1990), p. 106.

EPILOGUE

1. This epilogue was written on the heels of recent events, and, as with all scholarship, is a reflection on their times. There is a risk in analysing current events as they happen, but I believe that there is a greater danger in allowing this rhetoric to go unchallenged.
2. Dana Milbank and Dan Balz, 'Bush Negotiates a Rhetorical Minefield', *Washington Post* 20 September 2001, p. A24.
3. See statements by Jay Leno, David Letterman, Conan O'Brien, John Stewart and the online e-zine *The Onion* on the impossibility of dissent within American popular discourse.
4. Fawas Gerges, *America and Political Islam: Clash of Cultures or Clash of Interests?* (New York: Cambridge University Press, 1999).
5. Samuel P. Huntington, 'The Age of Muslim Wars', *Newsweek International*, Special Edition (December 2001–February 2002), p. 8.
6. *Ibid.*, p. 13.
7. Edward W. Said, 'Israel's Dead End', *Al-Ahram Weekly*, No. 565 (20–26 December 2001).
8. Colin Powell, 'President urges readiness and patience', Office of the Press Secretary, 15 September 2001.
9. Huntington, 'The Age of Muslim Wars', p. 9.
10. *Ibid.*, p. 8.
11. John Merscheimer, 'Why We Will Soon Miss the Cold War', *The Atlantic Monthly*, Vol. 266, No. 2 (August 1990), pp. 35–50; Kenneth N. Waltz, 'The Emerging Structure of the International Politics', *International Security*, Vol.18, No. 2 (Fall 1993), pp. 44–79.
12. George W. Bush, '"Islam is peace," says President', Office of the Press

Secretary, 17 September 2001. www.whitehouse.gov/news/releases/2001/09/print/20010917-11.html.

13. Samuel P. Huntington, 'The Clash of Civilizations?', *Foreign Affairs*, Vol. 72, No. 3 (Summer 1993), pp. 22–49.

14. Samuel P. Huntington, *Clash of Civilization and the Remaking of World Order* (New York: Simon and Schuster, 1996), p. 211.

15. Robert D. Kaplan, 'The Coming Anarchy', *The Atlantic Monthly*, Vol. 360, No. 31 (1994), p. 75.

16. Huntington, *Clash of Civilization*, p. 321.

17. John E. Coleman, 'Ancient Greek Ethnocentricism', *Greeks and Barbarians: Essays on the Interactions Between Greeks and Non-Greeks in Antiquity and the Consequences for Eurocentricism,* ed. John E. Coleman and Clark A. Waltz (Bethesda, MD: CDL Press, 1997), p. 178.

18. Christopher Coker, 'The New World (Dis)Order', *The International System after the Collapse of the East–West Order,* ed. Armand Cleese, Richard Cooper and Yoshikazu Sakamoto (London: Martinus Nijhoff, 1994), p. 37.

Bibliography

Acharya, Amitav. 'The Periphery as the Core', *Critical Security Studies*, ed. Keith Krause and Michael C. Williams (Minneapolis: University of Minnesota Press, 1997), pp. 299–328.

Agnew, John and Corbridge, Stuart. *Mastering Space: Hegemony, Territory, and International Political Economy* (New York: Routledge, 1995).

Ahluwalia, Pal and Sullivan, Michael. 'Edward Said and the World', Paper presented at the Annual Convention of the International Studies Association, Toronto, 18–22 March 1997.

Ajami, Fouad. 'The Summoning', *Foreign Affairs*, Vol. 72, No. 4 (September/October 1993), pp. 2–9.

Anderson, Benedict. *Imagined Communities: Reflections on the Origin and Spread of Nationalism*, 2nd edition (London: Verso, 1991).

Appiah, Anthony. 'The Uncompleted Argument: Du Bois and the Illusion of Race', *Critical Inquiry*, Vol. 12 (Autumn 1985), pp. 21–37.

Arendt, Hannah. *The Origins of Totalitarianism* (New York: Harcourt Brace Javonavich, 1973).

Aristotle. 'Politics', *Basic Works of Aristotle*, ed. Richard McKeon (New York: Random House, 1941).

Arneil, Barbara. *John Locke and America: The Defence of English Colonialism* (Oxford: Clarendon Press, 1996).

Arnold, David. 'Inventing Tropicality', *The Problem of Nature* (Oxford: Blackwell, 1996), pp. 141–68.

Arnold, Matthew. *Culture and Anarchy* (New Haven: Yale University Press, 1960 [1869]).

Ashcroft, Bill, Griffiths, Gareth and Tiffin, Helen. *The Empire Writes Back: Theory and Practice in Post-Colonial Literatures* (New York: Routledge, 1989).

Ashley, Richard K. 'The Geopolitics of Geopolitical Space: Toward a Critical Social Theory of International Politics', *Alternatives*, Vol. 12, No. 3 (1987), pp. 403–34.

Bacon, Helen. *Barbarians in Greek Tragedy* (New Haven: Yale University Press, 1961).

Baldick, Chris. *The Concise Oxford Dictionary of Literary Terms* (Toronto: Oxford University Press, 1990).

Balibar, Etienne. 'Racism and Nationalism', *Race, Nation, Class: Ambigious Identities*, trans. Chris Turner (London: Verso, 1990), pp. 71–85.

Barber, Benjamin R. *Jihad vs. McWorld: How Globalism and Tribalism Are Reshaping the World* (New York: Ballantine Books, 1995).

—— 'Jihad vs. McWorld', *Atlantic Monthly*, Vol. 269, No. 3 (March 1992), pp. 53–63.

Bartelson, Jens. *A Genealogy of Sovereignty* (Cambridge: Cambridge University Press, 1995).

Bartov, Omer. 'Savage War', *Confronting the Nazi Past: New Debates on*

Modern German History, ed. Michael Burleigh (London: Collin & Brown, 1996), pp. 125–39.

———— *Hitler's Army: Soldier, Nazis, and War in the Third Reich* (New York: Oxford University Press, 1992).

———— *The Eastern Front, 1941–45: German Troops and the Barbarisation of Warfare* (London: Macmillan, 1985).

Baudrillard, Jean. *The Gulf War Did Not Take Place*, trans. Paul Patton (Bloomington: Indiana University Press, 1995).

Bauman, Zygmunt. *Modernity and the Holocaust* (Ithaca, NY: Cornell University Press, 1989).

Behdad, Ali. *Belated Travelers: Orientalism in the Age of Colonial Dissolution* (Durham, NC: Duke University Press, 1994).

Benedict, Burton. 'Rituals of Representation: Ethnic Stereotypes and Colonized Peoples at World's Fairs', *Fair Representations: World's Fairs and the Modern World*, ed. Robert W. Rydell and Nancy Gwinn (Amsterdam: VU University Press, 1994), pp. 28–61.

Bhabha, Homi K. 'Of Mimicry and Man: The Ambivalence of Colonial Discourse', *The Location of Culture* (New York: Routledge, 1994), pp. 85–92.

———— 'The Other Question: Stereotype, Discrimination and the Discourse of Colonialism', *The Location of Culture* (New York: Routledge, 1994), pp. 66–84.

Blaney, David and Naeem Inayatullah. 'Prelude to a Conversation of Cultures in International Society? Todorov and Nandy on the Possibility of Dialogue', *Alternatives*, Vol. 19 (1994), pp. 23–51.

Bloom, Allan. *The Closing of the American Mind* (Toronto: Simon and Schuster, 1987).

Bloom, William. *Personal Identity, National Identity and International Relations* (Cambridge: Cambridge University Press, 1990).

Bond, Brian. *War and Society in Europe 1870–1970* (Montreal: McGill-Queen's University Press, 1998).

Bozeman, Adda B. 'The International Order in a Multicultural World', *The Expansion of International Society*, ed. Hedley Bull and Adam Watson (Oxford: Clarendon Press, 1984), pp. 387–406.

———— *Conflict in Africa: Concepts and Realities* (Princeton, NJ: Princeton University Press, 1976).

———— *Politics and Culture in International History* (Princeton, NJ: Princeton University Press, 1960).

Broszat, Martin. 'The Third Reich and the German People', *The Challenge of the Third Reich: The Adam von Trott Memorial Lectures*, ed. Hedley Bull (Oxford: Clarendon Press, 1986), pp. 77–94.

Brown, Chris, *International Relations Theory: New Normative Approaches* (London: Harvester Wheatsheaf, 1992), pp. 43, 73–5.

Bull, Hedley. 'European States and African Political Communities', *The Expansion of International Society*, ed. Hedley Bull and Adam Watson (Oxford: Clarendon Press, 1984), pp. 99–114.

———— 'The Challenge of the Third Reich: Introduction', *The Challenge of the Third Reich: The Adam von Trott Memorial Lectures*, ed. Hedley Bull (Oxford: Clarendon Press, 1986), pp. 3–16.

———— 'The Emergence of a Universal International Society', *Expansion of International Society*, ed. Hedley Bull and Adam Watson (Oxford: Clarendon Press, 1984), pp. 117–26.

———— 'The Revolt against the West', *Expansion of International Society*, ed. Hedley Bull and Adam Watson (Oxford: Clarendon Press, 1984), pp. 217–28.

———— *The Anarchical Society: A Study of Order in World Politics* (London: Macmillan, 1977).

———— 'International Theory: The Case for a Classical Approach', *Contending Approaches to International Politics*, ed. K. Knorr and J. Rosenau (Princeton, NJ: Princeton University Press, 1969), pp. 20–38.

Bull, Hedley and Watson, Adam. 'Conclusion', *Expansion of International Society*, ed. Hedley Bull and Adam Watson (Oxford: Clarendon Press, 1984), pp. 425–36.

———— 'Introduction', *The Expansion of International Society*, ed. Hedley Bull and Adam Watson (Oxford: Clarendon Press, 1984), pp. 1–9.

Burleigh, Michael D. *Ethics and Extermination: Reflections on Nazi Genocide* (New York: Cambridge University Press, 1997).

Burleigh, Michael. *Germany Turns Eastward: A Study of Ostforschung in the Third Reich* (New York: Cambridge University Press, 1988).

Burleigh, Michael and Wippermann, Wolfgang. *The Racial State: Germany 1933–45* (Cambridge: Cambridge University Press, 1991).

Burton. Richard F. *Personal Narrative of a Pilgrimage to Al-Madinah and Meccah*. ed. Isabel Burton (New York: Dover Publications, 1964).

Bush, George W. '"Islam is peace" Says President', Office of the Press Secretary (17 September 2001) www.whitehouse.gov/news/releases/2001/09/print/20010917-11.html.

Butler, Judith. *Gender Trouble: Feminism and the Subversion of Identity* (New York: Routledge, 1990).

Buzan, Barry. *People, States and Fear: An Agenda for International Security Studies in the Post-Cold War Era*, 2nd edition (Boulder, CO: Lynne Rienner, 1991).

Campbell, David. *Writing Security: United States Foreign Policy and the Politics of Identity*, 2nd edition (Minneapolis: University of Minnesota Press, 1998).

———— 'Politics Prosaics, Transversal Politics and the Anarchical World', *Challenging Boundaries: Global Flows, Territorial Identities*, ed. Michael J. Shapiro and Hayward R. Alker (Minneapolis: University of Minnesota Press, 1996).

———— *Politics without Principle: Sovereignty, Ethics, and the Narratives of the Gulf War* (Boulder, CO: Lynne Rienner, 1993).

———— *Writing Security: United States Foreign Policy and the Politics of Identity* (Manchester: Manchester University Press, 1992).

Campbell, David and Michael J. Shapiro, 'Introduction: From Ethical Theory to Ethical Relation', *Moral Spaces: Rethinking Ethics and World Politics* (Minneapolis: University of Minnesota Press, 1999), p. xi.

Cardoso, Fernando Henrique and Faletto, Enzo. *Dependency and Development in Latin America*, trans. Marjory Mattingly Urquidi (Los Angeles: University of California Press, 1979).

Carr, E.H. *The Twenty Years' Crisis, 1919–1939: An Introduction to the Study of International Relations*, 2nd edition (Toronto: Macmillan Press, 1966).

——— *International Relations Between the Two World Wars, 1919–1939* (London: Macmillan Press, 1947).

——— *International Relations Between the Two World Wars: 1919–1939* (London, Macmillan Press, 1942).

——— *Conditions of Peace* (New York: Macmillan Press, 1942).

——— *Propaganda in International Politics* (Oxford Pamphlets on World Affairs) (Oxford: Clarendon Press, 1939).

Césaire, Aimé. *Discourse on Colonialism*, trans. Joan Pinkham (New York: Monthly Review Press, 1972).

Chan, Stephen. 'Too Neat and Under-Thought a World Order: Huntington and Civilisations', *Millennium: Journal of International Studies*, Vol. 27, No.1 (1997), pp. 136–7.

Charmley, John. *Churchill's Grand Alliance: The Anglo-American Special Relationship 1940–57* (New York: Harcourt Brace and Co., 1995).

Chase, Allan. *The Legacy of Malthus: The Social Costs of the New Scientific Racism* (Chicago: University of Illinois Press, 1980).

Cheyfitz, Eric. *The Poetics of Imperialism: Translation and Colonization from The Tempest to Tarzan*, expanded edition (Philadelphia: University of Pennsylvania Press, 1991), p. 89.

Clark, Ian. *The Hierarchy of States: Reform and Resistance in the International Order* (Cambridge: Cambridge University Press, 1989).

Clarke, I.F. 'Introduction: The Paper Warriors and their Fights of Fantasy', *The Tale of the Next Great War, 1871–1914: Fictions of Future Warfare and the Battles Still-to-Come*, ed. I.F. Clarke (Syracuse, NY: Syracuse University Press, 1995), pp. 1–26.

Clarke, J.J. *Oriental Enlightenment: The Encounter Between Asian and Western Thought* (New York: Routledge, 1997).

Coker, Christopher. 'The New World (Dis) Order', *The International System after the Collapse of the East–West Order*, eds. Armand Cleese, Richard Cooper and Yoshikazu Sakamotom (London: Martinus Nijhoff, 1994), pp. 29–40.

——— *The Twilight of the West* (Boulder, CO: Westview Press, 1998).

——— *War and the 20th Century: A Study of War and Modern Consciousness* (London: Brassey's, 1994).

Coleman, John E. 'Ancient Greek Ethnocentrism', *Greeks and Barbarians: Essays on the Interactions between Greeks and Non-Greeks in Antiquity and the Consequences for Eurocentrism*, ed. John E. Coleman and Clark A. Waltz (Bethesda, MD: CDL Press, 1997).

Collingwood, R.G. *The New Leviathan: or Man, Society, Civilisation and Barbarism*, ed. David Boucher (Oxford: Clarendon Press, 1992).

Conklin, Alice L. *A Mission to Civilize: The Republican Idea of Empire in France and West Africa, 1895–1930* (Stanford: Stanford University Press, 1997).

Connolly, William E. *Identity/Difference: Democratic Negotiations of Political Paradox* (Ithaca, NY: Cornell University Press, 1991).

——— 'Taylor, Foucault, and Otherness', *Political Theory*, Vol. 13, No. 3 (1985), pp. 365–76.

Conversi, Daniele. 'Reassessing Current Theories of Nationalism: Nationalism as Boundary Maintenance and Creation', *Nationalism and Ethnic Politics*, Vol. 1, No. 1 (Spring 1995), pp. 73–85.

Cox, Robert W. 'Civilizations: Encounters and Transformations', *Studies in Political Economy*, Vol. 47 (Summer 1995), pp. 7–31.

Crabb, Cecil V. *The Elephants and the Grass: A Study of Nonalignment* (New York: Praeger, 1965).

Curtin, Philip. *Imperialism* (New York: Harper and Row, 1971).

Darby, Philip. *The Fiction of Imperialism: Reading Between International Relations and Postcolonialism* (London: Cassell, 1998).

Darby, Philip and Paolini, A.J. 'Bridging International Relations and Postcolonialism', *Alternatives*, Vol. 19 (1994), pp. 371–97.

Davies, Merryl Wyn, Nandy, Ashis and Sardar, Ziauddin. *Barbaric Others: A Manifesto on Western Racism* (Boulder, CO: Pluto Press, 1993).

Deibert, Ronald J. *Parchment, Printing, and Hypermedia: Communication in World Order Transformation* (New York: Columbia University Press, 1997).

Denon, Vivant. *Travels in Upper and Lower Egypt*, Vols I–III, trans. Alan Aikin (New York: Arno Press, 1973).

Der Derian, James ed. *The Virilio Reader* (New York: Blackwell, 1998).

———— 'Spy versus Spy: The Intertextual Power of International Intrigue', *International/Intertextual Relations: Postmodern Readings of World Politics*, ed. James Der Derian and Michael J. Shapiro (Toronto: Lexington Books, 1989), pp. 163–88.

———— *On Diplomacy: A Genealogy of Western Estrangement* (Oxford: Basil Blackwell, 1987).

Derrida, Jacques, 'Structure, Sign and Play in the Discourse of the Human Sciences', *Writing and Difference*, trans. Alan Bass (Chicago: University of Chicago Press, 1978), pp. 278–93.

Dillon, Michael. *Politics of Security: Towards a Political Philosophy of Continental Thought* (London: Routledge, 1996).

Dossa, Shiraz. 'Philosophical History and the Third World: Hegel on Africa and Asia', *European Values in International Relations*, ed. Vilho Harle (New York: Pinter, 1990), pp. 90–109.

Doty, Roxanne Lynn. *Imperial Encounters: The Political Representation in North–South Relations* (Minneapolis: University of Minnesota Press, 1996).

———— 'The Bounds of "Race" in International Relations', *Millennium: Journal of International Relations*, Vol. 22, No. 3 (Summer 1993), pp. 443–61.

———— 'Sovereignty and the Nation: Constructing the Boundaries of National Identity', *State Sovereignty as a Social Construct*, ed. Thomas J. Biersteker and Cynthia Weber (Cambridge: Cambridge University Press, 1996), pp. 121–47.

Dreyfus, Hubert L. and Rabinow, Paul. *Michel Foucault: Beyond Structuralism and Hermeneutics*, 2nd edition (Chicago: University of Chicago Press, 1983).

du Bois, W.E.B. 'To the Nations of the World', *W.E.B. du Bois: A Reader* ed. David Levering Lewis (New York: Holt and Company, 1995)

du Preez, Peter. *Genocide: The Psychology of Mass Murder* (New York: Boyars/Bowerdean, 1994).

Dyer, Gwynne. *War – Past, Present, and Future* (New York: Crown, 1985).

The Economist, 29 November 1997.

The Economist, 20 December 1997.

Eksteins, Modris. *Rites of Spring: The Great War and the Birth of the Modern Age* (Toronto: Lester and Orpen Dennys, 1989).

Elshtain, Jean Bethke. 'Freud's Discourse of War/Politics', *International/ Intertextual Relations: Postmodern Readings of World Politics*, ed. James Der Derian and Michael J. Shapiro (Toronto: Maxwell Macmillan, 1989), pp. 49–67.

Ensor, R.C.K. *Herr Hitler's Self-Disclosure in Mein Kampf* (Oxford Pamphlets on World Affairs, No. 3) (Oxford: Clarendon Press, 1939).

Fallows, James. 'How the World Works', *Atlantic Monthly*, Vol. 272, No. 6 (December 1993), pp. 61–87.

Fanon, Frantz. *A Dying Colonialism*, trans. Haakon Chevalier (New York: Grove Press, 1965).

——— *Black Skin, White Masks*, trans. Charles Lam Markmann (New York: Grove Press, 1967).

——— *The Wretched of the Earth*, trans. Constance Farrington (New York: Grove Press, 1963).

Fausett, David. *Images of the Antipodes in the Eighteenth Century: A Study in Stereotyping* (Amsterdam: Rodopi B.V., 1994).

Febvre, Lucien. 'Civilisation: Evolution of a Word and a Group of Ideas', *A New Kind of History*, ed. Peter Burke, trans. K. Folca (New York: Harper and Row, 1973).

Federici, Silvia. 'The God that Never Failed: The Origins and Crises of Western Civilization', *Enduring Western Civilization: The Construction of the Concept of Western Civilization and Its 'Others'*, ed. Silvia Federici (London: Praeger, 1995).

Ferro, Marc. *Colonization: A Global History*, trans. K.D. Prithipaul (New York: Routledge, 1997).

Finlay, David J., Holsti, Ole R. and Fagen, Richard R. *Enemies in Politics* (Chicago: Rand McNally, 1967).

Fiske, John. *Reading the Popular* (Boston: Unwin Hyman, 1989).

Flaubert, Gustave. *Flaubert in Egypt: A Sensibility on Tour*, ed. Francis Steegmuller, trans. Francis Steegmuller (Toronto: Bodley Head, 1972).

Förster, Jürgen. 'The Relation between Operation Barbarossa as Ideological War of Extermination and the Final Solution', *The Final Solution: Origins and Implementation*, ed. David Cesarani (New York: Routledge, 1994), pp. 85–102.

Foucault, Michel. 'Governmentality', *The Foucault Effect: Studies in Governmentality*, ed. Graham Burchell, Colin Gordon, and Peter Miller (Chicago: University of Chicago Press, 1991), pp. 8–104.

——— 'Body/Power' *Power/Knowledge: Selected Interviews and Other Writings, 1972–1977*, ed. Colin Gordon, trans. Colin Gordon, Leo Marshall, John Mepham and Kate Soper (Brighton: Harvester Press, 1980), pp. 55–62.

——— 'Two Lectures', *Power/Knowledge: Selected Interviews and Other Writings, 1972–1977*, ed. Colin Gordon, trans. Colin Gordon, Leo Marshall, John Mepham and Kate Soper (Brighton: Harvester Press, 1980), pp. 78–108.

——— 'Truth and Power', *Power/Knowledge: Selected Interviews and Other Writings, 1972–1977*, ed. Colin Gordon trans. Colin Gordon, Leo Marshall, John Mepham and Kate Soper (Brighton: Harvester Press, 1980), pp. 109–33.

———— 'Nietzsche, Genealogy, History', *Language, Counter-Memory, Practice: Selected Essays and Interviews*, ed. Donald F. Bouchard, trans. Donald F. Bouchard and Sherry Simon (Ithaca, NY: Cornell University Press, 1977), pp. 139–64.

———— *Discipline and Punish: The Birth of the Prison*, trans. Alan Sheridan (New York: Vintage, 1977).

Fox, Richard G. 'East of Said', *Edward Said: A Critical Reader*, ed. Michael Sprinker (Cambridge: Blackwell Press, 1992), pp. 144–55.

Freud, Sigmund. 'An Autobiographical Study', *Sigmund Freud: Historical and Expository Works on Psychoanalysis*, ed. Albert Dickson, trans. James Strachey. (London: Penguin Books, 1986).

———— 'On the History of the Psychoanalytic Movement', *Sigmund Freud: Historical and Expository Works on Psychoanalysis*, ed. Albert Dickson, trans. James Strachey. (London: Penguin Books, 1986).

———— 'Thoughts for the Times on War and Death', *Sigmund Freud: Civilization, Society and Religion*, ed. Albert Dickson, trans. James Strachey (New York: Penguin Books, 1985).

———— 'Civilization and Its Discontents', *Sigmund Freud: Civilization, Society and Religion*, ed. Albert Dickson, trans. James Strachey (New York: Penguin Books, 1985).

———— 'Group Psychology and the Analysis of the Ego', *Sigmund Freud: Civilization, Society and Religion*, ed. Albert Dickson, trans. James Strachey (New York: Penguin Books, 1985).

———— 'The Future of an Illusion', *Sigmund Freud: Civilization, Society and Religion*, ed. Albert Dickson, trans. James Strachey (New York: Penguin Books, 1985).

———— 'Thoughts for the Times on War and Death', *Sigmund Freud: Civilization, Society and Religion*, ed. Albert Dickson, trans. James Strachey (New York: Penguin Books, 1985).

———— 'Why War?', *Sigmund Freud: Civilization, Society and Religion*, ed. Albert Dickson, trans. James Strachey (New York: Penguin Books, 1985).

Fukuyama, Francis. 'The Trouble with Names', *Foreign Policy*, Vol. 119 (Summer 2000).

———— *The End of History and the Last Man* (New York: Avon Books, 1992).

Füredi, Frank. *The Silent War: Imperialism and the Changing Perception of Race* (London: Pluto Press, 1998).

Fussell, Paul. *The Great War and Modern Memory* (New York: Oxford University Press, 1975).

Gaddis, John Lewis. 'International Relations and the End of the Cold War', *International Security*, Vol. 17, No. 3 (1992), pp. 5–58.

Garret, Stephen A. 'Political Leadership and "Dirty Hands": Winston Churchill and the City Bombing of Germany', *Ethics of Statecraft: The Moral Dimensions of International Affairs*, ed. Cathal J. Nolan (London: Praeger, 1995).

Gay, Peter. *The Cultivation of Hatred: The Bourgeois Experience from Victoria to Freud* (New York: Norton, 1993).

George, Jim. 'Of Incarceration and Closure: Neorealism and the New World Order', *Millennium: Journal of International Studies*, Vol. 22, No. 2 (Winter 1993), pp. 197–234.

———— *Discourses of Global Politics: A Critical (Re)Introduction to International Relations* (Boulder, CO: Lynne Rienner, 1994).

Gerges, Fawas. *America and Political Islam: Clash of Cultures or Clash of Interests?* (New York: Cambridge University Press, 1999).

Gerhart, Gail. 'Africa: Books Reviewed in 1997' (September/October 1997). URL: http://www.foreignaffairs.org/envoy/books/africa/ bk_africa97.html.

Gilbert, Martin. *The Second World War* (Toronto: Stoddart, 1989).

Goertz, Gary. *Contexts of International Politics* (Cambridge: Cambridge University Press, 1994).

Goldgeier, James M. and Michael McFaul, 'A Tale of Two Worlds: Core and Periphery in the post-Cold War Era', *International Organization*, Vol. 46, No. 2 (Spring 1992), pp. 467–91.

Goldhagen, Daniel Jonah. *Hitler's Willing Executioners: Ordinary Germans and the Holocaust* (New York: Alfred A. Knopf, 1996).

Goldschmidt, Arthur Jr. *Modern Egypt: The Formation of a Nation-State* (Boulder, CO: Westview Press, 1988).

Gong, Gerrit W. *The Standard of 'Civilization' in International Society* (Oxford: Clarendon Press, 1984).

Gray, Chris Hables. *Postmodern War: The New Politics of Conflict* (New York: Guilford Press, 1997).

Gregg, Robert W. *International Relations on Film* (Boulder, CO: Lynne Rienner, 1998).

Grundlingh, Albert. *Fighting Their Own War: South African Blacks and the First World War* (Johannesburg: Ravan Press, 1987).

Hall, Stuart. 'New Ethnicities', *Stuart Hall: Critical Dialogues in Cultural Studies*, ed. David Morely and Kuan-Hsing Chen (London: Routledge, 1996), pp. 441–9.

———— 'When was the 'Post-Colonial'? Thinking at the Limit', *The Post-Colonial Question: Common Skies, Divided Horizons*, ed. Iain Chambers and Lidia Curti (New York: Routledge, 1996), pp. 242–60.

———— 'Who Needs Identity?' *Questions of Cultural Identity*, ed. Stuart Hall (London: Sage, 1996), pp. 1–17.

Hannaford, Ivan, *Race: The History of an Idea in the West* (Baltimore: Johns Hopkins University Press, 1996).

Hansen, Lene. 'R.B.J. Walker and International Relations: Deconstructing a Discipline', *The Future of International Relations: Masters in the Making*, ed. Iver B. Neumann and Ole Wæver (London: Routledge, 1997), pp. 316–36.

Harbsmeier, Michael. 'Early Travels to Europe: Some Remarks on the Magic of Writing', *Europe and its Others, Vol. I. Proceedings of the Essex Conference on the Sociology of Literature, July 1984*, ed. Francis Barker, Peter Hulme, Margaret Iverson, Diana Loxley (Colchester: University of Essex, 1985).

Haste, Cate. *Keep the Home Fires Burning: Propaganda in the First World War* (London, Penguin Books, 1977).

Headrick, Daniel R. *The Tools of Empire: Technology and European Imperialism in the Nineteenth Century* (New York: Oxford University Press, 1981).

Hegel, Georg Wilhelm Friedrich. *The Philosophy of History*, trans. J. Sibree (New York: Dover Publications, 1956).

Hennessy, Bernard C. 'Psycho-Cultural Studies of National Character:

Relevances for International Relations', *Background: Journal of the International Studies Association*, Vol. 6, No. 1 (Fall 1962), pp. 27–48.

Herman, Arthur. *The Idea of Decline in Western History* (Toronto: The Free Press, 1997).

Hitler, Adolf. 'Last Order of the Day, 16 April 1945', *The War, 1939–45: A Documentary History*, ed. Desmond Flower and James Reeves (New York: Da Capo Press, 1997), p. 1003.

———— 'Planning for National Suicide, March 1945', *The War, 1939–45: A Documentary History*, ed. Desmond Flower and James Reeves (New York: Da Capo Press, 1997), p. 856.

———— 'Most Secret. Directive No. 1 for the Conduct of War: 31 August', *The War, 1939–45: A Documentary History*, ed. Desmond Flower and James Reeves (New York: Da Capo Press, 1997), pp. 449–50.

———— *Nazi Culture: Intellectual, Cultural and Social Life in the Third Reich*, ed. George L. Mosse, trans. Salvator Attanasio (New York: Grosset and Dunlap, 1966).

———— *Hitler's Tabletalk 1941–44*, trans. Norman Cameron and R.H. Stevens (Oxford: Oxford University Press, 1953).

———— *Mein Kampf*, trans. Helmut Riperger (New York: Reynal and Hitchcock, 1939).

Hobsbawm, Eric. 'The Invention of Tradition', *Nationalism*, ed. John Hutchinson and Anthony D. Smith (Oxford: Oxford University Press, 1994), pp. 76–83.

———— *The Age of Capital, 1848–1875* (New York: Random House, 1975).

Hobson, J.A. *Imperialism: A Study* (Ann Arbor: University of Michigan Press, 1965).

Hodson, H.V. 'Race Relations in the Commonwealth', *International Affairs*, Vol. 26, No.3 (July 1950), pp. 305–15.

Holsti, K.J. *The State, War, and the State of War* (Cambridge: Cambridge University Press, 1996).

———— 'Governance without Government: Polyarchy in Nineteenth-Century European International Politics', *Governance without Government*, ed. James Rosenau and Ernst-Otto Czempiel (Cambridge: Cambridge University Press, 1992), pp. 30–57.

———— *Peace and War: Armed Conflicts and International Order 1648–1989* (Cambridge: Cambridge University Press, 1991).

———— *The Dividing Discipline: Hegemony and Diversity in International Theory* (Boston: Unwin Hyman, 1985).

———— 'National Role Conceptions in the Study of Foreign Policy', *International Studies Quarterly*, Vol. 14, No. 3 (September 1970), pp. 233–309.

———— *International Politics: A Framework for Analysis* (Toronto: Prentice Hall, 1967).

Homer-Dixon, Thomas F. 'On the Threshold: Environmental Changes as Causes of Acute Conflict', *International Security*, Vol. 16, No. 2 (Fall 1991), pp. 76–116.

Howard, Michael. 'The Military Factor in European Expansion', *Expansion of International Society*, ed. Hedley Bull and Adam Watson (Oxford: Clarendon Press, 1984), pp. 33–42.

Hudson, Valerie M. 'Culture and Foreign Policy: Developing a Research

Agenda', *Culture and Foreign Policy*, ed. Valerie M. Hudson (Boulder, CO: Lynne Rienner, 1997), pp. 1–24.

Huntington, Samuel P. 'The Age of Muslim Wars', *Newsweek International* (December 2001–February 2002), pp. 8–13.

———— 'The Lonely Superpower', *Foreign Affairs*, Vol. 78, No. 2 (March/April 1999), pp. 35–49.

———— 'The Erosion of American National Interests', *Foreign Affairs*, Vol. 76, No. 5 (September 1997), pp. 28–49.

———— *The Clash of Civilizations and the Remaking of the World Order* (New York: Simon and Schuster, 1996).

———— 'The Clash of Civilizations?' *The International System After the Demise of the East/West Conflict*, ed. Armand Cleese, Richard Cooper and Yoshikazu Sakamotom (London: Martinus Nijhoff, 1994), pp. 7–27.

———— 'The Clash of Civilizations?' *Foreign Affairs*, Vol. 72, No. 3 (Summer 1993), pp. 23–49.

———— 'If Not Civilizations, What?' *Foreign Affairs*, Vol. 72, No. 5 (November/December 1993), pp. 186–94.

———— *Political Order in Changing Societies* (New Haven: Yale University Press, 1968).

Hyam, Ronald. *Britain's Imperial Century, 1815–1914: A Study of Empire and Expansion* (London: Macmillan Press, 1993).

Inayatullah, Naeem. 'Beyond the Sovereignty Dilemma: Quasi-States as Social Construct', *State Sovereignty as a Social Construct*, ed. Thomas J. Biersteker and Cynthia Weber (Cambridge: Cambridge University Press, 1996), pp. 50–80.

Inayatullah, Naeem and David L. Blaney. 'Knowing Encounters: Beyond Parochialism in International Relations Theory', *The Return of Culture and Identity in IR Theory*, ed. Yosef Lapid and Friedrich Kratochwil (Boulder, CO: Lynne Rienner Publishers, 1996), pp. 64–84.

Isaacs, Harold R. 'Color in World Affairs', *Foreign Affairs*, Vol. 47, No. 2 (January 1969), pp. 235–50.

Jäckel, Eberhard. *Hitler's Weltanschauung: A Blueprint for Power*, trans. Herbert Arnold (Middleton: Wesleyan University Press, 1972).

Jackson, Patrick Thaddeus. '"Civilization" on Trial', *Millennium: Journal of International Studies*, Vol. 28, No. 1 (Spring 1999), pp. 141–53.

———— 'Occidentalism: The Symbolic Technology of German Reconstruction', Unpublished Doctoral Dissertation, Columbia University.

Jackson, Robert H. *Quasi-States: Sovereignty, International Relations, and the Third World* (Cambridge: Cambridge University Press, 1990).

———— 'Quasi-States, Dual Regimes and Neoclassical Theory: International Jurisprudence and the Third World', *International Organization*, Vol. 41, No. 4 (1987), pp. 519–49.

Jahoda, Gustav. *Images of Savages: Ancient Roots of Modern Prejudice in Western Culture* (New York: Routledge, 1999).

James, Paul. 'Postdependency?' *At the Edge of International Relations: Postcolonialism, Gender and Dependency*, ed. Philip Darby (New York: Pinter, 1997), pp. 61–83.

Johannsen, G. Kurt and Kraft, H.H. *Germany's Colonial Problem* (London: Thornton Butterworth, 1937).

Johnston, Alastair Iain. 'Thinking about Strategic Culture', *International Security*, Vol. 19, No. 4 (1995), pp. 32–64.

Kaplan, Robert D. *The Ends of the Earth: From Togo to Turkmenistan, From Iran to Cambodia – a Journey to the Frontiers of Anarchy* (New York: Vintage Press, 1996).

———— 'The Coming Anarchy', *Atlantic Monthly*, Vol. 274, No. 2 (February 1994), pp. 44–76.

Katzenstein, Peter J. 'Introduction: Alternative Perspective on National Security', *The Culture of National Security: Norms and Identity in World Politics*, ed. Peter J. Katzenstein (New York: Columbia University Press, 1996), pp. 1–32.

Kaufmann, Walter. *Nietzsche: Philosopher, Psychologist, Antichrist*, 4th edition (Princeton, NJ: Princeton University Press, 1974; first published 1956).

Keegan, John. *A History of Warfare* (London: Pimlico, 1993).

Keene, Edward G. 'International Theory and Practice in the Seventeenth Century: A New Interpretation of the Significance of the Peace of Westphalia', Presented at International Studies Association Annual Meeting (1997).

Kennedy, Paul. *Preparing for the Twenty-First Century* (Toronto: HarperCollins, 1993).

———— *The Rise and Fall of the Great Powers: Economic Change and Military Conflict from 1500 to 2000* (London: Fontana, 1988).

Keohane, Robert O. 'Realism, Neorealism and the Study of World Politics', *Neorealism and its Critics*, ed. Robert O. Keohane (New York: Columbia University Press, 1986), pp. 1–26.

Kiernan, V.G. *Colonial Empires and Armies, 1815–1960* (Kingston: McGill-Queen University Press, 1982).

———— *European Empires from Conquest to Collapse, 1815–1960* (Montreal: McGill-Queen University Press, 1998).

———— 'Colonial Africa and its Armies', *Imperialism and Its Contradictions*. ed. Harvey J. Kaye (New York: Routledge, 1995).

———— 'Noble and Ignoble Savages', *Exoticism in the Enlightenment*, ed. G.S. Rousseau and Roy Porter (New York: Manchester University Press, 1990), pp. 86–116.

———— *The Lords of Human Kind: Black Man, Yellow Man, and White Man in an Age of Empires* (New York: Columbia University Press, 1986).

Kirkpatrick, Jeanne J., 'The Modernizing Imperative: Tradition and Change', *Foreign Affairs*, Vol. 72, No. 4 (September/October 1993).

Kissinger, Henry. *Diplomacy* (London: Simon and Schuster, 1994).

Klein, Bradley. 'The Textual Strategies of the Military: Or Have You Read Any Good Defense Manuals Lately?', *International/Intertextual Relations: Postmodern Readings of World Politics*, ed. James Der Derian and Michael J. Shapiro (Toronto: Lexington Books, 1989), pp. 97–112.

Knutsen, Torbjörn L. *A History of International Relations Theory: An Introduction* (New York: Manchester University Press, 1992).

Kratochwil, Friedrich. 'The Embarrassment of Changes: Neorealism as the Science of *Realpolitik* without Politics', *Review of International Studies*, Vol. 19, No. 1 (Spring 1993), pp. 69–80.

Kristeva, Julia. *Strangers to Ourselves*, trans. Leon S. Roudiez (New York: Columbia University Press, 1991).

Kuczynski, R.R. 'Livings-Space' and Population Problems (Oxford Pamphlets on World Affairs No. 8) (Oxford: Clarendon Press, 1939).

Kuhn, Thomas. The Structure of Scientific Revolutions (Chicago: Chicago University Press, 1962).

Kupchan Charles A. and Kupchan, Clifford A. 'Concerts, Collective Security, and the Future of Europe', International Security, Vol.16, No. 1 (Summer 1991), pp. 114–61.

Kurth, James. 'The Real Clash', National Interest (Fall 1994), pp. 3–15.

Lacan, Jacques. 'The Field of the Other and Back to the Transference', The Four Fundamental Concepts of Psychoanalysis, ed. Jacques-Alain Miller, trans. Alan Sheridan (New York: Norton, 1977), pp. 203–15.

Laffey, John. Civilization and Its Discontented (Montreal: Black Rose Books, 1993).

Lane, Edward William. An Account of the Manners and Customs of the Modern Egyptians Written in Egypt during the Years 1833–1835 (London: East-West Publications, 1978).

Langer, William L. 'Farewell to Empire', Foreign Affairs, Vol. 41, No. 1 (October 1962), pp. 115–30.

——— The Diplomacy of Imperialism (New York: Alfred A. Knopf, 1951).

Lapid, Yosef. 'Culture's Ship: Returns and Departures in International Relations Theory', The Return of Culture and Identity in IR Theory, ed. Yosef Lapid and Friedrich Kratochwil (Boulder, CO. Lynne Rienner Publishers, 1996), pp. 3–20.

——— 'The Third Debate: On the Prospect of International Theory in a Post-Positivist Era', International Studies Quarterly, Vol. 33, No. 3 (1989), pp. 235–54.

Lasswell, Harold D. Propaganda Technique in the World War (New York: Alfred A. Knopf, 1927).

Lewis Martin W. and Wigen, Kären E. The Myth of Continents: A Critique of Metageography (Berkeley: University of California Press, 1997).

Lippmann, Walter. Public Opinion (New York: Free Press, 1997).

Livi-Bacci, Massimo. A Concise History of World Population, 2nd edition, trans. Carl Ipsen (New York: Blackwell, 1997).

Lloyd, T.O. The British Empire 1558–1995, 2nd edition (Oxford: Oxford University Press, 1996).

Locke, John. 'An Essay Concerning the True Original, Extent and End of Civil Government', Treatise of Civil Government and A Letter Concerning Toleration, ed. Charles L. Sherman (New York: Appleton-Century-Crofts, 1937).

Lowe, Lisa. Critical Terrains: French and British Orientalisms (Ithaca, NY: Cornell University Press, 1991).

Lunn, Joe Harris. 'Kande Kamara Speaks: An Oral History of the West African Experience in France 1914–18', Africa and the First World War, ed. Melvin E. Page (London: Macmillan Press, 1987), pp. 28–53.

Mahbubani, Kishore, 'The Dangers of Decadence', Foreign Affairs, Vol. 72, No. 4 (September/October 1993).

Malthus, Thomas Robert, 'An Essay on the Principle of Population (1798)', The Works of Thomas Robert Malthus. Vol. I, ed. E.A. Wrigley and David Souden (London: William Pickering, 1986).

Mann, Michael. 'Authoritarian and Liberal Militarism: A Contribution from Comparative and Historical Sociology', *International Theory: Positivism and Beyond*, ed. Steve Smith, Ken Booth and Marysia Zalewski (Cambridge: Cambridge University Press, 1996), pp. 221–39.

Manzo, Kathryn A. *Creating Boundaries: The Politics of Race and Nation* (Boulder, CO: Lynne Rienner, 1996).

Marshall, P.J. and Williams, Glyndwr. *The Great Map of Mankind: British Perceptions of the World in the Age of Enlightenment* (Toronto: J.M. Dent & Sons, 1982).

Mayall, James. 'International Society and International Theory', *The Reason of States*, ed. Michael Donelan (London: Allen and Unwin, 1978), pp. 122–41.

Mazrui, Ali A. 'The Moving Cultural Frontier of World Order: From Monotheism to North–South Relations', *Culture, Ideology and World Order*, ed. R.B.J. Walker (Boulder, CO: Westview Press, 1984), pp. 24–43.

———— *The African Condition: A Political Diagnosis* (Cambridge: Cambridge University Press, 1980).

———— *Towards a Pax Africana: A Study of Ideology and Ambition* (London: Weidenfeld and Nicolson, 1967).

Mazrui, Ali A. and Tidy, Michael. *Nationalism and New States in Africa from about 1935 to the Present* (London: Heinemann, 1984).

McClintock, Anne. *Imperial Leather: Race, Gender and Sexuality in the Colonial Contest* (New York: Routledge, 1995).

McFarlane, S.N. 'Quasi-States: Sovereignty, International Relations and the Third World – Book Review', *American Political Science Review*, Vol. 87, No. 1 (March 1993), pp. 254–56.

McGowan, Patrick J. 'African and Non-Alignment: A Comparative Study of Foreign Policy', *International Studies Quarterly*, Vol. 12, No. 3 (September 1968), pp. 262–95.

Meek, Ronald L. *Social Science and the Ignoble Savage* (New York: Cambridge University Press, 1976).

Mellehthin, General Von. 'The Battle of Kursk, 4 July 1942', *The War, 1939–45: A Documentary History*, ed. Desmond Flower and James Reeves (New York: Da Capo Press, 1997). p. 829.

Merscheimer, John J. 'Back to the Future: Instability in Europe after the Cold War', *International Security*, Vol. 15, No. 1 (Summer 1990), pp. 5–56.

———— 'Why We Will Soon Miss the Cold War', *Atlantic Monthly*, Vol. 266, No. 2 (August 1990), pp. 35–50.

Milbank, Dana and Balz, Dan. 'Bush Negotiates a Rhetorical Minefield', *Washington Post* (20 September 2001), p. A24.

Mill, John Stuart. 'Civilization', *Essays on Politics and Culture*, ed. Gertrude Himmelfarb (Garden City, NY: Anchor Book, 1962), p. 49.

Mitchell, Timothy. 'Orientalism and the Exhibitionary Order', *Colonialism and Culture*, ed. Nicholas B. Dirks (Ann Arbor: University of Michigan Press, 1992), pp. 289–317.

———— *Colonising Egypt* (New York: Cambridge University Press, 1988).

Montaigne, Michel de. 'On the Cannibals', *Essays*, trans. J.M. Cohen (London: Penguin Books, 1958), pp. 105–19.

Montesquieu, *Persian Letters*, trans. C.J. Betts (London: Penguin Books, 1993).

Moore-Gilbert, Bart. *Postcolonial Theory: Contexts, Practices, Politics* (New York: Verso, 1997).

Moraes, Frank. 'The Importance of Being Black: An Asian Looks at Africa', *Foreign Affairs*, Vol. 43, No. 1 (October 1964), pp. 99–111.

Morgenthau, Hans, J. *Politics among Nations: The Struggle for Power and Peace* (New York: Alfred Knopf, 1948; 2nd edition 1954; 5th edition 1978).

———— 'Critical Look at the New Neutralism', *Crisis and Continuity in World Politics*, ed. George Lanyi and Wilson McWilliams (New York: Random House, 1966), pp. 611–18.

Mosse, George L. 'Introduction', *Nazi Culture: Intellectual, Cultural and Social Life in the Third Reich*, ed. George L. Mosse, trans. Salvator Attanasio (New York: Grosset and Dunlap, 1966).

Mphahlele, Ezekiel. 'The Fabric of African Cultures', *Foreign Affairs*, Vol. 42, No. 2 (July 1964), pp. 614–27.

Müller, Rolf-Dieter and Ueberschär, Gerd R. *Hitler's War in the East, 1941–45: A Critical Assessment*. trans. Bruce D. Little (Providence: Berghahn Books, 1997).

Nandy, Ashis. *The Intimate Enemy: Loss and Recovery of Self under Colonialism* (Delhi: Oxford University Press, 1983).

Necipoglu, Gulru. *Architecture, Ceremonial, and Power: The Topakapi Palace in the Fifteenth and Sixteenth Centuries* (Cambridge, MA: MIT Press, 1991).

Neufeld, Mark. 'Reflexivity and International Relations Theory', *Millennium: Journal of International Studies*, Vol. 22, No. 1 (1993), pp. 53–76.

Neumann, Iver B. *Uses of the Other: 'The East' in European Identity Formation*. (Minneapolis: University of Minnesota Press, 1999).

Neumann Iver B. and Wæver, Ole, eds. *The Future of International Relations: Masters in the Making* (New York: Routledge, 1997).

Neumann, Iver B. and Welsh, Jennifer M. 'The Other in European Self-definition: An Addendum to the Literature on International Society', *Review of International Studies*, Vol. 17, No. 1 (1991), pp. 327–48.

Nietzsche, Friedrich. 'Twilight of the Idols', *Twilight of the Idols and The Anti-Christ*, trans. R.J. Hollingdale (New York: Penguin Books, 1990).

———— *Beyond Good and Evil: Prelude of a Philosophy of the Future*, trans. R.J. Hollingdale (London: Penguin Books, 1990).

———— *The Gay Science with a Prelude in Rhymes and an Appendix of Songs*, trans. Walter Kaufmann (New York: Random House, 1974).

———— *The Will to Power: An Attempt at a Revaluation of all Values*, ed. Walter Kaufmann trans. Walter Kaufmann and R.J. Hollingdale (New York: Vintage, 1967).

———— *Thus Spoke Zarathustra: A book for all and none*, trans. Walter Kaufmann (London: Penguin Books, 1966).

———— 'The Genealogy of Morals', *The Birth of Tragedy and The Genealogy of Morals*, trans. Francis Golffing (New York: Doubleday, 1956), pp. 147–299.

O'Hagan, Jacinta. 'Conceptions of the West in International Relations Thought: From Oswald Spengler to Edward Said', Unpublished PhD Dissertation, Australia National University, 1998.

———— 'Civilisational Conflict? Looking for Cultural Enemies', *Third World Quarterly*, Vol. 16, No. 1 (1995), pp. 19–39.

Ohmae, Kenichi. 'Rise of the Region State', *Foreign Affairs*, Vol. 72, No. 2 (Spring 1993), pp. 78–87.

Olson, William and Groom, A.J.R. *International Relations Then and Now: Origins and Trends in Interpretation* (New York: HarperCollins, 1991).
Organski, A.F.K. *World Politics*. 2nd edition (Toronto: Random House, 1968).
Osterhammel, Jürgen. *Colonialism: A Theoretical Overview*, trans. Shelley L. Frisch (Princeton: Markus Wiener, 1997).
Page, Melvin E. 'Black Men in a White Men's War', in Pge, ed., *Africa and the First World War* (London: Macmillan Press, 1987), p. 1–27.
Pandya, Gitesh. www.boxofficeguru.com/intl.html Accessed 20 March 1999.
Paolini, A.J. *Navigating Modernity: Postcolonialism, Identity, and International Relations*, ed. Anthony Elliot and Anthony Moran (Boulder, CO: Lynne Rienner, 1999).
Parsons, Jack. *Population Fallacies* (London: Unwin, 1977).
Pasic, Sujata Chakrabarti. 'Culturing International Relations Theory: a Call for Extension', *The Return of Culture and Identity in IR Theory*, ed. Yosef Lapid and Friedrich Kratochwil (Boulder, CO: Lynne Rienner Publishers, 1996), pp. 85–104.
Pick, Daniel. *War Machine: The Rationalisation of Slaughter in the Modern Age* (New Haven: Yale University Press, 1993).
———— *Faces of Degeneration: Aspect of a European Disorder 1848–1918* (Cambridge: Cambridge University Press, 1993).
Powell, Colin. 'President Urges Readiness and Patience', Office of the Press Secretary (15 September 2001).
Pratt, Mary Louise. *Imperial Eyes: Travel Writing and Transculturation* (London: Routledge, 1992).
Pred, Allan. *ReCognizing European Modernities: A Montage of the Present* (New York: Routledge, 1995).
Press Conference by President Clinton and President Mandela, Garden of Tuynhius Cape Town, Office of the Press Secretary, 27 March 1998.
Ribbentrop, Count von 'German Ambassador in Moscow, 21 June 1941', *The War, 1939–45: A Documentary History*, ed. Desmond Flower and James Reeves (New York: Da Capo Press, 1997).
Rosecrance, R.N. 'A New Concert of Powers', *Foreign Affairs*, Vol. 71, No. 2 (Spring 1992), pp. 64–82.
Rosenau, James N. 'Governance, Order and Change in World Politics', *Governance without Government: Order and Change in World Politics*, ed. James N. Rosenau and Ernst-Otto Czempiel (Cambridge: Cambridge University Press, 1992), pp. 1–29.
Rousseau, Jean-Jacques. *Émile: or On Education*, trans. Allan Bloom (New York: Basic Books, 1979).
———— 'Essay on the Origin of Languages', *On the Origin of Language*, trans. John H. Moran (Chicago: University of Chicago Press, 1966), pp. 5–83.
Sadowski, Yahuda. *Theorists of Global Chaos* (Washington, Brookings Institute, 1997).
Said, Edward W. 'Israel's Dead End', *Al-Ahram Weekly*, No. 565 (20–26 December 2001).
———— 'Response', *Social Text*, Vol. 40 (1994), pp. 20–4.
———— *Culture and Imperialism* (New York: Random House, 1993).

—————— *Orientalism* (New York: Random House, 1978).

Salter, Arthur. *The Dual Policy* (Oxford Pamphlets on World Affairs No. 11) (Oxford: Clarendon Press, 1939).

Sarup, Madan. *Identity, Culture and the Postmodern World*, ed. Tasneem Raja (Athens, GA: University of Georgia Press, 1996).

Sattin, Anthony. *Lifting the Veil: British Society in Egypt 1768–1956* (London: J.M. Dent, 1988).

Sayyid, Bobby S. *A Fundamental Fear: Eurocentrism and the Emergence of Islam* (London: Zed Books, 1997), p. 47.

Schmidt, Brian C. 'Lessons form the Past: Reassessing the Interwar Disciplinary History of International Relations', *International Studies Quarterly*, Vol. 42, No. 3 (September 1998), pp. 433–59.

Schuman, Frederick L. *International Politics: The Western State System and the World Community*, 6th edition (Toronto: McGraw-Hill, 1958).

—————— *International Politics: An Introduction to the Western State System* (New York: McGraw-Hill, 1933).

Schumpeter, Joseph A. *Imperialism and Social Classes*, ed. Paul M. Sweezy, trans. Heinz Norden (New York: Augustus M. Kelly, 1951).

Schwarzenberger Georg, *Power Politics: A Study of World Society*, 3rd edition (London: Stevens and Sons, 1964 [1941]).

—————— *Power Politics: An Introduction to the Study of International Relations and Post War Planning* (London: Camelot Press, 1941).

Shapiro, Michael J. *Violent Cartographies: Mapping Cultures of War* (Minneapolis: University of Minnesota Press, 1997).

—————— 'Introduction to Part I', *Challenging Boundaries: Global Flows, Territorial Identities*, ed. Michael J. Shapiro and Hayward R. Alker (Minneapolis: University of Minnesota Press, 1996).

—————— 'Moral Geographies and the Ethics of Post-Sovereignty', *Perspectives on Third-World Sovereignty: The Postmodern Paradox*, ed. Mark E. Denham and Mark Owen Lombardi (New York: St. Martin's Press, 1996), pp. 39–59.

—————— *The Politics of Representation: Writing Practices in Biography, Photography, and Policy Analysis* (Madison: University of Wisconsin Press, 1988).

Sheehan, Bernard W. *Savages and Civility: Indians and Englishmen in Colonial Virginia* (New York: Cambridge University Press, 1980).

Shelling, Thomas C. *The Strategy of Conflict* (Cambridge, MA: Harvard University Press, 1963).

Singer, Max and Wildavsky, Aaron. *The Real World Order: Zones of Peace and Zones of Turmoil* (Chatham: Chatham House Press, 1993).

Smith, Anthony D. *National Identity* (Las Vegas: University of Nevada Press, 1991).

Smith, Anthony. 'Towards a Global Culture?', *Theory, Culture, and Society*, Vol. 7 (1990), pp. 171–91.

Spengler, Oswald. *The Decline of the West*, ed. Helmut Werner, trans. Sophie Wilkins (New York: Alfred A. Knopf, 1962).

Stalin, Joseph. 'Stalin on Foreign Policy', in Morganthau, *The Struggle for Power* (New York: Alfred Knopf, 1978).

Stoler, Ann Laura. *Race and the Education of Desire: Foucault's History of Sexuality and the Colonial Order of Things* (Durham, NC: Duke University Press, 1995).

———— 'Rethinking Colonial Categories: European Communities and the Boundaries of Rule', *Colonialism and Culture*, ed. Nicholas B. Dirks (Ann Arbor: University of Michigan Press, 1992), pp. 319–52.

Strang, David. 'Contested Sovereignty: The Social Construction of Colonial Imperialism', *Sovereignty as a Social Construct*, ed. Thomas J. Biersteker and Cynthia Weber (Cambridge: Cambridge University Press, 1996), pp. 22–49.

Szymanski, Albert. *The Logic of Imperialism* (New York: Praeger, 1981).

Tamarkin, Mordechai. 'Culture and Politics in Africa: Legitimizing Ethnicity, Rehabilitating the Post-Colonial State', *Nationalism and Ethnic Politics*, Vol. 2, No. 3 (Autumn 1996), pp. 360–80.

Taylor, Philip M. *Munitions of the Mind: A History of Propaganda from the Ancient World to the Present Era* (New York: St. Martin's Press, 1995).

Teitelbaum Michael S. and Winter, Jay M. *The Fear of Population Decline* (Toronto: Academic Press, 1985).

Thompson, Kenneth W. *Masters of International Thought: Major Twentieth Century Theorists and the World Crisis* (Baton Rouge, LA: Louisiana State University, 1980).

Tinker, Hugh. *Race, Conflict and the International Order: From Empire to United Nations* (London: Macmillan Press, 1977).

Todorov, Tzvetan. *The Conquest of America: The Question of the Other*, trans. Richard Howard (Norman, OK: University of Oklahoma Press, 1999).

Touré, Sékou. 'Africa's Future and the World', *Foreign Affairs*, Vol. 41, No. 1 (October 1962), pp. 141–51.

Toynbee, Arnold. 'The Psychology of Encounters', *Civilization on Trial and The World and the West* (New York: Meridian Books, 1958), pp. 227–88.

———— *A Study of History*, Vol. IX (London: Oxford University Press, 1954).

———— *Study of History*, ed. D.C. Somervell (New York: Dell, 1946).

———— *Survey of International Affairs 1933* (Oxford: Oxford University Press, 1934).

Trevorton, Gregory F. 'Finding an Analogy for Tomorrow', *Orbis*, Vol. 37, No. 1 (Winter 1993), pp. 1–20.

Vadney, T.E. *The World Since 1945*, 2nd edition (London: Penguin Books, 1992).

Vasquez, John A. *The War Puzzle* (Cambridge: Cambridge University Press, 1993).

Vincent, R.J. 'Race in International Relations', *Culture, Ideology and World Order*, ed. R.B.J. Walker (Boulder, CO: Westview Press, 1984), pp. 44–59.

———— 'Racial Equality', *The Expansion of International Society*, ed. Hedley Bull and Adam Watson (Oxford: Clarendon Press, 1984), pp. 239–54.

Volkan, Vamik D. *Psychodynamics of International Relationships: Vol. I: Concepts and Theories*, ed. Vamik D. Volkan, Demetrios A. Julius, Joseph V. Montville (Toronto: Lexington Books, 1990).

———— *The Need to Have Enemies and Allies: From Clinical Practice to International Relations* (Northwale, NJ: Jason Aronson Press, 1988).

Waite, Robert G.L. *The Psychopathic God: Adolf Hilter* (New York: Da Capo Press, 1977).

Walker, R.B.J. *Inside/Outside: International Relations as Political Theory* (Cambridge: Cambridge University Press, 1993).

——— 'Quasi-States: Sovereignty, International Relations and the Third World', *Canadian Journal of Political Science* (25 December 1992), pp. 804–5.

——— 'The Concept of Culture in the Theory of International Relations', *Culture and International Relations*, ed. Jongsuk Chay (New York: Praeger, 1990), pp. 3–17.

——— 'Culture, Discourse, Insecurity', *Towards a Just Peace: Perspectives from Social Movements*, ed. Saul Mendlovitz and R.B.J. Walker (Toronto: Butterworths, 1987), pp.171–90.

——— 'East Wind, West Wind: Civilizations, Hegemonies, and World Orders', *Culture, Ideology and World Order*, ed. R.B.J. Walker (Boulder, CO: Westview Press, 1984), pp. 2–22.

——— 'World Politics and Western Reason: Universalism, Pluralism, Hegemony', *Culture, Ideology and World Order*, ed. R.B.J. Walker (Boulder, CO: Westview Press, 1984), pp. 182–212.

Wallerstein, Immanuel. 'The Construction of Peoplehood: Racism, Nationalism, Ethnicity', *Race, Nation, Class: Ambiguous Identities* (London: Verso, 1991), pp. 71–85.

Walsh, Thomas. *Journal of the Late Campaign in Egypt: Including Descriptions of that Country* (London: Hansard, 1803).

Waltz, Kenneth N. 'The New World Order', *Millennium: Journal of International Studies*, Vol. 22, No. 2 (Summer 1993), pp. 187–96.

——— 'The Emerging Structure of International Politics', *International Security*, Vol. 18, No. 2 (Fall 1993), pp. 44–79.

——— 'Anarchic Orders and Balances of Power', *Neorealism and its Critics*, ed. Robert O. Keohane (New York: Columbia University Press, 1986), pp. 98–130.

——— *Man, the State and War: A Theoretical Analysis* (New York: Columbia University Press, 1959).

Walzer, Michael. *Just and Unjust Wars: A Moral Argument with Historical Illustrations* (New York: Basic Books, 1977).

Wan, Marilyn. 'Naturalized Seeing/Colonial Vision: Interrogating the Display of Races in Late Nineteenth Century France', Master's Thesis, Fine Arts, University of British Columbia, 1992.

Watson, Adam. *The Evolution of International Society: A Comparative Historical Analysis* (New York: Routledge, 1992).

——— 'European International Society and Its Expansion', *Expansion of International Society*, ed. Hedley Bull and Adam Watson (Oxford: Clarendon Press, 1984), pp. 13–32.

Weatherford, Jack. *Savages and Civilization: Who Will Survive?* (New York: Crown Publishers, 1994).

Weber, Max. 'The Uniqueness of Western Civilization', *Max Weber on Capitalism, Bureaucracy and Religion*, ed. and trans. Stanislav Andreski (London: Allen and Unwin, 1983), pp. 21–9.

——— 'The Economic Foundations of 'Imperialism', *From Max Weber: Essays in Sociology*, ed. and trans. H.H. Gerth and C. Wright Mills (New York: Oxford University Press, 1958), pp. 162–79.

Weeks, Albert L. 'Do Civilizations Hold?' *Foreign Affairs*, Vol. 72, No. 4 (September/October 1993), pp. 24–5.

Weindling, Paul. 'Understanding Nazi Racism: Precursors and Perpetrators', *Confronting the Nazi Past: New Debates on Modern German History*, ed. Michael Burleigh (London: Collin & Brown, 1996).

Wendel, Else. 'On Leave from Russia', *The War, 1939–45: A Documentary History*, ed. Desmond Flower and James Reeves (New York: Da Capo Press, 1997).

Wendt, Alexander. 'Anarchy is What States Make of It: The Social Construction of Power Politics', *International Organization*, Vol. 41, No. 2 (1987), pp. 391–25.

Wendt, Alexander. 'Identity and Structural Change in International Politics', *The Return of Culture and Identity in IR Theory*, ed. Yosef Lapid and Friedrich Kratochwil (Boulder, CO: Lynne Rienner Publishers, 1996), pp. 47–64.

White, Hayden. *Tropics of Discourse: Essays in Cultural Criticism* (Baltimore: Johns Hopkins University Press, 1978).

Wight, Martin. 'De systematibus civitatum', *Systems of States*, ed. Hedley Bull (Leicester: Leicester University Press, 1997), pp. 21–45.

——— *International Theory: The Three Traditions*, ed. Gabriele Wight (Leicester: Leicester University Press, 1991).

Wolff, Larry. *Inventing Eastern Europe: The Map of Civilization on the Mind of the Enlightenment* (Stanford: Stanford University Press, 1994).

Yengoyan, Aram A. 'Culture, Ideology and World's Fairs', *Fair Representations: World's Fairs and the Modern World*, ed. Robert W. Rydell and Nancy Gwinn (Amsterdam: VU University Press, 1994), pp. 62–85.

Young, Robert J.C. *Colonial Desire: Hybridity in Theory, Culture and Race* (London: Routledge, 1995).

Zimmern, Alfred. *The Prospects of Civilization* (Oxford Pamphlets on World Affairs, No. 1) (Oxford: Clarendon Press, 1939).

——— *The Study of International Relations: An Inaugural Lecture delivered before the University of Oxford on 20 February 1931* (Oxford: Clarendon Press, 1931).

Index

Compiled by Sue Carlton